ATTENTION
SELECTIVE PROCESSES IN
VISION AND HEARING

ATTENTION
SELECTIVE PROCESSES IN
VISION AND HEARING

NEVILLE MORAY
SENIOR LECTURER IN PSYCHOLOGY,
UNIVERSITY OF SHEFFIELD

 HUTCHINSON EDUCATIONAL

HUTCHINSON EDUCATIONAL LTD
178–202 Great Portland Street, London W1

London Melbourne Sydney Auckland
Bombay Toronto Johannesburg New York

First published 1969

© Neville Moray 1969

*This book has been set in Times, printed in Great Britain
on Smooth Wove paper by Anchor Press, and
bound by Wm. Brendon, both of Tiptree, Essex*

09 099250 4

For my parents

ACKNOWLEDGMENTS

Among the many people with whom I have had the pleasure of discussing matters concerning attention I would like especially to thank Dr. D. Broadbent and Dr. A. Treisman, for help and stimulation ever since I first became interested in this work. I would also like to thank all my colleagues at Sheffield University who have patiently listened to accounts of some of the ideas expressed in this book and through the fire of whose criticism, along with that of the members of the Experimental Psychology Society, the experiments and theories have passed. To what extent the fires have succeeded in refining that material is uncertain.

Special thanks are also due to Professor H-L. Teuber of the Department of Psychology and Professor W. Rosenblith of the Research Laboratory of Electronics of the Massachusetts Institute of Technology for their kindness in arranging for me to spend a year at M.I.T., during the course of which this book was written. I must also thank all my American colleagues who so generously invited me to visit them and discussed my ideas with patience and interest, and who helped me with the experimental research carried out during the year at M.I.T., in particular, L. Braida and Dr N. Durlach of the Communications Biophysics Laboratory and the secretaries of the C.B.L. who helped prepare the typescript. Professor J. Senders provided much help and stimulation in connection with visual attention and theoretical problems. The secretaries of the Sheffield Department typed the final text for which help I am very grateful.

Throughout the years that I have been interested in these matters the support and encouragement given by Professor Harry Kay of the Sheffield Department of Psychology has been unfaltering, and I would like to express my very deep gratitude to him. And lastly I must thank my wife Gerta for applying the critical eye of an art historian to the mundane task of detecting errors in the proofs of the text.

The publishers have allowed the insertion of some new material at proof stage. This has been included at the end of relevant chapters (with bibliographical references).

Neville Moray
Massachusetts Institute of Technology and
University of Sheffield

CONTENTS

ILLUSTRATIONS

EDITORIAL FOREWORD

In 1908 Pillsbury wrote of attention:

> The manifestations of the state which we commonly call attention are protean. No part of the individual is untouched by them. They extend to every part of the physical organism, and are amongst the most profound facts of mind. So numerous and varied are the ramifications of attention, that we find it defined by competent authorities as a state of muscular contraction and adaptation, as a pure mental activity, as an emotion or feeling, and as a change in the clearness of ideas.

The very ubiquity of the concept, coupled with methodological inadequacies of the introspective approach, led to its demise as a central problem in psychology. Beginning in the 1950's there was a resurgence of interest in the problem of attention and the application of rigorous experimental techniques resulted not only in its rehabilitation as a respectable concept in psychology but also to its assuming a position of great importance; indeed it provides a paradigm case for the efficacy of experimental psychology. The theoretical significance of work on attention is considerable both in psychology and neurophysiology, the practical implications of this research are also extensive. Neville Moray was one of a small and highly successful band of psychologists responsible for the development in this field over the past decade, his own extensive studies have made an important contribution to our understanding of the mechanisms of attention.

At a time when scientists from all disciplines are in danger of being submerged under the plethora of scientific publications it would seem appropriate to offer a word of justification for a new series of monographs. Despite the many learned journals, whose numbers are increasing almost daily, and the many books published on psychological topics, there remain a number of gaps. This series it is hoped will serve to stop some of those gaps. It is our aim to publish critical evaluations of important areas of research which have not hitherto been the subject of such treatment; *Attention* is one of these. They are not 'telephone directory' reviews nor are they definite texts but rather a 'state of the art' analysis by an expert who is able not only to assess our present knowledge but also to offer some creative synthesis. In addition to providing an assessment of the field we hope they will give some insight into a scientist's reflections on his area of special interest.

Kevin Connolly

1 ATTENTION ANCIENT AND MODERN

The summer of 1967 saw what may have been the first ever international symposium devoted explicitly to problems of Attention, when Sanders (1967) arranged a meeting at the Institute for Perception at Soesterberg in the Netherlands. This meeting put the seal of respectability on the prodigal who had been reintroduced to polite psychological society in 1958 by Broadbent, in his book *Perception and Communication*. Despite an auspicious beginning, research on attention had fallen into disrepute during the out-and-out Behaviourist period.

Since Broadbent's book work on attention has begun to pour from an ever increasing number of laboratories. It seems a suitable occasion, ten years later, to summarise what we now know, and it is to that task that this monograph is dedicated. It attempts to survey the behavioural research in vision and hearing which throws light on how we share and divert attention, to make some general methodological recommendations, to review current theories, and to provide a guide to the relevant physiological work. As far as possible, work on memory has been omitted. A bibliography of the major work to the spring of 1968 is included.

The early years of modern experimental psychology were marked by a considerable amount of research on attention. The laboratories of Wundt, Titchener, and Helmholtz carried out experiments in the field. For Wundt it was attention which turned perception into apperception, and so played a central role in the account of sensation and perception. Titchener was concerned both with particular researches into such problems as 'prior entry' as a function of attention, and also the more general role of attention in the determination of 'sensory clearness' in introspective reports. Indeed in his book *The Psychology of Feeling and Attention* (1903) there is a lengthy systematic listing of those factors which catch the attention and a discussion of their role in perception. These factors include intensity, extension (in space), duration, 'certain qualitative characteristics' (by which he seems to have in mind emotionally toned stimuli, for he elsewhere describes them as '. . . intimate, worrying, wicked things . . .'), repetition, suddenness, movement, novelty, association with ideas already present, accommodation of sense organs and the cessation of the stimulus. As we shall see later, there is surprisingly little that modern work would wish to add to such a list, although the actual definition of the various qualities would be given with rather more precision, and the conceptual framework of the list would differ markedly. In particular, interest would centre on differing probabilities of response categories, rather than on intro-spective judgments of 'sensory clearness'. Not surprisingly the all-embracing work of William James likewise had a section on attention, although it compares rather poorly in this case with the experimental precision of Titchener. Attention, for James, was

the taking possession by the mind, in clear and vivid form, of one out of what seem simultaneously possible objects or trains of thought.

Focalisation, concentration of consciousness are of its essence. It implies

withdrawal from some things in order to deal effectively with others, and is a condition which has a real opposite in the confused, dazed, scatterbrained state which in French is called 'distraction' and 'Zerstreutheit' in German.

There was also a considerable body of experimental work devoted to the so-called 'span of attention' or 'span of appre-hension', by such men as Hamilton and Jevons, work concerned with the question of how many things could be held in the mind simultaneously or could be taken in at a glance. This field of study has had a surprising renaissance in the last five years, and the recent publication by Bakan (1967) of extracts from the original sources now makes them readily available.

It is all the more odd, therefore, to see the way in which re-search on attention disappeared virtually completely from about 1920 onwards, except for references to span of apprehension experiments, some work of the Gestalt school, and the unfruitful definitions of McDougall (1928),

Attention is merely conation or striving considered from the point of view of its effect upon the cognitive processes.

Otherwise, not until the 1950's were references to the phenomena again made explicitly by name. One of the first was Broadbent's paper (1954) *The role of auditory localisation in attention and memory span,* and the seal of respectability was finally put upon the field by his book already referred to above. As several authors have remarked, the reason for the disappearance of a field of research as important as it is entertaining (a combination comparatively rare in research topics) was probably due to the methods and conceptual framework within which the early workers investigated it.

It fell into bad odour because of the inability of introspective psychologists to agree with one another, or to provide objective evidence to back their assertions. (Broadbent, 1958, p. 109)

Even the definition adopted by Hebb as late as 1949 would not have caused transports of delight in a Watsonian Behaviourist,

When an experimental result makes it necessary to refer to 'set' or 'attention' the reference means, precisely, that the activity that controls the form, speed, strength, or duration of the response is not immediately preceding excitation of the receptor cells alone.

though Hebb himself had described the early work, with some justification, as treating of,

... various properties of mind, undefinable and impossible to understand. (op cit.)

It was probably due to the inability of the introspectionist methodology to come to terms with the attack of Behaviourism that attention so nearly disappeared from the scene for a quarter of a century. It is certainly true, when you must depend upon instructions which are impossible to obey, such as 'pay attention as strongly you can', together with a request for judgments about the relative clarity of sensations and perceptions, that experiments become extremely difficult to control or interpret. Anyone will know this who has tried to repeat even the most straightforward of Titchener's experiments, such as the demonstration of 'prior entry'. Furthermore, this approach ruled out the use of animals completely, and therefore further removed attention from the notice of the rapidly growing Behaviourist school. It is interesting to see that this barrier has been the last of all to be overcome, and that only within the last four or five years has the concept of attention appeared once again in the experimental systematic study of animal behaviour.

Berlyne (1960) stated the position well:

> The problems of stimulus selection are mostly ones that are just beginning to be taken seriously by behaviour theory. There are good reasons why they had to be neglected in favour of problems of response selection for a long time, but a concerted attack on them will be necessary before behaviour theory is equipped for complex and realistic forms of behaviour, especially in human beings. In the guise of questions about awareness, some of the aspects of stimulus selection figured prominently in the writings of the early, introspective experimental psychologists, but they were shelved when the behaviourist revolution took place, largely because the principal preoccupations of the psychologists of that period masked them. Some aspects of stimulus selection have continued to interest the psychology of perception, which has been dealing with questions of prime importance for behaviour theory but has often been carried on in a language that harks back to the days when psychologists were mainly occupied with conscious experience and consequently does not always dovetail neatly into the terminology favoured by behaviour theorists. During the last ten years, however, efforts to merge the study of perceptual phenomena with behaviour theory have been rapidly increasing and some topics, like exploration and curiosity, that psychologists have never really done much about are being eagerly taken up.

The renaissance of interest in attention seems to be connected with three developments. Firstly, the use of operational definition couched in stimulus-response language has become accepted to a degree which allows us to undercut the difficulties of the appeal to introspection, and to put the 'objects' of attention and the process itself on a more 'external' or 'public' footing, with all the advantages in research which that invariably brings. Secondly, towards the end of the Second World War a number of important problems arose for which answers were required from applied psychologists, and which were, whatever they were called at the time, clearly to do with attention. Communications systems in ships, planes and air-traffic control centres all produced situations in which there was a very high flow of information, and in which the human operator might be required to do two things at once. The classical problem of the division of attention needed a solution. Furthermore the growing number of semiautomatic control processes, in which the human operator was required to perform rather little physical exertion, but had to handle great quantities of information displayed on dials and other forms of information readout, again drew attention to the need for a study of how observers handle simultaneously received signals, and how fast they can switch from one task to another. There are few things more likely to overcome a theoretical prejudice against the possibility of certain kinds of research than an urgent practical need for solutions, especially in the sphere of military operations. Hence attention began to find its way back into the laboratory at long last. The third important factor in the rise of such research has been the development of new kinds of apparatus and techniques which have made the control of experiments very much more easy. In the field of auditory research it is impossible to overestimate the importance of the tape-recorder, and indeed the last decade has perhaps seen too heavy an emphasis on auditory research at the expense of visual work, a balance which is just now beginning to be restored. The importance of striking a balance between the two kinds (and indeed others also) of research is emphasised if one compares the views about the design of the brain found in Hebb's (1949) *Organisation of Behavior,* which draws mainly on visual research for its data and Broadbent's (1958) *Perception and Communication,* which is mainly based on auditory work.

The present monograph takes as its starting point *Perception and Communication* and will mainly be concerned with work which has been done since its publication. But whereas in 1958 Broadbent was able to achieve an almost exhaustive coverage of the field a similar complete review would only be possible now in a very large book. Not merely has work that is relevant to the nature of attention increased enormously but there is also the problem of the idea of attention. 'Attention' is a word with a great many very varied meanings, applicable to a very wide range of phenomena, many of them obviously central to an understanding of a human and animal behaviour and probably even to the design of intelligent artifacts. Among the distinct subdivisions of the concept we may at least distinguish the following broad categories.

1 Mental concentration
The person concentrates on some particular task, such as mental arithmetic, and tries to exclude all incoming stimuli which might interfere with the performance of the specified task.

2 Vigilance
A situation where nothing much is happening, but the observer is paying attention in the hope of detecting some event whenever it does happen (watch keeping).

3 Selective attention
'The Cocktail Party Problem' faced by a person who is receiving several messages at once and is trying to select only one of them to accept and respond to.

4 Search
A set of signals is presented and the observer hunts among them for some subset or single signal.

5 Activation
'Sit up and pay attention.' In other words, get ready to deal with whatever happens next. This is an everyday version of the 'orientation reflex'.

6 Set
A preparation to respond in a certain way, either cognitively (as in perceptual defence and context effects in signal/noise discrimination) or by overt motor responses (motor preparatory set). In connection with this use of the word we may notice that as long ago as the early 1940's Gibson (1941) had already catalogued a dozen uses of the word and argued that it was becoming so extended in its meaning as to be losing its usefulness.

7 Neisser (1967) has recently argued strongly that attention refers to a process which seems almost identical with what is usually called 'analysis-by-synthesis'.

Looking over the above list one is struck rather by the complete disparity among the tasks which it includes than by any features which all the uses have in common. 'Attention' indeed might almost act as a paradigm for Wittgenstein's (1953) theory of the relation of words to their use:

> We see a complicated network of similarities overlapping and criss-crossing: sometimes overall similarities, sometimes similarities in detail. . . .

I can think of no better expression to characterise these resemblances than 'family resemblances'.

That some of the resemblances are more apparent than real in the case of attention, and that there may well be the need for as many different small scale theories as there are subdivisions of use in the research field, is indicated by the following experiment by the author.

Wittenborn (1943) on the basis of a factor analytic study proposed two tests of 'attention' which he claimed were relatively free from the influence of such things as practice effect, rote learning ability, vocabulary size, and so on. They were heavily loaded with a factor which he identified as 'mental concentration', or attention. Performance on the two tests was highly correlated. The easiest way to describe the tests is to quote the instructions to subjects taking part in the experiments:

TEST 11 You will hear sets of three digits. Some of the digits will require no response. Some will be responded to by marking a + in the answer space. This will be in one of two conditions:
(1) When the first number is the largest and the second the smallest.
(2) When the third number is the largest and the first the smallest.

TEST 12 Lists of letters selected from the alphabet will be read. You will respond to some letters by marking a plus. You will respond to others by marking a minus. Others will require no response. Mark a vowel following a consonant +, a consonant following a vowel −, and when two vowels or two consonants occur together, mark the next letter + no matter what it is.

These two tests were carried out by Moray (1958, unpublished) and were combined with the results of another investigation (Moray and Taylor, 1958) on speech shadowing—an experiment which entails repeating a message while hearing it. The object was to examine the relation between Wittenborn's 'attention' and selective listening.

The first test was presented at a rate of 96 digits per minute with a pause equal to one digit between each group of three digits. Twelve groups of three digits were given in a run, and there was a one-second pause between successive runs. Ten runs were given in succession. The second test used a presentation rate of 66 letters per minute, with a pause of four seconds between each run of fourteen letters. Ten runs of letters were given in succession.

The lists were prepared using random number tables and were pre-recorded, together with instructions, on a tape-recorder. Subjects were tested singly. They were given a pro-forma with spaces to make the relevant marks, and with the instructions written at the top. They were allowed five minutes to study the instructions to be sure that they understood them. The forms had two sample lists correctly filled in which the listeners checked off while listening to those two lists presented over the tape-recorder. This was followed by three practice runs in the first test and four in the second. The score sheets were checked against a key which had been prepared in advance.

TABLE 1   *Data from experiment using Wittenborn's Tests*

Subject	Mean omissions from shadowing	Mean mistakes	Total errors on Wittenborn digits	Wittenborn letters
J.R.	8·3	3·8	43	14
M.R.	7·6	1·8	13	13
P.E.	7·4	1·8	37	26
J.M.	6·3	5·8	41	40
J.T.	4·0	4·6	3	4
M.C.	3·6	2·0	18	34
K.C.	3·1	3·5	41	27
G.B.	2·5	2·9	2	5
C.C.	2·0	2·8	28	37

TABLE 2   *Table of correlations*

Omissions vs Mistakes	$r = +0·04$
Digit Test vs Letter Test	$r = +0·62*$
Mistakes vs Letter Test	$r = +0·07$
Mistakes vs Digits Test	$r = +0·23$
Omissions vs Letter Test	$r = -0·10$
Omissions vs Digit Test	$r = +0·40$

* Only the Digit Test vs Letter Test correlate at the 0·05 level of significance. No other correlations approach this level.

The subjects were undergraduates and research workers at Oxford University who had previously taken part in the experiment on speech shadowing. The responses in the shadowing task were recorded and scored for omission and commission errors.

For reasons which we need not discuss here, the arithmetic mean of the commission errors and the geometric mean of the omission errors were used. The results were correlated with the performance of the subjects on the Wittenborn tests, and the results are shown in tables 1 and 2. Correlations between performance on the two kinds of attention are negligible.

This monograph will largely be concerned with selective attention in the modalities of vision and hearing. One particular set of experiments will not be considered in detail since it has recently been reviewed fully elsewhere; therefore the so-called 'split span' experiments in which a memory span list is given simultaneously to the two ears will be omitted (Broadbent, 1954; see Moray, 1969a for the review referred to). No attempt will be made to cover the literature on vigilance, which requires an entire book on its own and has recently been the subject of a symposium edited by Buckner and McGrath (1963). Little work has been done recently on the Wittenborn kind of test, and most of the work on the 'orientation reflex' and arousal has either been slanted towards physiological models or is directly physiological; interested readers are referred to a review by Gray (1966) which explicitly is devoted to work on attention in Russia.

For those unfamiliar with modern work on attention and its past history the following references may be found useful: Bakan (1966) has recently edited a small selection of readings covering some of the oldest and newest material and providing a ready access, among other things, to the classical work of Titchener. Worden (1967) and Sanders (1963) both include historical reviews as part of their respective monographs (the former monograph dealing primarily with modern physiological work and the latter with visual attention). Broadbent's (1958) *Perception and Communication* remains of course a *sine qua non* for anyone entering the field, while Neisser (1967) provides a wide ranging review covering many related topics for the period since Broadbent's book and including a number of topics related to attention. Gray (1966), as already mentioned, provides a good review of recent Russian work.

Norman has published a review of the relation of attention and memory experiments which is eminently readable and contains some really classical work (from ancient Greece): (Norman, D., 1969, *Memory and Attention*, Wiley, N.Y.). A book of readings edited by Mostofsky is shortly expected, and the proceedings of the third 'Attention and Performance' symposium (ed. Sanders, North-Holland Press) will appear in 1970.

2 THE DESIGN, ANALYSIS AND CONCEPTUAL FRAMEWORK OF EXPERIMENTS ON ATTENTION

Due to the adoption of information theory by psychology, and especially to the popularity of the model developed for the human operator by Broadbent (1958), work in the last decade has frequently made use of the idea of the 'channel' over which messages arrive, and has described attention as the selection of one 'channel' and the rejection of another 'channel'. Because many of the experiments were auditory and since there has been particular interest in dichotic stimulation (where the listener receives one message through one ear and another message through the other ear) this seemed conceptually reasonable. However, later work has led to increasing confusion in the use of this word as pyschologists have used a large number of 'channels', some of which are very difficult to define in terms either of physical identity or even functional capacity. It is reasonable at first sight to talk of the left and right ears as providing two input channels. But supposing that more than two positions in space are used as sources (Triesman, 1964b; Moray, Bates and Barnett, 1965), is each one a channel? Is a language, for example, French, a different channel from English, if the two messages are merely translations of one another and come from the same location and are spoken by the same voice? (Treisman, 1964a) Is voice quality a channel in this sense? (Moray and Barnett, 1965)

Although the term 'channel' is still in use to describe the presentation of different messages, and while it is a convenient indeed almost irresistible shorthand for those familiar with the field, it seems that a more sophisticated treatment is now needed. For example, describing an experiment in which the ability to select on the basis of type of stimulus material was measured, Broadbent and Gregory (1964a) write

> . . . a different kind of attention, to a class of item rather than to a source of stimulation.

This chapter will be concerned to offer a comprehensive framework within which any experiment on attention may be described, regardless of the material involved, what 'channels' are used and so on. In doing so, the necessary controls for these experiments will emerge as part of the logic of the experimental design, and a terminology will appear. The point of departure is from the suggestion,

> It may be desirable to think of the stimuli used in any experiment as having positions in an 'information space' made up of all the dimensions discriminable by the sense organs. (Broadbent, 1958, p. 78)

We shall say that any signal or event which occurs at or after the receptors in a sensory pathway may be described as occurring in some region of 'signal space'. When dealing with the initial reception and transduction of signals we will call this the 'input space', and when dealing with the organisation and initiation of responses we will call it the 'output space'.

Input space can be thought of as a space of many dimensions. Any stimulus may be defined as a point or region in this space, specified by the co-ordinates along all the dimensions on which it can be categorised. The dimensions may be as simple as position in (physical) space, loudness, colour, size, etc.; or as complex as grammatical class, meaningfulness or frequency of use of words. We therefore will have to have metrics for dimensions some of which are continuous, others discontinuous. The problem of defining a dimension is itself difficult; but if the experimenter alters some characteristic of the stimulus in a way detectable by the subject, and if, in so doing, it is possible to avoid altering any other characteristic as far as the subject is concerned, then the type of alteration is on a dimension orthogonal to any other dimension. (There may be dimensions which are not orthogonal in this sense but where there is some degree of independence of stimulus position nonetheless.)

A signal is therefore presented in some region of input space, and in a typical attention experiment another will be presented simultaneously in another region of input space. The observer's task is therefore to select one region of input space and to discriminate between the signals (identify the signals) which occur in that region. If he can succeed, and in particular if he can enhance his discrimination of signals in that region and reduce the discriminability of signals in a neighbouring region, then we say that he can pay attention to that region.

Notice that it is a separate question whether he can pay attention to one out of a class of signals, and also that it may turn out on occasion that he can discriminate between the two regions of input space, and increase his chance of detecting in which region the signals arrived, but not be able to use this knowledge to enhance the identification of the signals occurring in that region. In such a case we might want to say that he can pay attention to the region (what used to be called a 'channel'), but cannot make use of this ability to pay attention to signals in that region.

Output space is perhaps a slightly more novel idea, although there are certain experiments which imply its existence as a concept in the mind of those who have done the experiments. (In particular there are the experiments on 'stimulus-response compatibility' by Fitts and Deininger, 1954; Leonard, 1959; and Davis et al., 1961). The assumption is made that an accurate response requires the selection of motor units and their integration from among the very large number of options provided by the motor cortex. One might think that two movements for the initiation of which there is no overlapping of motor units (such as the left and right index fingers) should be more discriminable in this space than, say, the middle and index fingers of the right hand, which share common muscles in the groups which control them. Stimulus-response compatibility, then, is a matter of mapping points in the input space on to points in the output space.

The analysis of attention may be thought of as an enquiry into what dimensions of input and output space may be selected by a human subject, what kinds of signals may be selected within such spaces, and whether such selection can be used to enhance the detectability of signals and the efficiency of information transmission by the human operator. Figure 1 indicates some ways in which the examination might proceed. It is *not* intended as a flow diagram of the sequential order in which selection occurs.

We need a systematic terminology to use in such a discussion. We have already noted that the terminology of information theory has been extended to a point where it becomes confusing rather than enlightening, except as a rough and ready short-hand. A channel has now come to mean almost any criterion which might be used to select a message. We need to be able to

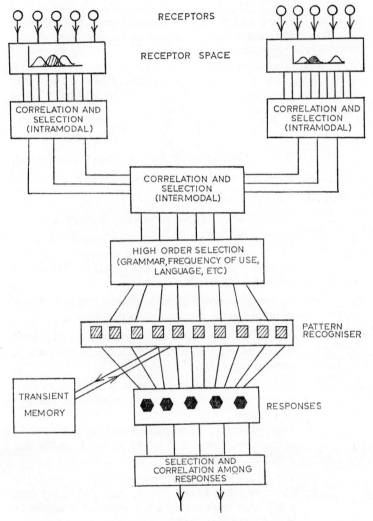

FIG. 1. Modes of selectivity

differentiate between regions of signal space, classes of signals, individual signals, etc., as possible candidates for attentional selection. We need to distinguish voluntary paying of attention from cases where attention is caught. And we need some idea of how to relate measurement to decisions about the success of paying attention. There follows an attempt to develop a notation which allows us to classify the performances which are found in experiments on attention using human subjects and behavioural methods.

Notation

S	is the subject on whom the experiment is performed.
a, b . . . j	are events which can occur in signal space.
A, B . . . J	are regions of signal space.
{]	denotes that the signal space is an input space.
[}	denotes that the signal space is an output space. Thus I{a] is to be read, 'Event a occurs in region I of input space,' where I might be the left half of the visual field, the right ear, etc.
R_I	denotes the correct identification of region I when a stimulus has been presented in that region.
r_a	denotes the response required to event a, and is used where the response is very direct, e.g. pressing a key, or repeating a heard word.
a^r	denotes a transform of a, such as 'add 17 to each number and speak the sum', or 'translate the message into French'. Thus [r_a}J is to be read 'Response r_a is output to output space region J' where J might be the left hand, flexor pollicis brevis, tongue, etc.
|	The 'conditional probability' symbol. Thus $p(r_a)|I\{a]$ is to be read, 'the probability that S will give response r_a when stimulus a occurs in region I of input space'.
$\bar{a}$	Overbar is negation: 'not event $-a$'.
I{a+b]	'Both event a and event b occur in region I of input space.'

T, t   are subscripts meaning 'at time T' or 'at time t'. Thus $p(r_a)_{T+t}|I\{a\}_T$ is read as 'the probability that S will give response r_a at time $T+t$ if event a occurs in region I of signal space at time T'.

$>, <, =, \sum$ have their usual meanings.

$\underset{\uparrow}{I}$:   'S tries to pay attention to region I.'

$\underset{\uparrow}{a}$:   'S tries to pay attention to signal event a.'

a, b   The sets of events $(a_1, a_2, \ldots a_m)$, $(b_1, b_2, \ldots b_n)$

$\underline{\underline{a_{t \to T}}}$ 'Event a is stored from t to T before being output. Thus $p(r_a)_T|\underline{\underline{a_{t \to T}}}|I\{a\}$ is to be read 'The probability of S giving response r_a at time T if signal a has been stored from t to T after being input to region I.'

The application of this rather cumbersome notation will bring out the fact that much of the experimental work of the last few years, while being suggestive is by no means decisive as to possible mechanisms. One finding of past research is that the successful paying of attention does not seem to 'turn off' a rejected message but merely reduces in some way the probability that it will be perceived and cause a response. It is therefore necessary to give all the experimental paradigms in terms of relative probability levels, whatever the final interpretation of these may be. Ordering levels of performance is relatively easy, however, even if at present exact prediction of absolute values is not.

Consider two stimulus events, *a* and *b*, which call respectively for the responses r_a and r_b.

Let *a* be presented by itself in region I of input space, and S be required to say when it has occurred. Similarly let *b* be presented in region I by itself, and S asked to say when it has occurred. Then we may measure the accuracy of S's performance on the two tasks respectively by

$$p(r_a)|I\{a\} \tag{1}$$

and $$p(r_b)|I\{b\} \tag{2}$$

In general, where *a* and *b* are well above threshold and there is little noise, we may expect

$$p(r_a)|I\{a] \simeq p(r_b)|I\{b] \simeq 1\cdot 0 \qquad (3)$$

Now let us present a and b simultaneously in region I. Several things may happen, and by considering the various outcomes we may clarify the meaning of the experiment.

If
$$p(r_a)|I\{a+b] < p(r_a)|I\{a] \qquad (4)$$

and
$$p(r_b)|I\{a+b] < p(r_b)|I\{b] \qquad (5)$$

then the evidence suggests that each signal is masking the other.

If however (4) and (5) are both true, but in addition

$$\overset{a}{\underset{\uparrow}{}}: \acute{p}(r_a)|I\{a+b] > p(r_a)|I\{a+b] \qquad (6)$$

and
$$\overset{b}{\underset{\uparrow}{}}: p(r_b)|I\{a+b] > p(r_b)|I\{a+b] \qquad (7)$$

then we might conclude that neither signal was masking the other completely, but rather they were competing for attention.

If, on the other hand, (4), (5), and (6) were true, but

$$\overset{b}{\underset{\uparrow}{}}: p(r_b)|I\{a+b] = p(r_b)|I\{a+b] \qquad (8)$$

then we could conclude that while the presence of b competes with a for S's attention a actually masks b.

As a measure of the efficacy of attention as a means of enhancing performance we might use either the difference

$$\left(\overset{a}{\underset{\uparrow}{}}: p(r_a)|I\{a+b] - p(r_a)|I\{a+b] \right) \qquad (9)$$

or the ratio

$$\left(\frac{\left(\overset{a}{\underset{\uparrow}{}}: p(r_a)|I\{a+b] - p(r_a)|I\{a+b] \right)}{p(r_a)|I\{a+b]} \right) \times 100 \qquad (10)$$

The second is probably preferable.

There is one more possible outcome of our hypothetical experiment. Again suppose that (4), (5), and (6) were true, but that in addition

$$\overset{a}{\underset{\uparrow}{}}: p(r_b)|I\{a+b] > p(r_b)|I\{a+b] \qquad (11)$$

This implies that in trying to pay attention to a S is in fact behaving as if he were attending to I, the region. That is, the attempt to pay attention to a is causing a higher degree of attention to the experiment as such, to both messages, rather than to the signal event specified by the experimenter.

If on the other hand

$$\underset{\uparrow}{a}: p(r_b)|I\{a+b] < p(r_b)|I\{a+b] \tag{12}$$

then we have strong reason for saying that S can in fact pay attention to a at the expense of b.

Let us now consider a more 'typical' experiment on attention, the design of which is rather similar to the many two channel listening studies which have until recently provided the backbone of research in this area.

S is presented with event a in region I of input space, and with event b simultaneously in region J of input space.

We will assume that in isolation

$$p(r_a)|I\{a] \simeq p(r_b)|J\{b] \simeq 1·0 \tag{13}$$

Furthermore, we run a pilot experiment in which S is asked to say in which region of input space a signal has occurred without identifying it, with the result that

$$p(R_I)|I \simeq p(R_J)|J \simeq 1·0 \tag{14}$$

(Notice that here we are distinguishing response to what is usually called a 'channel' from response to an event. This particular check has almost never been made in an experiment on attention.)

We can now combine (13) and (14) to get an overall measure of performance,

$$(p(r_a)|I\{a]) \cdot (p(R_I)|I) = p(r_aR_I)|I\{a] \tag{15}$$

and similarly for the other region and the other event set. Equation (15) is the probability of giving response r_a and ascribing it to region I, given that it actually occurred in that region. The scores usually used in dichotic listening experiments are implicitly of this kind.

We now turn to the main experiment, and find that

$$p(r_aR_I)|I\{a]\&J\{b] < p(r_bR_J)|I\{a]\&J\{b] < p(r_bR_J)|J\{b] \tag{16}$$

indicating that when both are presented neither set of events is discriminated as well as in the absence of the other, but that, J{b] appears to dominate I{a] as far as attracting attention is concerned.

A supplementary analysis, or an extra experiment, might show that

$$p(R_J)|J\{b] = p(R_I)|I\{a]\&J\{b]$$
$$= p(R_J)|I\{a]\&J\{b] = p(R_I)|I\{a] \tag{17}$$

Now (16) and (17) together indicate that in competitive situations the regions remain as distinguishable as ever, but that signal event *b* dominates signal event *a*. This might be because of a genuine attentional effect, or be merely on account of masking. We can distinguish these alternatives by asking S to pay attention deliberately to some aspect of the situation. We might, for example, find that when he tries to pay attention to signal event *a*, we get

$$\overset{a}{\uparrow}: p(r_a)|I\{a]\&J\{b] > p(r_a)|I\{a]\&J\{b] \tag{18}$$

which indicates that at worst the masking component is a minor one. The masking effect itself can be estimated from

$$\left(p(r_a)|I\{a] \right) - \left((p(r_a)|I\{a]\&J\{b]) - (\overset{a}{\uparrow}: p(r_a)|I\{r_a]\&J\{b]) \right) \tag{19}$$

Other possible outcomes of extra analyses or experiments, taken with (16) above, show how alternative explanations of the phenomena may be characterised and eliminated. These are examples only, not a completely exhaustive account of all possible outcomes, and are intended to draw attention to the complexities of experiments on attention and how seldom these have been taken into account *explicitly* in the past.

Equation (16) gives us

$$p(r_aR_I)|I\{a]\&J\{b] < p(r_bR_J)|I\{a]\&J\{b] < p(r_bR_J)|J\{b] \tag{16}$$

and equation (14) gives us

$$p(R_I)|I \simeq p(R_J)|J \simeq 1\cdot0 \tag{14}$$

Suppose that we also find

$$\overset{I}{\uparrow}: p(r_aR_I)|I\{a]\&J\{b] > p(r_aR_I)|I\{a]\&J\{b] \tag{20}$$

$$\overset{I}{\uparrow}: p(R_I)|I\{a]\&J\{b] > p(R_I)|I\{a]\&J\{b] \tag{21}$$

$$\underset{\uparrow}{\mathbf{I}}: p(r_a)|I\{a]\&J\{b] = p(r_a)|I\{a]\&J\{b] \tag{22}$$

This combination of results shows that while S can select a region of input space and ignore another, to do so does not aid the detection of signal events occurring in that region of input space.

Instead of those results we might find the following:

$$\underset{\uparrow}{\mathbf{I}}: p(r_aR_I)|I\{a]\&J\{b] > p(r_aR_I)|I\{a]\&J\{b] \tag{23}$$

$$\underset{\uparrow}{\mathbf{I}}: p(R_I)|I\{a]\&J\{b] > p(R_I)|I\{a]\&J\{b] \tag{24}$$

$$\underset{\uparrow}{\mathbf{I}}: p(r_a)|I\{a]\&J\{b] > p(r_a)|I\{a]\&J\{b] \tag{25}$$

which would indicate that S can both attend to the region in input space where the signals are occurring, and also make use of that ability to enhance signal event detection.

Finally, consider the following set of results from the same experiment. (14) and (16) are assumed to be true as before, and in addition

$$\underset{\uparrow}{\mathbf{I}}: p(r_aR_I)|I\{a]\&J\{b] < p(r_aR_I)|I\{a]\&J\{b] < p(r_bR_J)|I\{a]\&J\{b] \tag{26}$$

$$\underset{\uparrow}{\mathbf{I}}: p(r_a)|I\{a]\&J\{b] < p(r_a)|I\{a]\&J\{b] \tag{27}$$

$$\underset{\uparrow}{\mathbf{I}}: p(R_I)|I\{a]\&J\{b] < p(R_I)|I\{a]\&J\{b] \tag{28}$$

$$\underset{\uparrow}{\mathbf{I}}: p(r_b)|I\{a]\&J\{b] > p(r_b)|I\{a]\&J\{b] \tag{29}$$

$$\underset{\uparrow}{\mathbf{I}}: p(R_J)|I\{a]\&J\{b] > p(R_J)|I\{a]\&J\{b] \tag{30}$$

Taken together these results indicate that the regions of input space can be discriminated by the nervous system and can be used by the observer for enhancing and depressing the detectability of signal events, despite the fact that voluntarily S cannot make use of the discriminability of the regions of input space. Although trying to pay attention to region I and detect signal *a*, S in fact pays attention to region J and detects signal *b*.

B

Rather than continue to multiply hypothetical examples in this way, we will look at only three more problems explicitly. These are to do with classes of events, timing, and attention to output rather than input.

We noted that Broadbent and Gregory (1964a) raised the question of attention not to sensory channels but to classes of stimuli. For example we might say to a subject, 'the numerals 0–9 will appear on one side of the field, and the letters r–z on the other side. Can you pay attention to the numbers and ignore the letters?' Consider the case where there is a set of events which occur in region I, defined as

$$a = (a_1, a_2, \ldots a_m)$$

and similarly a set of events

$$b = (b_1, b_2, \ldots b_m)$$

which occur in region J.

This is, in fact, the most common experimental design: see, for example, Cherry (1953), Moray (1959) and Treisman (1960). Two prose messages are presented to a listener and he is required to respond to one and ignore the other, the messages arriving in different regions of auditory space. Obviously such an experiment can be treated in terms of a rather than a with a great saving of computation and experimental time. So we can compute

$$p(raR_I)|I\{a]$$

just as we computed $\qquad p(r_aR_I)|I\{a]$

with the following equation giving the mean probability of response over the entire set.

$$p(raR_I)|I\{a]$$
$$= \frac{\sum(p(r_{a1})|I\{a_1] + p(r_{a2})|I\{a_2] + \ldots + p(r_{am})|I\{a_m])}{m} \quad (31)$$

However, we must now consider the following possible outcome of an experiment. Suppose that in a pilot experiment we establish that

$$p(ra)|I\{a] \simeq p(rb)|I\{b] \simeq 1 \cdot 0 \quad (32)$$

and then find, in the main experiment, that

$$p(ra)|I\{a\}\&I\{b\} < \underset{\uparrow}{I}: p(ra)|I\{a\}\&I\{b\} < p(ra)|I\{a\} \quad (33)$$

may we conclude, as is usually done, that $\underset{\uparrow}{I}$: results in an enhancement of the detectability of the single set? Obviously not! Suppose
we look at the data in a more fine-grained way, analysing the
individual members of the event set a. Although unlikely, it is
possible that the following table of probabilities might appear:

	a_1	a_2	a_3	a_4	a_5	
$p(r_a)|I\{a\}$	0·5	0·5	0·1	0·1	0·4	$p(ra) = 0·32$
$\underset{\uparrow}{I}: p(r_a)|I\{a\}$	0·8	0·2	0·4	0·0	0·3	$p(ra) = 0·34$

Clearly the probability of the individual members of the signal
event set should be checked. At the time of writing there seems to
be no experiment in the literature where this has been done. It is
probably true that in many of the experiments it can be assumed
that the distribution of probabilities among the members of the
two sets of signals does in fact remain stationary with time (for
example when the messages are prose chosen at random from the
works of an individual author, or when strings of random numbers
are used). The fact remains, however, that the problem of
differences in the relative detectability of the members of a set
ought to be treated explicitly in experiments on attention, either
by doing the control experiment, or by explicitly justifying the
lack of its necessity. Given this proviso, then calculations of

$$p(raR_1)|I\{a\}$$

provide a convenient short cut at some stages in the development
of the experimental design.

Questions of timing are of universal importance in experiments
on attention and have not received the treatment they deserve. The
establishment of the maximum rate at which attention may be
switched, or at least the explicit description of the effects of
different relative times of onset of signals, etc., seems to be one of
the most important outstanding problems. Let us consider the

following hypothetical experiment. We again find equations (13) and (16) to be satisfied, so that we have

$$p(r_aR_I)|I\{a\}\&J\{b\} < p(r_bR_J)|I\{a\}\&J\{b\} < p(r_bR_J)|J\{b\} \quad (16)$$

and let us assume an extended version of equation (14) also satisfied

$$p(R_I)|I\{a\}\&J\{b\} = p(R_J)|I\{a\}\&J\{b\} = p(R_I)|I \quad (14)$$

Now we add condition I: but instead of finding

$$\underset{\uparrow}{I}: p(r_a)|I\{a\}\&J\{b\} > p(r_a)|I\{a\}\&J\{b\} \quad (25)$$

throughout the experiment, we find that on odd numbered trials

$$\underset{\uparrow}{I}: p(r_a)|I\{a\}\&J\{b\} > p(r_a)I|\{a\}\&J\{b\}$$

and

$$\underset{\uparrow}{I}: p(r_b)|I\{a\}\&J\{b\} < p(r_b)|I\{a\}\&J\{b\}$$

while on even numbered trials

$$\underset{\uparrow}{I}: p(r_a)|I\{a\}\&J\{b\} < p(r_a)|I\{a\}\&J\{b\}$$

and

$$\underset{\uparrow}{I}: p(r_b)|I\{a\}\&J\{b\} > p(r_b)|I\{a\}\&J\{b\}$$

Dealing with performance *overall* we would decide that S cannot pay attention, since he was in one region half the time and the other region the other half. But consider the two cases where overall

$$\underset{\uparrow}{I}: p(r_a)|I\{a\}\&J\{b\} = p(r_b)|I\{a\}\&J\{b\} = 0.5 \quad (34)$$

In one there are some occasions where both responses are given, some where neither is given, and some where either one or the other but not both are given. In another experiment (34) holds true overall, but in half the trials the signals from region I are correctly identified and those from region J are incorrectly identified, and in half the trials the opposite is true, so that both the following are true for 50% of the run:

$$\underset{\uparrow}{\overset{I}{\uparrow}}: p(r_a)|I\{a]\&J\{b] = 1\cdot0$$

and

$$\underset{\uparrow}{\overset{I}{\uparrow}}: p(r_b)|I\{a]\&J\{b] = 0\cdot0 \tag{35}$$

$$\underset{\uparrow}{\overset{I}{\uparrow}}: p(r_a)|I\{a]\&J\{b] = 0\cdot0$$

and

$$\underset{\uparrow}{\overset{I}{\uparrow}}: p(r_b)|I\{a]\&J\{b] = 1\cdot0 \tag{36}$$

From the first version it appears that S cannot pay attention nor can the brain select one region at the expense of the other, since there is no systematic connection between trials and responses, except that overall only 50% of the signal events are identified. In the second case, however, (35) and (36) together may be interpreted to mean that, while voluntary attention appears to be effective in half the trials attention is involuntarily switched on the other half. In such a case we need to combine the two expressions to give a complete description of the experiment. Averaging overall will not do. Then,

$$\begin{cases} \underset{\uparrow}{\overset{I}{\uparrow}}: p(r_a)_T|I\{a]\&J\{b] > \underset{\uparrow}{\overset{I}{\uparrow}}: p(r_b)_T|I\{a]\&J\{b] \\ \underset{\uparrow}{\overset{I}{\uparrow}}: p(r_a)_t|I\{a]\&J\{b] < \underset{\uparrow}{\overset{I}{\uparrow}}: p(r_b)_t|I\{a]\&J\{b] \end{cases} \tag{37}$$

where the brace is used to indicate that the two expressions refer to the same experiment, T and t may be given numerical values to indicate particular times, and a complete analysis requires that it be established that the switch from r_a to r_b and back cannot be put down to masking, as outlined earlier. There is also the possibility that in certain experiments a value of 0·5 or some other fractional value for the probability of correct response might be used to indicate a partially correct response (for example the word 'cattle' for 'chattel' in a shadowing experiment); and the possibility of partially correct responses also requires explicit treatment, which will not be gone into here.

A final class of experiment is mentioned in order to introduce a part of the notation which has not been used so far. In these experiments, S is required to act as a generator and to emit signals without receiving any stimuli, according to some specified rule, while being required to monitor incoming information which is irrelevant to the generator task. (For example, see Baddeley, (1966).) Suppose that the detection task alone, and the generator task alone, are each errorless, but that when performed together

$$p(r_a R_I)|I\{a\}\&[b]J = p(r_a R_I)|I\{a\} \tag{38}$$

and

$$p(r_b R_J)|I\{a\}\&[b]J < p(r_b R_J)|[b]J \tag{39}$$

The expressions would describe the effect of the input on the output task.

Although the above notation is cumbersome it does emphasise the complexities and controls required in untangling the nature of selective attention. S may respond to a signal, a class of signals or a region of space, may store or transform the signals before output, and may generate signals for which there is no input set. Thinking about the implications of such a notation it will be apparent where the ambiguities in some of the attention experiments arise, and also why 'channel' has suffered the fate of 'set' as an over-extended term. This was noted of the latter word many years ago (Gibson, 1941). Furthermore it will be apparent to those who are familiar with the field that there are hardly any experiments which have included the full range of control experiments indicated. This may account to some extent for the amount of disagreement about the meaning of the experiments, which is evidenced by the use of identical experiments to support rival theories. Often it can be shown that assumptions are justified even if not explicitly stated. But the fact remains that while we are able to make some broad qualitative generalisations about attention we are sadly lacking in precise quantitative predictions.

There are a few more general problems of methodology which must be mentioned. The first is to do with the description of a signal event or signal space. A crucial factor in the ability of S to pay attention to a signal event or a region of signal space is the similarity of that signal event to others which are presented, and the similarity of one region of signal space to another. Separability is inversely related to similarity. We therefore need a measure of similarity. Two obvious candidates are correlation and confusion functions. If the signals are continuous wave forms their similarity over some given interval of time can be expressed as the correlation between the wave forms. If, on the other hand, the signals are discrete there are various functions which might be used to describe their mutual confusability, for example Crossman's function (Crossman, 1955). Since measures of the second kind may readily be applied also to continuous signals, while the reverse is not true, it may turn out to be best to standardise on some confusion function for all experiments on attention. It would be best if the measure could be applied both to the similarity between signals and also to the similarity between regions of signal space.

The next problem is one of terminology. It is perhaps not too harsh to say that, with the gradual extension to cover wider fields of language originally intended to apply to a fairly restricted information theoretical model of the human operator, terminology is at best confusing and at worst a mess. Words such as channel, line, dimension, message and so on appear almost indiscriminately from one writer to another, and often from one paper to another by a single author, applied apparently to one and the same aspect of an experiment. This is not so much a reflection of the quality of the experiments as it is due to the very rapid expansion of research, which has burst the banks of the original theory and flooded the surrounding conceptual countryside, leaving only here and there the tip of a recognisable and identifiable concept showing. Perhaps the following might be acceptable as a start towards clarification.

If S produces r_a when a is presented, let us say that S *identifies* a correctly.

If
$$\underset{\uparrow}{a} : p(r_a)|a > p(r_a)|a \tag{40}$$

we shall say that paying attention to a increases the probability of the correct identification of a, or increases the efficiency of identifying a.

To deal with the difference between voluntary and involuntary attention, we shall make use of the following inequalities:

if
$$\underset{\uparrow}{a} : p(r_a)|a > p(r_a)|a \tag{40}$$

then S is *paying attention* (can pay attention) to message (signal) a.

If
$$\underset{\uparrow}{I} : p(R_I)|I > p(R_I)|I \tag{41}$$

then S is *paying attention* (can pay attention) to region I of signal space.

And if $\quad\quad\quad \underset{\uparrow}{I}: p(r_a)|I\{a] > p(r_a)|I\{a]$ $\quad\quad\quad\quad$ (42)

then S can increase the efficiency of identifying *a* by paying attention to I of signal space region.

Consider now the case where S cannot make any difference to his performance by $\underset{\uparrow}{I}$:, but nonetheless there is a difference in the efficiency of identifying signals in different regions. (As an example consider binocular rivalry, where S cannot control which eye he is using to see at any given moment, but where identification of items appearing in the momentarily dominant eye will be better than those in the momentarily non-dominant eye: more generally the problem of attention being caught despite the application of $\underset{\uparrow}{a}$: or $\underset{\uparrow}{I}$:). In such cases, 'the brain can pay attention but its owner cannot'. Rather than settle for such a bizarre formulation we will say that where selection occurs but is not under the control of S, the S *can be tuned* to a certain region, signal or class of signals, or that S's *attention is caught by* such a region, signal or class of signals.

Finally we will use the word *detect* to imply the identification of the presence of a signal, class of signals or region of signal space when S cannot identify it: 'There is something there but I can't tell what it is.'

In summary then we have the terms *detect* and *identify* to describe the relation of response to signal, and *tuning* and *attention* to describe the involuntary and voluntary modes of that selectivity with which attention research concerns itself.

The final problem of method seems almost too obvious to mention, but is extremely important. It is the degree of sophistication of the people used as subjects. There is now some formal evidence (Moray and Jordan, 1966) to suggest that practice can markedly alter the capacity of subjects to select and to switch between channels. Furthermore, although this has not been mentioned in much of the published work, those who are experimenters in this field quite certainly reach levels of performance in time sharing tasks which are an order of magnitude or so better than naive subjects. This factor has not been mentioned in any theories so far. Our theories are theories for unpractised subjects.

When large scale parametric studies begin to appear it will be difficult to compare their outcome to those experiments which have already been published, because in the course of many trials the subjects will not stay in a steady state but alter progressively. There is a great need for explicit study in this area. Furthermore in many cases an experiment may ruin an observer as a subject for future experiments on attention. If for example he is told to ignore one message which is only to distract him, and he is then asked about that message at the end of the run, it is extremely difficult for him to ignore it on subsequent runs: he will tend to time share. The only obvious way around these problems is to ensure an adequate supply of subjects, and for experimenters to keep as detailed a log as possible of each subject's past experimental history, *and report this when publishing the research,* including total number of hours and approximate number of signals. Finally, there is good reason to believe that altering payoffs may be very important, and that the way in which subjects interpret instructions may make very large differences to experiments such as these.

Kinschler has recently reported on 'Attention Operating Characteristic' with interesting properties which represents a further step towards quantifying attentional measures, and takes into account false alarms, which were not discussed in this section. See Kinschler, R., 1970, in *Attention and Performance III*, ed. Sanders, A. North-Holland Publishing Co., Amsterdam.

3 A REVIEW OF CURRENT THEORIES
OF ATTENTION

There are at present some six theories of selective attention current in the literature, of which three allow a detailed examination of their predictions. These theories will be presented before the review of experimental data so that the reader can remind himself of the position of the theorists while reading about experiments designed to support or test them. After presenting the experimental data in subsequent chapters we shall return to an evaluation of the theories.

Broadbent's theory

In the closing chapters of *Perception and Communication* Broadbent (1958) summarised the conclusions he had reached in the form of a flow diagram model, the so-called 'Filter Theory' of attention. Figure 2 is based on his formulation. Although he has subsequently modified it somewhat, the model will here be presented in its original form, and the main difference between the earlier and later versions noted in passing.

Information enters the system through a number of parallel sensory channels. In addition to obvious channels such as the left and right auditory nerves the visual pathways, etc., a channel may also be a position in auditory space or a wave envelope of a particular fundamental frequency or similar *functional* channels. These are presumed to have a distinct neural representation somewhere in the brain, which allows messages to be selected on the basis of their pitch, loudness, and spatial position characteristics. Later in the system there is a limited capacity channel, in the information theory sense, whose capacity is very much smaller than the total capacity of the initial parallel input lines. Hence there must be either a loss of information between the parallel inputs and the later parts of the system, or some form of recoding

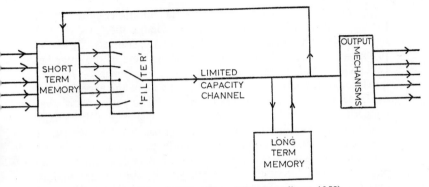

FIG. 2. Broadbent's filter theory (after Broadbent, 1958)

is required to overcome the bottleneck. Broadbent postulates a short term memory store at the inner end of the parallel input lines, followed by the filter. The filter has the ability to select one of the input lines and allow its information direct access to the limited capacity channel. Lines which are not so selected will hold their messages in the short term memory store for a period 'of the order of seconds', during which time the representation becomes progressively degraded so that signals which remain in the store for some time before being allowed into the further parts of the system will, when they eventually do enter it, be liable to be read erroneously.

It will be observed that this system allows a parallel to serial recoding of messages, so that overloading of the limited capacity channel is prevented by serialising the input to it. There is provision for returning signals which have passed through the limited capacity channel to the short term store again ('rehearsal' whether conscious and deliberate or unconscious), and there is access to and from the long term store of learnt associations ('long term memory') at the end of the limited capacity channel. At the downstream end of the channel there is also access to the motor response system. The part of the system which is concerned with the analysis of particular patterns, such as heard words, and with the conscious perception of the signals by the observer is not made explicit. It seems likely from the description of the system as a whole that this is the limited capacity channel itself, since the recognition of an incoming signal necessarily implies access to long term memory.

Several suggestions are made as to the conditions under which the filter will switch channels. These include the sudden arrival of new signals on a hitherto unoccupied channel, contextually highly probable signals, and so on. The switching time of the filter between channels is to be of the order of 0·25 seconds.

Although the model is based on the whole of the experimental evidence reviewed in the book, a crucial experiment is that concerned with the handling of messages consisting of three pairs of digits, one member of each pair being presented to one ear at the same time that the other member of the pair is presented to the opposite ear (Broadbent, 1954). It is on this experiment that the parallel to serial recoding strategy, and its timing, are mainly based. (This experiment has come to be called the 'split span' experiment.)

The major alteration to the model has been the generalisation of the notion of channel. Owing to the work of Gray and Wedderburn (1960), Treisman (1964) and his own later work (Broadbent and Gregory (1964)), Broadbent now considers that the channels which the filter may select are much more varied in kind than originally envisaged; they include verbal classes, languages, etc.

Treisman's theory

The main source of Treisman's theory is the series of experiments (Cherry, 1953; Moray, 1959; Treisman, 1960; 1964a, b, and c) using the technique of speech shadowing and dichotic presentation. Usually the dichotomy has been between a message presented to one ear and another message presented to the other ear. Shadowing consists of asking a listener to repeat a prose message while he hears it, rather than waiting until it finishes. It therefore approaches a steady state as regards the loading of the perceptual system and is very powerful technique for locking a subject's attention on to the required message.

Several versions of Treisman's model are available: the version presented in Figure 3 is a composite of them.

The general outline of the model owes much to Broadbent's formulation, but can be thought of as making more explicit the selection rules governing the action of the filter, and also the problem of identifying particular signals when they occur.

Information again flows into the organism through a number of parallel channels. The messages reach some part of the nervous system where they are analysed for crude physical properties, such as loudness, pitch, position, colour, brightness, etc. The information resulting from this analysis is available to conscious perception and for reporting by the subject, regardless of what happens to the message beyond this point. As well as extracting such characteristics the mechanism can act to attenuate the signal strength of the output from these analysers, and it is in this way

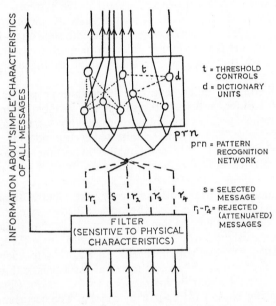

FIG. 3. Treisman's input selection

that the filter operates. If a listener has been told to listen to one ear then all other output lines from the position analyser pass only weakened signals; if selection is of a male voice, then the lines from the 'voice quality' (first formant pitch?) analyser will attenuate any signals which do not have the requisite quality. Signals are in essence sorted along the various dimensions which the filter can select, and the output lines run from different positions along the dimensions.

The weakened messages and the one unweakened message pass deeper into the nervous system and eventually reach the pattern recogniser. This consists of a large number of 'dictionary units'. It was conceived as an adaptive, self-organising pattern recogniser with properties similar to those proposed by Uttley (1955). Messages entering it traverse a logical tree with probabilistic nodes; when they reach the end of the tree a single dictionary unit 'fires' and the word is recognised by the observer. It appears from the model that the firing of a dictionary unit and the conscious perception of the word are the same event (given that the necessary level of overall arousal, etc., is present in the system), although this is not made explicit. It is on the basis of the firing of the dictionary unit that the response is made, although again it is not explicit whether the dictionary units are themselves also response units, or whether they trigger other units on the output side of the mechanism.

The dictionary units have two important properties. Their thresholds differ, and their thresholds are variable. Some units have thresholds which are always considerably lower than those of the majority. The dictionary units which respond to the occurrence of biologically (or emotionally) important signals have permanently lowered thresholds. Therefore, even if such a signal has arrived along a line whose signal strength has been attenuated by the filter it will trigger its dictionary unit. Neutral signals will will not be able to trigger their appropriate dictionary units owing to their signal strength having been attenuated by the filter; but unattenuated signals will be able to do so and hence the message which they compose will be heard. In addition to such semi-permanent threshold differences transient variations in thresholds may be brought about by instructions to the subject ('listen for the following kind of words'), or by context. The occurrence of a particular signal will, if it triggers a dictionary unit, lower the threshold for other signals which in the past have occurred in association with it. Therefore, highly probable signals arriving over an attenuated channel will be able to trigger the dictionary units. Characteristics such as the language to which a message belongs are extracted only at the level of this dictionary.

It will be seen that this theory postulates selection during input by the attenuation of incoming rejected messages, and that attention is in fact a two stage process, since first there is filtering on the basis of the channel characteristics, and second by the threshold settings of the dictionary units. No account is given of switching times of either the filter or the dictionary settings.

The theory of Deutsch and Deutsch

Drawing on exactly the same experimental data as Treisman, Deutsch and Deutsch (1963) have proposed what is often called a 'response selection' theory of selective attention. Their main criticism of Treisman's model is that it is redundant, and that by suitably altering the properties of the dictionary the lower level filter is made unnecessary. It is important to examine this model with great care, since there are one or two details which are vital to

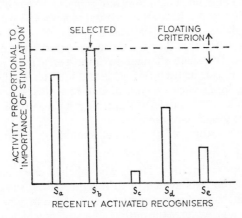

FIG. 4. Deutsch and Deutsch's selection model (after Deutsch and Deutsch, 1963)

understanding its predictions. As a flow diagram it could be represented by the same diagram as that used for Treisman's model, except that the filter for physical characteristics would be omitted and the input lines run without interruption directly to the dictionary. However we also require Figure 4, based on the Deutschs' own diagram, to describe the workings of the dictionary.

At the dictionary each signal is analysed and recognised for the particular signal which it is. The output activity of the recogniser which has fired is proportional to the *importance* of the signal to the organism; the dictionary unit fires the more strongly the more important the stimulus is, not necessarily the more strongly it is stimulated. The importance weighting is a function of past experience. All signals pass this stage. The output from the dictionary is inspected, and the unit firing most strongly is allowed to transmit to the further stages of the mechanism; thus the most important stimulus captures the attention. Only if another unit begins to fire more strongly will the first be displaced; otherwise it will continue to occupy the output lines until its stimulation by the incoming signal ceases. Thus the most important signal both captures the system and in a sense sets the criterion for any other signal to surpass. In addition, access for the output from the dictionary to further stages of the mechanism is limited by the general level of arousal. If the general level of arousal is very low (as in sleep) only the most important signals will be able to trigger the output lines. As the level of arousal increases so will more and more signals be able to have access to the response side of the system, providing that they are the most important at the moment they occur. Transient changes in importance may be brought about by context, instructions, etc., and long term differences by learning as in Treisman's system, but here linked conceptually to Deutsch's (1960) model for learning by means of which the 'importance weightings' are altered.

One more feature of the model should be carefully noted. Deutsch and Deutsch (1963) say

> If we suppose that only signals whose height corresponds to the height of the level switch in further processes, such as motor output, memory storage, and whatever else it may be that leads to awareness, we have the outline of a system which will display the type of behaviour we associate with attention.

That is, the most important message produces an output whose level is matched to a corresponding level in an output mechanism, which then transmits the message *to the level where the subject is consciously aware of the nature of the signal.* So in this theory recognition by the pattern recognising mechanisms of the brain of the precise nature of an incoming signal occurs at an earlier stage than that at which the observer is conscious of the nature of the signal. Pattern recognition precedes conscious perception and is not identical with it. Rather, perception is a response to the output of the pattern recogniser. The fact that the observer is not aware of what signal was presented is not, on this model, evidence that that signal has not been analysed. This feature makes for certain difficulties in designing crucial experiments to distinguish it from Treisman's but these can probably be overcome. Those interested in the full implications of the model should consult the earlier book (Deutsch, 1960) to understand the way in which the importance weightings become attached to the stimuli.

Deutsch (personal communication, 1968) does not agree that their model is a response selection model, but regards it as selecting incoming signals in the same sense in which Treisman's model does.

We turn now to three theories which are less precisely stated than those so far discussed.

Reynolds' theory

Reynolds (1964) proposed another response selection theory. His work is interesting in that he drew both on visual and on auditory work in formulating the model, which is not true of the models so far discussed. He divides previous theorising into three classes: stimulus orientated (filter theory), organismic (expectancy theory) and response theory, and proceeds to elaborate the latter. Starting from a consideration of stereopsis, and considering the fact that if one eye is presented with a red field and the other with a green field the most common effect is rivalry, he concludes,

> Even though stimuli were presented simultaneously to the subject, he responds to them successively. This is not due to some verbal impediment resulting from the inability of the subject to say red and green simultaneously, but reflects a genuine perceptual process which involves a temporary inhibition of response.

This last mentioned 'temporary inhibition of response' is in fact Reynolds' theory. It will be obvious that while probably true in some sense it has little explanatory or predictive value. It is not even entirely clear that Reynolds is consistent throughout in his adoption of a response orientated theory. For example when speaking of the fact that a listener will tend to hear his own name when it is presented in an unattended message (Moray, 1959) he says that a response to one's own name is more readily elicitable than a response to other signals. Other irrelevant messages are not heard because they are not potent elicitors of responses, and, in fact,

> ... the experimenter has told the subject to disregard that part of the stimulus input.

which is surely the description of an organismic rather than a response directed model.

A final quotation will serve to underline the weakness of Reynolds' approach.

> When the subject is presented with an 'easy' situation . . . the response pattern flows smoothly with few delays or errors in response. At 'harder' levels the subject either attempts some organisation of stimulus inputs . . . or some selection of response output based on the potency of the eliciting response pattern; in both cases delays in response (temporary inhibition of response) are involved, *almost by definition* (italics mine).

The problem is that the italicised phrase is all too true throughout Reynolds' paper, and like all theories which are true by definition it loses in explanatory power what it gains in internal consistency. The theory, in fact, merely redescribes the phenomena at the same level of language.

Egeth's review

It would not be fair to criticise Egeth's (1967) paper on the grounds of inadequate theorising, since he himself makes no claim to be putting forward a complete theory. Rather he is concerned to review the field of data available. However, he does in the end draw attention to the ideas of Lawrence (1963) and the formulation of the reception of stimuli in terms of the 'stimulus-as-coded'. He seems to imply that the understanding of attention lies in the discovery of the coding and decoding rules which are applied from moment to moment by the observer who is being bombarded with information; and that attention is in fact the application of such coding rules, arranged in a hierarchy through which data is transferred and transformed until finally recognition and response are obtained.

> As it stands now, the coding-response hypothesis is a rather general qualitative theory of behaviour; one of the important tasks of future research is the exact specification of the coding responses which enable subjects to respond selectively to specified portions of complex stimuli. (Egeth, 1967)

These ideas seem intuitively rather important and are perhaps best seen as convergent to the problems more usually attacked in attention research. It is to be hoped that Egeth will be able to elaborate them more fully, for they bear relations to several other theories and are clearly relevant to some of the most striking features of attentional phenomena. They are closely related to the ideas put forward by Miller, Galanter and Pribam (1960) in *Plans and the Structure of Behaviour,* and mark the realisation that in adaptive systems, such as human beings, information flow models will only be applicable if a great deal more is known about the mechanisms which control the flow of information through the system. One thing that recent research, using information theory, has shown clearly is that concentration on the communication channel itself as if it were an entirely passive transmission line is inadequate for an understanding of the limits of performance (Moray, 1967).

Neisser's theory

Neisser (1967) has published what is to date the most extensive review since *Perception and Communication,* not only of the attention literature but also of fields which border upon attention, and in particular emphasising the active cognitive aspects of selection. For Neisser, as for many earlier psychologists, the problems raised by the selective and adaptive response of the observer to the arrival of large amounts of information are central to psychology. However, the particular kind of work with which the present monograph is concerned is dismissed by Neisser as 'preattentional selection'. The name 'attention' is reserved for a complex, active process of analysis-by-synthesis which Neisser regards as the central ability of the cognitive mechanisms of the brain. It is too early to say whether his approach will prove fruitful, but there is no doubt that it raises some interesting questions. We shall see later that there is abundant evidence that attention mechanisms act as if making the 'best bet' over the interpretation of certain kinds of rejected signals, and an explanation of this ability to handle very noisy situations, or degraded messages, might well benefit from invoking something akin to Neisser's ideas. There does not, however, at present seem to be a basis for a predictive model of selective attention, despite the large amount of space which he gives in the book to the relevant work. The book is however an outstanding review of recent literature and a provocative and interesting synthesis of that work. It would seem that in one respect his insistence on the constructive character of recognition (a position which he shares with Sayre, 1965) would lead him to reject outright the Deutsches insistence on complete analysis below the perceptual level; even Treisman's position does not fit the analysis-by-synthesis model particularly well.

This ends the review of current theories. The three most important are the older ones, those of Broadbent, Treisman and the Deutsch's. Of these most discussion has been of the latter two, although many people working in the rather different fields of reaction times, skills, and short term memory still refer directly to Broadbent's original formulation. Perhaps the other two theories may best be seen as attempting to provide the contents of the 'black box' labelled 'filter' in Broadbent's model. It will be noted that all the theories discussed are qualitative ones, usually flow diagram models. There has yet to emerge a general theory of selectivity which is quantitative, although as we shall see there are one or two limited successes in this endeavour. Probably the time is not yet ripe for a large scale quantitative model, but there seems to be enough work in existence to hold out the hope that in the not too distant future, perhaps within five or ten years, one may be constructed and that eventually a chapter such as this will be reviewing an equally large array of quantitative models.

Two more recent books should now be consulted. The first is *Memory and Attention*, Norman, D., 1969, Wiley, N.Y. The second is *Attention in Learning*, Trabasso, T., and Bower, G., 1969, Wiley, N.Y. The latter provides the first example of a quantitative functional model as distinct from the qualitative, structural models outlined in this chapter. See also a chapter in *Ann. Rev. Psychol.* 1970 by Swets, J. and Kristofferson, A.

In this chapter and later ones the question with which we are essentially concerned is this: under what conditions can an observer increase the probability of receiving one message at the expense of others which may be present at the same time? In terms of the notation developed in Chapter 2, given that we are conducting an experiment which may be described by

$$\underset{\uparrow}{I}: p(r_a R_I)|I\{a\} + J\{b\} > p(r_a R_I)|I\{a\} + J\{b\}$$

what sorts of signals may constitute a and what regions of signal space may be the location of I?

Available evidence about selective listening may be divided roughly into two classes on the basis of the relation between the presentation of the signals and the way in which and time in which an answer is required. The first group of experiments was comprehensively reviewed by Broadbent (1958). It consists of experiments, frequently inspired by real life situations such as the reception of messages by air traffic controllers and the like, in which listeners first hear several messages simultaneously and then are asked to reply by repeating or answering the messages of one or more of them. Because of the excellent coverage by Broadbent this work will only be outlined; the interested reader should consult *Perception and Communication* for a fuller treatment and also an extensive bibliography. The second class of experiments are those conducted by Cherry (1953), Moray (1959 et seq.) and Treisman (1960 et seq.) and others. And it is on these that much of the recent theorising has been based. These comprise the 'shadowing' experiments in which the listener is asked to repeat back relatively long messages while receiving them. They have sometimes been called 'verbal tracking' experiments, a name which aptly describes their essential features.

Listen and answer experiments

Certain dimensions of a stimulus are properties which could refer to signal space defined within a single sense organ. If we think of the most general description of an auditory signal, a complex series of longitudinal pressure waves received at a single ear, we can, of course, describe it in terms of its Fourier components and their frequency, amplitude, and phase; and subjectively in terms of its pitch and loudness. We might then ask whether a listener can select one of two messages on the basis of its frequency or loudness. It seems fairly clear that two pure sine waves cannot be distinguished monaurally only on the basis of phase differences, although, of course, if presented simultaneously the phase differences may be recognisable as differences of loudness or timbre. The same questions may be asked of most such signals when they occur in the fused binaural space which is produced by feeding identical signals to the two ears. Indeed it seems that in certain cases, such as extreme lateralisation of a binaural sound image, it may not be possible to distinguish a monaural from a binaural input. However, in so far as there are some parts of the nervous system which receive only unilateral direct representation of an incoming message, and contralateral information only via one or more interneurones, it is possible in theory that selection could occur prior to any interaction, within the signal space of the sense organ itself. (Hernandez-Peon et al. (1956) indeed argued on the basis of physiological evidence that such selection was possible, claiming to have a recorded it directly. We shall see there are very grave objections to thus interpreting their experiments.)

There is rather surprisingly little work of this kind using pure tone and other simple signals. The literature on auditory psychophysics is, of course, very large indeed; but where more than one signal has been presented the experiments have usually been concerned with the masking of one tone or other signal by a second; and as we saw in Chapter 2, such 'selectivity' is not to be confused with voluntary selective attention; there are straightforward methods for distinguishing one effect from another. It is, however, unfortunate that little work on attention has used simple signals. If there is indeed tuning or attention at the most peripheral levels the most likely way for it to occur would be by the selective tuning of some part of the basilar membrane and the receptors connected with it. It is known that centrifugal fibres run right out to the cochlea itself (Galambos, 1955) although the details of their function in normal intact animals is as yet uncertain. It is not beyond the bounds of possibility, although at present beyond the bounds of evidence, that in attending to the lower of two tones, for example, one end of the basilar membrane might be selectively inhibited. It may be that a close scrutiny of the work on critical bands and masking would be able to throw light on such a possibility. If the critical bands are not centred on absolute values (as are the filters in, say, an octave band analyser) but have peaks which may be moved this would be evidence for the possibility of direct tuning at or near the cochlea. While the decisive evidence does not seem to exist, there is some evidence that there may be such tuning at the level of the cochlear nucleus (Allanson & Whitfield, 1956).

Swets (1963) has noted that many of the experiments on the critical band model of hearing imply some degree of voluntary control over the sensitivity of the auditory mechanisms for pure tone analysis. An observer performs better in signal detection tasks when he has prior information about the physical characteristics of the signal, and his behaviour alters in a way which suggests that the changes are brought about on the receptive side of the system. If signals of two frequencies are used, on each trial only one of them being present, and the order of presentation randomised, then detection is improved by telling the listener before each trial which signal may be next presented, although telling him afterwards does not help. Cues about frequency, loudness, time of arrival, etc., when given in advance can raise human performance to within 3 dB of that predicted for an ideal observer, whereas complete uncertainty lowers performance to about 12–15 dB below the ideal observer. Swets discusses several approaches to the question of voluntary tuning and how it might occur.

There are two experiments on divided attention using pure tones, which yielded rather surprising results. Odenthal (1961) measured the DL for pitch when the standard tone was presented to one ear and the comparison tone to the other. He claimed that below 1000 Hz the DL is about 14 Hz, and that it then rises steadily until with the standard at about 1500 Hz the DL is some 60 or 70 Hz. This would seem to suggest that separation of the signals reduces the accuracy with which they can be compared, for the corresponding binaural DL below 1500 Hz is fairly constant in the range of 3–5 Hz. If Odenthal's results are correct, then clearly the separation of input would be expected to aid the selection and separation of messages, since where we find that two messages cannot be efficiently compared with one another, we may reasonably expect that the opposite will hold—they will be readily separable. However, Odenthal's experiment has several rather peculiar features, and it needs to be replicated before its results can be accepted. For example, it is not clear why when the separation of frequencies was very small the listeners did not hear very marked changes in the quality of the signals, shifts of lateralisation, binaural beats and so on, which would have provided very strong cues for there being a difference between the signals arriving at the two ears. Odenthal makes no mention of such things.

The second experiment is one by Ingham (1957). Listeners were required to perform a DL for pitch on one ear and a DL for loudness on the other, under different conditions of attention. Ingham could find little or no difference in threshold with changes in the distribution of attention, depending on whether the listener was paying attention to or away from the message where the target signal occurred. This is at first sight rather remarkable, since intuitively one would expect that if attention has any effect it would be to alter thresholds. Otherwise why does one not attend to everything at once? However, workers in the shadowing field have found results which seem to confirm Ingham's report, and only very recently have any contradictory results begun to appear (Moray, 1969b, d). In shadowing experiments it is common to find that although the content of rejected messages cannot be reported their overall physical characteristics can be.

Partly due to the emphasis of much of the research on real life situations (where pure sinusoids are rare) and partly due to the necessary use of speech in shadowing experiments, we have extremely little data on the psychoacoustics of attention. Herman (1965) provides one exception, but apart from the experiments mentioned earlier and carried out primarily with other aims in mind the whole question of threshold changes under different conditions of attention must be regarded as being in a state of appalling inadequacy. This is the more unfortunate since it is becoming abundantly clear that such data must be the basis of a quantitative theory of attention.

Very few experiments exist even using speech, when we consider truly monaural, as distinct from single message, input. The majority of experiments on selection by means of pitch, loudness, voice quality, etc., have used binaural presentation, either over headphones or by means of a loudspeaker. There is one study, however, which systematically examined the difference between monaural and dichotic performance in some detail, and that is the set of experiments by Egan, Carterette and Thwing (1954). They investigated the effectiveness of spatial localisation, bandpass filtering, and the relative loudness of two messages as means of enhancing their separability. Two monaural studies were included. In the first, the listeners heard prose messages or pairs of short sentences preceded by call sign ('Langley Base we must all vote on Tuesday': 'Mitchell Field the fur of many cats is used'). The messages were recorded by a single male speaker, presented monaurally and began simultaneously. The experiment required the listeners to write down the message received from a specified source (Langley Base or Mitchell Field), and from their performance an articulation score was derived based on the per cent correct identification of the messages. High pass filtering of either the target message or the interfering message improved the articulation score, the improvement being greater when the interfering message was filtered. In the absence of filtering the articulation score was about 50%. Filtering the target message increased this to around 70%, and filtering the interfering message improved articulation score to over 90%.

In a second experiment the messages were differentiated by their respective loudness. When the target message was louder than the interfering message the articulation score rose rapidly, and a +10 dB difference in favour of the target message gave virtually perfect performance. Egan et al. noted that the curve relating performance to relative intensities appeared to have a sudden change of slope in the region where the messages were equally loud, and in fact from 0 to −10 dB signal to noise ratios there was almost no change in the articulation score. Outside this range on either side the slope was of the order of 4% change in articulation score per dB. As they observe, it is reasonable to interpret this to mean that any difference, even the fact that the target message is slightly quieter than the interfering one, allows the message and call sign to be identified as being part of one and the same stimulus sequence, and so the improved identification cues actually offset over a small range the increasing masking of the target by the interfering message.

These two results indicate clearly that selection of a message can be made on the basis of frequency spectrum differences and loudness differences in the case of monaural presentation. Confirmation comes from Spieth, Curtis and Webster (1954) for binaurally presented messages. It is, however, not immediately clear whether selection is with respect to the feature itself (loudness of spectrum difference) or with respect to the message, once the physical cues have allowed the message to be identified. The point was made in Chapter 2 that either the region of signal space or the message within that region might be the actual object of selection. There is some reason to think that in the experiments just described the difference in quality allows the message to be identified, and thereafter it is to the message that attention is paid. Broadbent (1952) in another call-sign experiment found that his listeners could select the message which began with a particular call-sign, even if the voice speaking that call-sign alternated from one trial to another. If it is the message which is being selected, then the experiments do not provide evidence for selection within monaural space in the sense referred to earlier in the chapter, for selection would involve the handling of the speech signals as such, a level of analysis which certainly requires the higher levels of the brain. Cherry (1953) emphasises the point. He played two messages recorded by the same speaker over a single channel at equal loudnesses to listeners who were asked to report what they heard. The messages were composed of strings of clichés taken from political speeches. It is characteristic of such material that it has very high redundancy within a cliché, but low transitional probability from one cliché to the next. Cherry's listeners were able, with practice, to identify the messages cliché by cliché, but were unable to separate the string of clichés which constituted one message from the string which constituted the other. While a message was identifiable as such it could be selected, but where there was ambiguity about what constituted the next part of the verbal sequence selectivity broke down. The point has been well summarised by Egan et al.:

A speech signal, whether it be a single word or a meaningful sentence, can be considered as made up of a series of events, suitably chosen, having certain conditional probabilities among them. These probabilities have relatively high values as compared with the conditional probabilities of the corresponding events in a random series. Furthermore, when speech is masked by noise the conditional probabilities between events in the speech series and the events in the noise series are relatively low in value.

The same applies, of course, to the probabilities of the events within one sentence compared with the probabilities of mutual occurrence of events within one sentence and the events within another unconnected sentence occurring simultaneously. As Broadbent, 1958, p. 14, has remarked:

> The listener is apparently making use of the transitional probabilities between words and phrases, a factor which is clearly not sensory.

It has been remarked by a number of workers (for example, Broadbent, 1952) that the greatest difficulty in these binaural multichannel experiments seems to be in identifying the relevant message. Once a listener has picked up the message which he is trying to hear, staying with it usually presents relatively little difficulty. We might also add that Tolhurst and Peters (1956) found that in either binaural or dichotic listening to two messages, where the listener was 'passive' and had no indication as to which he should select, there was a simple and direct relation between the relative intensities of the two messages, such that the louder of the two messages always showed the higher reception score.

The above evidence seems to indicate that features such as pitch, loudness and perhaps rhythm can help a listener to identify one of two or more messages which are presented either monaurally or binaurally; after this the structure of the message itself allows the listener to continue to select it. In other words, it is to the *message* that attention is being paid rather than to signals of a particular pitch or loudness:

$$\text{Instructions:} \quad \overset{I}{\underset{\uparrow}{}} : (r_a) | I\{a\} + J\{b\}$$

$$\text{Performance:} \quad \overset{a}{\underset{\uparrow}{}} : (r_a) | I\{a\} + J\{b\}$$

Although there are casual observations and implications from other experiments (e.g. Treisman, 1964a) the writer knows of no direct attempt to establish how well a listener can make use of or identify the actual characteristics of a message. We do not know whether a person can increase his chances of detecting the presence and content of a message of specified pitch or loudness by paying attention to that pitch and loudness, as distinct from paying attention to a message *of* that pitch and loudness. There are obvious methodological difficulties in such an investigation.

Frequency and loudness, then, can help in paying attention, if only by aiding the identification of a message to be received. However, the most effective dimension so far discovered along which a message may be located for selection is without doubt position in auditory space. The most effective way in which humans handle the 'cocktail party problem' (as Cherry has called it) in which one listens to one voice out of a number which are speaking at the same time, is undoubtedly by using the fact that the different sources occupy different positions in space.

The majority of recent work on auditory selectivity has used separation of the messages in auditory space, either by localisation or by lateralisation. Many of the studies on auditory control tower reception have emphasised the importance of the localisation

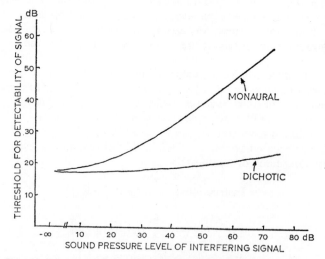

FIG. 5. Advantage of dichotic presentation for detecting a signal in competing noise (after Egan et al., 1954)

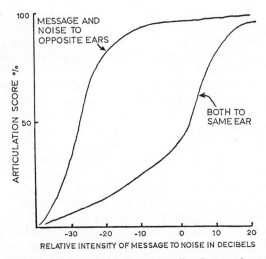

FIG. 6. Beneficial effect of dichotic presentation for speech reception
(after Egan et al., 1954)

variable in selection, both through the provision of 'pull-down' facilities, and also through investigations of the spacing of loudspeaker arrays. (See Broadbent, 1958, for references.) We may again look to the study by Egan et al. (1954) for a typical result. Figures 5 and 6 summarize their results. Figure 5 shows the detectability of the presence of one message in the presence of another; figure 6 the articulation score for one message in the presence of another. 'Dichotic' is the name for the condition in which one message is presented to one ear and the other to the opposite ear. Using this data we can establish that listeners can in theory listen to the ear, and not just to the message in the ear. From the work of Cherry and Sayers (1956) we can establish that when sound sources are separated by more than 10° there is a negligible chance of mistaking the direction from which a sound arrives. Furthermore, experiments on shadowing which we shall consider below show that a listener can disregard a change in the position of a message, and leave that message, retaining its position as the characteristic which determines reception (Treisman 1960). In this case the region of signal space itself, and not just the message in that region, is selectable. Broadbent (1958) has noted that spatial separation may not be advantageous if more than one of the messages calls for a response. This is in line with a general principle about selection: in so far as messages are confusable they may be both received; in so far as they are separable, and do not interfere with one another, they are difficult to handle simultaneously.

Some recent experiments have slightly complicated the picture of the way in which spatial selectivity works. Following on the demonstration by Sperling (1960) that post-stimulus cueing could lead to the retrieval of unusually large amounts of material in visual span of apprehension tasks, Moray et al. (1965) performed an analogous experiment in hearing. They presented lists of letters at a rate of two per second per channel, over each of four spatially separated sources, and required listeners to recall either all the letters that they could, or only the letters which came on immediately after the end of the last of the stimuli. They found that here again post-stimulus cueing restored its value to about eight. It seems from this result that wherever the mechanism operates to select a message from a region of auditory space it must be far enough into the nervous system for there to be at least a transitory store, perhaps what Neisser (1967) has called an 'echoic' store, prior to what is usually thought to be the post-perceptual short term memory store. We shall see later that there is abundant evidence that incoming rejected messages can pass information to very high levels in the nervous system.

As regards 'Listen and Answer' experiments, then, we may take it as established that the kinds of cues which intuitively seem reasonable candidates for the role can in fact assist attention. Differences in messages along the dimensions of pitch, loudness, semantic continuity and localisation all help and can be used by the attention mechanism. The obvious qualitative generalisation to which this leads is the plausible one that any feature which helps to distinguish one message from another will make it more probable that one message can be selected and another rejected. The task remains to establish the full range of differences which can be so used and to scale the signal space involved. In this respect it is interesting to consider another experiment by Broadbent (1955) which shows some cases where the differences are not sufficient. He presented to listeners a number of dichotic stimuli which were derived from single messages by means of various distortions. Using 18 listeners he found that 15 of them fused the sound of a metronome when the frequencies below 400 Hz were sent to one ear and the frequencies above 2000 Hz to the other. Eight listeners fused the sound of a male voice intoning the vowel /i/ when the two inputs were in random phase relationships and 10 when they were in phase. None fused speech filtered similarly to the metronome when the low frequencies followed the high frequencies by 0·25 seconds, and none fused a pure tone of 3000 Hz with one of 500 Hz.

This raises a kind of difference which we have not so far discussed, namely the timing of the messages. There is no doubt that, if all else is equal, the one of a pair of messages which starts earlier has a very high probability of being selected. During the period before the second message starts it is virtually, perhaps completely, impossible to avoid hearing the message which has begun. It is interesting to note that Schubert and Parker (1955) found that in listening to a message which was being switched between the ears it helped to have noise in the non-signal ear, as though it is easier to listen away from one message and to another than merely to a selected message; although it is also possible to interpret this result as relating to some kind of inhibitory effect of the end of a signal.

There are several studies of temporal priority, overlapping messages, etc., which show that the earlier of two messages, especially if also marked out by loudness or other differences, will tend to have priority (Broadbent, 1958; Spieth, Curtis and Webster, 1954; Poulton, 1956). Further, answering a prior question interferes with the reception of a second question, and messages which are interleaved (abababab), are harder to receive even at slow speeds than the same messages in sequential order (aaaabbbb) where the messages are sentences. Much of the work of temporal order using sentences or lists seems more related to short term memory effects than to the selective process as such, and therefore will not be extensively treated here. Interested readers may consult Broadbent (1958) for a review of the ealier work, and Moray (1969a) for some of the more recent work.

Selective listening and shadowing studies

We turn now to a series of experiments using the technique of speech shadowing. It is on these experiments that most of the recent theorising has been based. But it must be admitted that, while fascinating and having at least to some degree a 'real life' quality as distinct from the rather puritan stimuli of tone bursts and white noise frequently used in psychoacoustics, the experimental data perhaps cannot under close inspection really support the weight of the conceptual edifices which have been erected upon them.

Two papers published in 1953, one by Cherry, and one by Poulton, mark the beginning of speech shadowing, the technique of asking a listener to repeat aloud a continuous message while hearing it. Poulton found that his subjects spoke jargon when performing the required task, although under the impression that they were correctly repeating the messages which they heard. It is important to note this result. It is unique among the work on shadowing, in which it has generally been found that listeners can repeat the heard message perfectly well, even in the presence of a competing message. The reason for the discrepancy will be discussed in a later chapter. Cherry's results are more typical. He asked the listener to repeat a message heard through one ear while into the other a different, distracting message was played, which the listener was to disregard. He found that repetition of the accepted message was possible. When the listeners were asked what they could report about the rejected message their responses suggested that its semantic content had been completely blocked. They were able to say whether it had been speech or some other kind of signal, whether in a man's or woman's voice, often whether it was a list of words or continuous prose, but never could they report the content. Indeed the language of the rejected message could change from English to French to German to Latin to reversed English and back to English, and the listeners would not notice. Apparently there was a complete blocking of the message except for what have come to be called its 'general physical characteristics'. (The phrase is placed in quotes because there is now reason to think that this is a fallacious description of what occurs.) It seemed as though shadowing was an extraordinarily powerful way of locking a listener's attention on to the required message.

Cherry's paper attracted surprisingly little attention until the late 1950's when Moray and Treisman began a series of studies using the shadowing technique. Moray (1959) confirmed Cherry's finding with regard to the efficacy of the block for the content of the rejected message, but also drew attention to the first example of a way to break through the block. He asked a panel of judges to rate a list of words for their suitability to occur in a particular long prose passage, although in fact they did not occur in the passage. On this basis he made up three lists of seven words. The first list was of words which did actually occur in the passage. The other two were equally suitable but did not in fact occur in the passage. He then asked listeners to shadow the long passage at about 130 words per minute. During this time the second list of seven words was repeated thirty-five times in the rejected ear. Thirty seconds after the end of shadowing cards bearing the three lists of seven words were shuffled and dealt to the listener, who was required to say whether he had heard the word in either ear during shadowing. The deck of cards, therefore, contained seven words from the accepted message, seven from the rejected message, and seven which had been presented in neither message but which might well have occurred in the prose message on the basis of a panel of judges. The results were as follows:

Words recognised from the shadowed message   4·9 out of 7
Words 'recognised' from the rejected message   1·9 out of 7
Words 'recognised' when presented in neither ear 2·6 out of 7

The scores given are the mean recognition scores for eight subjects. All eight showed similar performance, and while the difference between the shadowed and the rejected message is highly significant, the difference between the rejected message and the control words is not. Although certain defects in the design are apparent (such as the thirty second delay between the end of shadowing and the start of the recognition test, due to the experiment originally being designed for a different purpose) the fact that 35 repetitions of seven plausible words led to no recognition certainly confirms Cherry's report. No further systematic studies have been reported varying the number of presentations of the rejected message and the delay before testing, but Norman has recently repeated it with a minimal delay between presentation of a target word in the rejected message and recall, and found good recall if the delay is less than two seconds.

    This complete failure to find any trace of the rejected message led Moray to ask what kinds of signals might actually be heard in it, if any. He had shown (Moray, 1958) that making the rejected message louder did not have any striking effect on its reception, at least as measured by the lack of switching to that

C

message when shadowing a different one. The increases of commission and omission errors which he did find when the rejected message was louder than the accepted message fitted quite well with the data on dichotic interference which we have already seen reported by Egan et al. (1954). What commission errors did occur did not appear to be importations from the rejected messages. Significantly, the major source of errors were omissions, which would seem to indicate not that the words were breaking through from the wrong ear to any extent, but that the unfavourable signal to noise ratio was making it harder to respond to the accepted message. If the two messages were equally loud or favoured the selected message there was little further decrease in errors in the latter, which were by that time less than 5%. It is possible that some of the interference was due to bone conduction between the ears since in the most unfavourable signal to noise ratio the rejected message was about 70 dB above threshold, and the results of Zwislocki (1953) would suggest at least 5 dB peripheral masking caused by bone conduction under those conditions.

Again the block appears to be very effective. Moreover, Moray (1959) failed to alter the listeners' performance by giving a set to receive a certain class of signals. Relatively short passages were used for shadowing, and they included four digits embedded in the message and four digits embedded in the rejected message. Even when the digits were the last four words on each channel, and when they alternated rather than coming together in simultaneous pairs, listeners did not report numbers from the rejected message when given a set to report numbers from both ears. On the other hand, Moray did find that a person's own name could attract his attention. If commands such as 'Stop now' or 'Change to this ear' were inserted into the non-shadowed message they were neither obeyed nor heard, but if the command was prefixed by the listener's own name ('John Smith change ears now') it was heard in about one third of the trials when listeners were not expecting it. Either the listener obeyed the instruction or he reported when asked that he had heard it but had not obeyed because he thought it was a special attempt to distract him.

We have, then, something of a paradox. On the one hand it appears that a listener cannot hear the content of a rejected message while shadowing a different message localised at the opposite ear. On the other hand some special signals can cause a change in behaviour, although in experiments with presentation rates of about 120–180 words per minute the attention does not normally wander at all. It is in the attempt to resolve this paradox that the various theories have been developed.

Moray and Taylor (1958) searched for conditions in which listeners would switch attention by requiring them to shadow statistical approximations to prose (Miller and Selfridge, 1950; Taylor and Moray, 1960; Moray, 1966) while the rejected message was normal prose. Contrary to initial expectations there was no evidence that words were imported from the rejected message as the shadowed message became less and less coherent. There were, however, strong relations between the order of approximation and performance of shadowing, which can be summarised by the equations,

Omissions = $26 \cdot 7 - 21$ ($\log_{10}$ Order of Approximation)
Commissions = $6 \cdot 5 - 0 \cdot 33$ (Order of Approximation)

The difference between omission and commission errors, and the fact that different functional relationships are required to relate them to the independent variable, is fairly common in these experiments, and presumably reflects two separate mechanisms. There is some reason to think that omissions may be caused by central factors and commissions by peripheral masking, but this deserves greater study (see also Moray and Barnett, 1965; and Moray, 1969a). Bearing in mind the way in which statistical approximations are constructed, the logarithmic relationship of omissions to order of approximation suggests that performance is related to the information load imposed on the listener by the accepted message. ('Information' here is used in the sense of the metric, developed by Shannon, relating to the relative probability of the signals (Shannon and Weaver, 1949)). Treisman later showed (Treisman, 1965) that if the rate of presentation were slowed down proportionately to the fall in redundancy of the material then the omission curve became flat. She estimated the information content by means of the 'cloze' procedure (Taylor, 1956) in which words were deleted from the statistical approximations and up to 200 subjects asked to guess what the missing words were. From these guesses an estimate of their probabilities within the vocabulary of the subculture from which the guessers came can be made and hence their average information content; and a recent check on the estimates by Harrison, Moray and

Treisman (in preparation) confirmed that the estimates were probably reasonably reliable for the passages as a whole, though not for the individual words. An interesting observation made by Moray and Taylor was that when shadowing low orders of approximation, where redundancy is much reduced and the normal transition probabilities of learnt language violated, subjects repeatedly showed a kind of transient dysphasia, blocking and making uncouth meaningless sounds. All such subjects spontaneously remarked that they had heard the words 'but couldn't get them out'. Some subjects began by listening to whole phrases and then speaking them, but at low orders of approximation all spontaneously dropped this strategy and began to close up on the stimuli until they were shadowing as close to them in time as they could manage. This suggests that, faced with the loss of ability to predict the next few words, and with a consequent rising information load, subjects were becoming seriously overloaded. This might be because of a motor set which was constantly making wrong predictions, necessitating a reorganising of output before making the response and an increasing lag behind the input until breakdown occurred; or because of an increase in reaction time caused by the less and less predictable signals, leading to the same effect. Whatever the reason it is noteworthy that even under overload the listeners' attention did not break down. Far from switching to the more easily predictable message they stuck grimly to the extremely difficult task of handling the nonsense which poured into their ear through the 'acceptable' channel.

This last is an important observation, for it casts light on the extraordinary tenacity with which shadowing allows a listener to hold on to the accepted message. Indeed it is from easy, rather than from difficult messages, that the attention wanders. If listeners are required to shadow unusually redundant materials, such as nursery rhymes or Christmas carols, they will tend to report material from the rejected passage. There is also some reason to think that whispering or *sotto voce* shadowing is a less efficient block than overt shadowing. Shadowing is efficient because it really does occupy the attention; it keeps the listener busy, and so the often errant attention is kept firmly on the job on hand.

Treisman has continued to make important contributions to this field, and we will now consider a series of experiments in which she explores the question of how much information reaches the depths of the nervous system and how much, in selection, is filtered out at a relatively peripheral level. The results in many respects parallel the findings of the earlier work using 'listen and answer' methods, since similarity, probability, voice quality, etc., all play an important role.

Cherry (1953) had asked listeners to shadow a message while into the other ear he played the same message displaced in time. Rather surprisingly it appeared that the listeners recognised the messages as being the same even when they were several seconds apart in time. Now it is apparent that there will be some separation at which the two messages will be so far apart in time that they will function as 'different' messages, and by systematically examining the effects of different delays we should be able to recognise how different a message must be before attention will break down. Treisman (1961) carried out the relevant experiment, and Moray (1960a) duplicated her results in part. Treisman investigated both the case where the accepted message led in time and where it lagged in time over the rejected message. There were striking differences. When shadowing the leading message the listeners realised that the messages were identical when they were as much as 10 seconds (some 20 words) apart. When the shadowed message lagged behind the rejected one, the messages were not recognised as being identical until they were within a second or so of one another.

The most obvious interpretation of these results would be that, when shadowing leads, even though the rejected message is not consciously being perceived by the listener the rejected input is correlated with messages which have been received by the accepted ear and also with the memory trace left by those messages. If the correlation between the trace and the incoming rejected signal is sufficiently high the brain cannot select one and reject the other. In this respect it is interesting to observe that both Cherry and Sayers (1956) and Licklider (1959) have postulated cross correlation mechanisms as the basis of auditory localisation. It is, of course, not necessary for the messages to be correlated for meaning; quite crude correlation of the overall wave envelope would be sufficient to establish their identity. Moreover, although these particular experiments involved correlation between messages in different positions of auditory space, it seems likely that such correlations are common, and may be a feature of many sensory and higher dimensions of signal space. Treisman was able to establish that both the time lag and also the number of intervening words contributed to the critical delay at which recognition occurred, and there was also interaction between the kind of material presented and the critical delay.

There are two possible explanations which may be offered for the difference between the leading and lagging cases. Firstly, it might be that the rejected message is blocked so peripherally that its information never reaches the memory store at all. In this case the reason why the two messages are recognised as the same at an interval of a second or so is that there are occasionally long words which are such that the second half of the word is still being presented to the rejected ear when the beginning of the word starts on the accepted ear, and that with such a degree of overlap there is a breakdown of attention. Secondly it could be that the rejected message is indeed stored, but that what is stored is such an imperfect representation of the signal (so attenuated, as Treisman would say) that it fades in memory, or becomes noisy so rapidly that the correlation with the accepted message is too weak to trigger the identification of the two messages. The experiment is not necessarily evidence that the rejected message does not enter the depths of the nervous system.

In another dichotic experiment Treisman (1960) asked listeners to repeat a message they heard through one particular ear, emphasising that their task was to keep to that ear rather than to the message in it. The two messages were completely different prose passages, and half way through the presentation they changed sides, so that the message which had been on the left ear was now on the right ear, and vice versa. She found that at the moment when the messages changed sides listeners would repeat one or two words from what was now the wrong ear, and then revert to the correct ear, although unaware of the fact that they had not kept to the same ear the whole time. She also controlled for the ability of the listeners to guess what the next words might be. She concluded that one of the occasions on which attention passed out of the listeners' control was when the signal in the rejected message was highly probable in the context of the signals just received on the accepted message. It was for this reason that the probabilistic changes in threshold of the 'dictionary units' were incorporated in her model. This provides one case in which we can say indeed that observers can select the actual region of signal space as well as the message which arrives in that region, and which therefore satisfies the demands made in Chapter 2 for distinguishing such alternatives experimentally.

The effect of linguistic features is shown in another of Treisman's experiments (Triesman, 1964a). The experiment is one which raises some difficulties for the view that there is a substantial loss of information early in the pathway. She played an English message to one ear and a translation of that message, delayed by 3·5 seconds, to the other. While listeners who spoke little French could select the English and reject the French with little difficulty, 50% of the bilinguals realised that the two messages had the same meaning. In a binaural mixing of two such passages (1964b), the bilinguals found it extremely difficult to select one message and reject the translation, sometimes giving an output in mixed languages, while those who spoke little of the second language were little affected by it. This result seems to indicate that information reaches a very high level in the nervous system even when presented in the rejected message, since it appears that meaning can be recognised as such. However, we shall see later on that there is at least one other possible way of accounting for this result.

Treisman (1961, 1964b) has also provided some semiparametric results concerning the way in which cues can be used by listeners to separate messages. As with 'Listen and Answer' tasks, by far the most efficient method of separation is auditory localisation. She used lateralisation of sound images by means of unbalanced intensities to achieve the separation of the sound sources. Using the figures given by Stewart and Hovda (1918) she estimated the angular separation of sound sources which would be equivalent to the degree of imbalance of loudness which she used, and obtained the following results:

	Equivalent separation in degrees				
	2–3	10	24	36	90+
Percentage of omissions from accepted message	58	44	22	21	11
Commission errors	4	6	4	6	4
Intrusions from wrong message	12	7	0	1	0

It is immediately clear that separation is very powerful as a means of selection.

Treisman also investigated the effect of more than one rejected message at a time. This experiment is very important, for it draws attention to a conceptual trap into which it is all too easy to fall in reading accounts of dichotic listening experiments. Since so many of these experiments use headphones to present stimuli, and present each message to one ear and to one ear only, it is often tempting to think of the apparent rejection of one of the messages as involving the turning off as it were of the ear as a whole; for instance, the listener shuts off his left ear and listens only with his right. Such a conclusion leads at once to rather *simpliste* physiological speculations involving centrifugal fibres as the obvious control mechanism. A few moments' thought should suffice to show how beset with unwarranted assumptions is such a view, and Treisman's experiment gives one direct refutation of the idea. She presented three messages. All the energy of one went to the right ear, all the energy of the second went to the left ear, and the signal energy of the third was equally divided between the two ears. The result was that three sound images were heard, one lateralised at the left ear, one at the right, and the third inside the head in approximately the mid-line. It was then possible to ask the listener to select the message in the middle and to reject the others. Clearly this is not done by turning off both ears in order to listen to the third message! Whatever switches, attenuators or what have you are postulated, one must keep it very clearly in mind that the evidence is to do with switching within signal space rather than between hypothetical afferent pathways, whose existence as specific localised entities handling a well defined class of signals becomes increasingly implausible as the categories of message which the listener is required to receive increase in complexity. Treisman found that if the two rejected messages were lateralised in the same position while the accepted message was lateralised some distance away there was less interference with shadowing than when all three messages were phenomenally separated. She was also able to show that the interference caused by two rejected messages was greater than that caused by only one, and that the effect could not entirely be attributed to increased masking, but appeared to be related to the information load imposed upon the system by the presence of three distinct messages. It was possible to shadow one of two messages lateralised in the same position in auditory space and, as might be expected, this was easier to do if the two messages were spoken in different voices, and easier still if the voices were also of speakers of different sexes. Other distinguishing features such as the rejected message being in a foreign language unknown to the speaker, or being in technical jargon, also make their rejection easier.

Treisman investigated various factors which increased the rate of information processing required of the listener (Treisman, 1965). She used different rates of presentation, stimulus materials of differing information content, and included also simultaneous translation. (It will be apparent that shadowing is in fact the degraded case of simultaneous translation in which the message is translated into itself.) It has become less fashionable of late to relate behaviour directly to information content. Chomsky (1957) has shown the inadequacy of a finite state theory of sentence generation, and even in such simple experiments as choice reaction times there is difficulty in appealing to information content to account for the observed differences. Our work has become less centred on the statistical structure of the stimulus and more upon the way in which the subject manipulates and operates upon the messages he receives. It is instructive to compare the orientation of say, Miller's (1951) *Language and Communication* with Miller et al.'s (1960) *Plans and the Structure of Behaviour*. The fact remains, however, that Treisman observed a very close relation between performance in selective listening tasks and the information content of the stimulus material. Hence, even if the reception and translation of messages is accomplished by mechanisms which are not explicable directly in terms of Shannon information, there will have to be some kind of combination of the various conceptual models involved. Figures 7 and 8 summarise Treisman's findings.

In attempting to account for the results reviewed above, Treisman produced the model which was described in Chapter 3. Several versions of it have been published (Treisman, 1960; 1966; 1967). It might be well for the reader at this point to refer back to Chapter 3 and compare the models of Treisman and the Deutsches (Figures 3 and 4). There is, it will be observed, a considerable degree of agreement between them. Indeed if we remove the first attenuating stage of Treisman's model we should have a system which was almost identical to that of the Deutsches. There is a

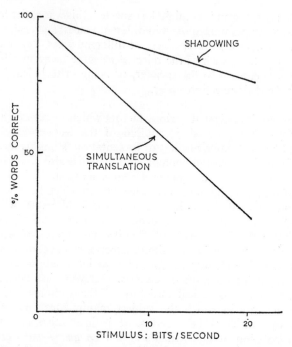

FIG. 7. Treisman's experiment on shadowing and translating

passage in one of Treisman's papers, 1966, which is almost indistinguishable from what one might expect to find in one of Deutsches papers:

> Since Nature has not guaranteed that all signals that are important to us or relevant to our interests should arrive at our senses with particular clarity and intensity, we have to adopt the alternative strategy of lowering our criteria for perceiving them, accepting them on the basis of less sensory evidence than we would a neutral or uninteresting stimulus. Now I suggested that *selective attention might have just this effect of reducing the sensory evidence for all unattended messages to just a trickle.* This would mean that perceptual questions asked about these reduced messages would be answered only if the subjects' criterion was lowered in their favour, if they were particularly relevant or important to him. (Italics mine).

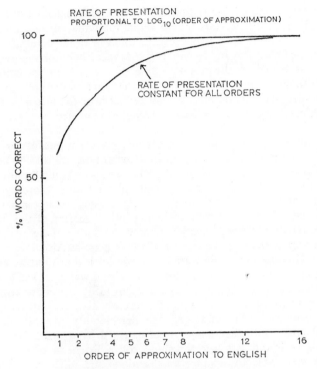

FIG. 8. Shadowing and information content

The crucial question is whether the incoming messages are in fact attenuated before they reach the level at which the full analysis of meaning takes place and whether the italicised sentence above is required. Without it we virtually have a description of Deutsch's model. The early experiments on shadowing outlined in this chapter will make it clear why the suggestion was made—by and large listeners simply do not hear the content of the rejected message, but do hear its general physical characteristics. A listener does hear a few verbal signals, and they are just the sort which might be expected to trigger a detector with an unusually low threshold, be it temporary (context effects) or permanent ('important' signals). This would be neatly explained by a mechanism such as Treisman's. The crux of the argument between Treisman and the Deutsches is over the claim that there is evidence that all the information about the nature of the message reaches the same high level of the nervous system where total analysis takes place, so that selection is of responses. It should be noted carefully that both the Deutsches and Reynolds (1964) speak of conscious awareness as being on the response side of the pattern recognition system, and their models are not therefore vulnerable to the rejoinder that 'the listeners do not in fact hear the message, so it can't reach the cortex or pattern recognition centre'.

Results apparently favouring the interpretation put forward by Deutsch and Deutsch are given by Howarth and Ellis (1961) and Oswald, Taylor, and Treisman (1960). The latter group monitored the EEG of sleeping subjects, while playing tape-recordings of names and other stimuli to the sleepers. They found (in a very well controlled experiment, including 'blind' scoring of the EEG records) that sleepers awoke more often in response to their own names than to the names of other people. Also they gave more K-complexes (which are indices of cortical arousal) to their own names than to other names even without waking. (The writer of the present monograph also gave strong GSR without waking or being aware of it to the name of a recently acquired girl friend!) Howarth and Ellis measured the detectability of a listener's own name and other names when masked by white noise, and similarly found a lower threshold for a listener's own name. They were able to advance an ingenious and fairly convincing argument that the three experiments (the two just mentioned and Moray's on hearing one's own name when shadowing) were all tapping one and the same mechanism. If they are right it seems that the incoming signals must reach the cortex in sufficient strength for the meaning of the signal to be extracted even when the listener does not hear the message. Further evidence in this direction comes from an unpublished experiment by the writer.

Following the discovery that a person's name is heard in the rejected message in a dichotic shadowing situation, but that voluntarily imposing a set to receive numbers did not seem effective, the writer attempted to make a neutral word affectively important by pairing it with shock. Thirty subjects were used, of whom 12 conditioned adequately. They were told that the experiment was concerned with the nature of conditioning in the presence of distracting stimuli. To establish the conditioned response single channel presentation was used, the messages being presented

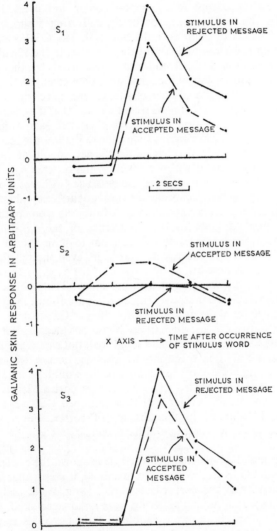

Fig. 9. Conditioned G.S.R. to an emotional stimulus

to their right ears. The messages were prose passages about 100 words long, each containing the word *country*. The experimenter monitored the output of the tape-recorder and pressed a key whenever the word *country* occurred, delivering a shock to the subjects' hands through an induction coil. The GSR was monitored visually on a moving spot galvanometer. In the 12 subjects a strong conditioned GSR to *country* occurred by the twelfth trial. Two more conditioning trials were then given, and the GSR again measured in the absence of shock. One more trial was then given with shock. The listeners were then told that they were going to be given a distraction message to their left ears which they were to disregard. They were to continue to shadow the message in their right ears. On the first trial under the new conditions the word *country* was presented without shock in the rejected ear. On the next trial it occurred in the accepted ear. The GSR was measured by recording the position of the moving spot at 2-second intervals, using an exogenous voltage source. All subjects who conditioned showed marked GSR to the occurrence of the word *country* in the accepted message, and three seem to have shown it also when it occurred in the rejected message, even though they did not hear it. All were aware by the end of the experiment of what word it was that was paired with the shock. The records of the three subjects on the first, the critical, trials are shown in Figure 9.

Bearing in mind the notorious difficulties of GSR work, and the rather primitive way in which the response was measured, it would be useful to have this experiment replicated. If it can be established that such a conditioned autonomic response occurs, without the listener being aware of the stimulus, it would be additional evidence that the rejected message reaches cortical levels, since there is considerable evidence that conditioned GSRs cannot be obtained in humans in the absence of cortex. For example, Duret-Cosyns and Duret (1956) have said:

Although Fauville and Schwartz have shown the existence o segmental GSR in the decerebrate animal, it seems that in man the integrity of the cortex is essential. Doig, Wolf, and Wolff working with a human suffering from a damaged skull, pathologically decerebrate, were unable to show any GSR response. We have studied 5 cases of confused and comatose patients reacting violently to cutaneous stimulation even when it is slight, by shouting, and withdrawal of the limbs, and have been unable by any means, including auditory, visual, tactile, electric, etc., to produce the slightest sign of GSR activity. (Translation by the present writer)

Even if we were to conclude that the incoming messages reach the cortex from the rejected channel this would not preclude the Treisman model, since there is no reason at present to say that this may not be a considerable distance functionally 'below' the level of awareness. But there seems to be an implication in the model that the attenuation should be rather 'lower down' than this, at a level where simple, but not complex, aspects of the stimulus may be analysed. An objection put forward by Norman (personal communication) and by Deutsch, Deutsch and Lindsay (1967) that attenuation of the incoming sign would affect both signal and noise alike, leaving their ratio the same, has been answered by Treisman (1967) with the obvious reply that if there is more than one level of synaptic activity between the attenuator and the analysers we may reasonably expect noise to be added to the weakened signal + noise, with the result that the signal does become relatively weaker.

On the basis of the experiments so far described there does not seem to be enough evidence to decide between the models of Treisman and the Deutsches. Four recent experiments add to the data and might at first sight be expected to clarify the picture, but there are reasons to think that they are open to more than one interpretation. At this time they will be reported and in the final chapter will be related to the problem of achieving an overall theory.

Broadbent and Gregory (1963) were the first to use the signal detection theory in a selective situation. They measured the detectability of signals in one ear, while the listener monitored the opposite ear for the occurrence of certain signals, and found that d' and not β was affected for the detection task. This would favour Treisman's suggestion that the rejected message strength is reduced rather than that response selection is altered. However, there is the objection that the tasks on the two channels were not exactly the same, and that having a memory component on one channel might alter the situation. Treisman and Geffen (1967) also obtained a change in d' not β in a shadowing experiment, although the way in which the analysis was performed adds even more assumptions to those inherently present in the use of signal detection theory, as they themselves point out.

The experiment they performed is very interesting. They attempted to set up a crucial experiment to distinguish between Treisman's model and the one proposed by Deutsch and Deutsch. In addition they hoped to get information as to which characteristics of the message were passed by their hypothetical attenuator. As usual listeners were asked to shadow a message presented to one ear, while a different message was presented to the other ear. The messages were 150 words in length and lasted about one minute. Embedded in the prose were certain target words which the listeners had to detect. These words were sometimes in context and sometimes not. Sometimes homophones or synonyms were present, and so on. The listeners had to shadow the selected message and in addition tap the table with a ruler whenever they heard the target word in *either* ear. The verbal responses, the stimulus passages and the tapping noises were all recorded and later scored for correct repetitions, taps and latencies. Perfect performance would therefore require the accurate repetition of the heard message, and tapping the table to the occurrence of a target word when it occurred in the accepted message or when it occurred (not simultaneously) in the rejected message.

The rationale of the experiment was as follows. There is a primary response (shadowing) and a secondary response (tapping). If there is a perceptual filter, but no limit on the number of responses which can be made, then both the primary and secondary responses can be made to the accepted message, but the secondary response to the second (rejected) message should be very inefficient. If both messages are fully analysed, and response competition occurs, then the primary message should be given efficiently, but the secondary response (tapping) should be very inefficient for both messages.

The results at first sight appear to uphold Treisman's theory. The vast majority of tapping responses were made to the target words in the accepted message (86·5% as compared with 8·1% to the secondary message). Next, target words received more responses when in context than when out of context in both messages (which agrees with Treisman's model but does not distinguish between it and the one of Deutsch and Deutsch). Thirdly, while tapping to target words in the accepted message interfered only slightly with repeating the primary message, tapping to the occurrence of target words in the rejected message caused a much greater disruption of performance. Conversely, 76% of primary message words which failed to receive a tap were not repeated. Treisman and Geffen say:

> Either the words were simply not perceived, or the two responses competed so strongly that neither could be made overtly.

Since the words which were missed in the secondary response caused no interference it suggests that they were not identified. Treisman and Geffen argue that the results strongly support perceptual selection:

> Since both stimulus and response are identical for the primary and secondary message (i.e. the target words—Moray) it is difficult to argue for a difference in importance, in response load, or in response bias, and the result seems best explained on the assumption that the secondary target words are much less likely to be identified than the primary ones. There is also some degree of response competition shown by the number of occasions when one response to the primary target word was given but not the other (19%). But in this task the response competition is much less dramatic than the perceptual competition.

Unfortunately, while this is a possible interpretation of the results it is by no means the only one. For one thing because of Deutsch and Deutsch's insistence that conscious perception is a response their finding that the 'words were simply not perceived' would be interpreted by the Deutsches as evidence for their model. Furthermore a completely different view might be taken of the experimental design. Perhaps the two responses which are competing are, in fact, on the one hand 'tap-while-repeating' to the primary message, and on the other 'tap-without-repeating' to the secondary message. After all it was found that the primary message taps and repetitions seemed to be very closely linked, as though they were a single act. Missing a primary tap usually meant missing a primary repetition, which did not happen when a secondary tap was missed. Tapping responses caused only a minute increase in errors when they were to primary responses, while tapping to targets in the secondary message caused a great increase in primary message errors. If one were to adopt the Deutschs' attitude to the experimental design it can be interpreted as evidence for their model. But the experiment is not in fact a crucial one as it stands for distinguishing between it and the model of Treisman.

It is interesting that when Lawson (1966a) in a similar experiment used tone bursts as targets, requiring a tapping response, she found that there was no difference between the detection of pips in the primary and secondary message. Unfortunately several important details are not given in the paper. For example there is no indication of the absolute intensity of the pips, and hence there is no guarantee that they did not contain substantially more acoustic energy than the mean time average for the speech signals among which they were interspersed. Indeed, since the pips were added to the prose, not interspersed with the words, there must have been at least a 3 dB increase in the power (6 dB SPL) in the critical band centred on 750 Hz, the frequency used. Moreover there is no indication that any kind of shaping circuit or electronic switch was used in order to avoid switching transients at the onset of the signal. It is quite possible therefore that there were high energy high frequency components which might have given the signals a disproportionate strength, and have resulted in their very high detectability. It is also important to notice that the signals were fairly long, 350 milliseconds' duration. The reaction time to the pips was rather long, over 500 msecs. On the other hand as the signal discrimination became more complex, performance on the secondary message became less efficient. When the listeners had to discriminate high from low pitched tone bursts reaction times were longer to the rejected message than to the accepted (primary) message. When the listeners were required to respond to the higher pitched tone burst on one ear and the lower pitched tone burst on the other, while shadowing one of the messages, Lawson obtained reaction times of over 800 msecs. All the errors in the final condition were false positives, comprising some 40 % of the total responses. There were also very large individual differences. It is to be hoped that this experiment will be repeated with better control of the stimulus materials.

The first of her findings, that tone bursts are equally detected on the primary and secondary messages, is quoted both by Treisman and Geffen and by Deutsch and Deutsch as evidence for their respective positions. As we have seen there has been general agreement until now that selection, however it may occur, seems to block the processing of verbal ('complex') signals and leave 'simple' signals relatively undisturbed. The later sections of Lawson's paper do not quite fit this picture, and we will see in a later chapter much stronger reasons for doubting this interpretation.

Recently Moray and O'Brien (1967) tried to extend the application of signal detection theory to selective listening. In theory a change in d' might be ascribable to attenuation of the signal, and thus support Treisman's position, while a change in β would reflect response bias and support Deutsch and Deutsch. Moray and O'Brien required listeners to receive a stream of 900 digits with 100 letters randomly interspersed among them, in the left ear, and another such list in the right ear, at a rate of two per ear per second. Of the letters, 25 in one ear occurred at the same moment that a different letter occurred in the opposite ear. Listeners were asked to press a response key with their left hand whenever they heard a letter on the left ear, another with their right hand whenever they heard a letter in their right ear, and both keys when they heard letters simultaneously in both ears. They were not required to shadow either of the messages, merely to listen. A monaural condition was used as a control to establish performance in the absence of competition.

d' did indeed alter. It was highest in the monaural control task. It was substantially lower, and equal for the two messages, when attention had to be equally divided between the two messages. When attention was directed towards one message and away from the other, d' rose for the accepted message and fell for the rejected message. Interestingly, if the hits, false positives, etc., were summed over the two messages before the statistics were calculated, there was no difference in d' when performance on (Accepted + Rejected) as a whole in the selective condition was compared with (Left + Right) as a whole from the shared condition. There were only slight changes in β and they were unsystematic. While the earlier conclusions favour Treisman's model, the fact that whatever detection mechanisms operate seem to have access to both messages, in such a way that the total performance remains constant while one message may be traded off against the other, might be taken to mean that both messages reach the central analysing devices. Changes in β are hard to interpret for, as Taylor (1967) showed, unless the form of the ROC curve is known estimates of β may be misleading and no ROC curve for this kind of performance has been obtained. Indeed the application of signal detection theory to this kind of stimulus material at all is extremely difficult. When certain words, or a class of words, are the targets, and the rest of the message the background against which they occur, we are saying, as it were, that 'spoken digits' are the noise distribution and 'spoken letters' the signal + noise distribution. While it is possible to construct an elaborate justification for such a usage it is obviously a rather strange dimension along which the distribution is moving, and at present there are rather grave doubts as to whether this kind of analysis should be attempted with these types of signals. While it seems intuitively plausible that signal detection theory measures should apply to attention experiments (see Broadbent and Gregory 1963) little systematic work has been done. Norman and Lindsey (1967) have provided an ROC curve in a selective attention experiment where a memory task was mixed with a detection task, and found that the detection task, but not the memory task, was affected; but to date no ROC curves have been provided for different conditions of attention, and there are considerable experimental difficulties involved. One attempt by the present writer failed to get adequate measurements for such a curve, owing to the difficulty of requiring a rapid rate of presentation and simultaneously a high proportion of targets. It seemed that both changes in d' and β occurred as different conditions of attention were required, but the pattern was not clear.

There is, however, a much more serious problem raised by the paper of Moray and O'Brien. When they tabulated the responses to the simultaneous occurrence of a target in both messages they found that the probability of detecting one of such a pair was extremely high (1·0 for three of their subjects), but the probability of detecting both of such a pair was extremely low (0·0 for some of their subjects). This looks very much more like an on-off switch than an attenuator. Moreover, consider the fact that what is obtained in all these experiments is a proportion, averaged over a run, of hits, false positives, misses and rejections. These can be analysed and interpreted in such a way as to suggest that, say, 75 % hits mean there is a probability of 0·75 that any individual target will be detected, and the argument for attenuation rather than complete switching off makes that assumption. Exactly the same statistics could be obtained in a case where the probability of detecting a signal is always either 1·0 or 0·0 (this is in fact the case; either a response is given or not; confidence ratings have not been recorded). Now there is no compulsion to move from the fact that on 75% of trials a hit is scored to the conclusion that on every trial the strength of the internal representation of the signal is 75% of what it is when there is 100% detection. To do so is to accept the attenuation model. However, exactly the same data might lead one to argue that the rejected message was switched off on 75% of the occasions, and the accepted message on 25% of the occasions when a target arrived on the accepted message. This is not a possibility that has been put forward since the qualitative formulation by Broadbent (1958), but we will return to it later, when we have seen that such a model seems to fit the visual modality, for example, rather well.

The situation in regard to selective listening seems, then, rather unsatisfactory. On the basis of the experiments so far quoted there is no way to distinguish between the models. In fact there is the one finding on simultaneous signals from Moray and O'Brien which at least hints that perhaps none of them are adequate. There are certainly very few cases where the full sequence of analyses suggested as paradigmatic in Chapter 2 have been implemented, although in the work on shadowing there is something which approaches it. We saw that Treisman found that spatial separation of the messages increased the efficiency of shadowing and reduced intrusions from the rejected message. Hence:

$$\overset{I}{\underset{\uparrow}{}}: p(r_a)|I\{a] + J\{b\} > \overset{I}{\underset{\uparrow}{}}: p(r_a)|I\{a + b\}$$

where I is spatial position and a the prose message in that position. From Cherry's experiments on clichés and Treisman's experiments on different kinds of prose materials we can conclude that the contextual continuity of a message is enough to allow its selection, so we also have,

$$\overset{a}{\underset{\uparrow}{}}: p(r_a)|I\{a + b\} > p(r_a)|I\{a + b\}$$

and we can say that both the position in space and the message in that position may be the object of selection. But detailed analysis of messages and responses signal by signal will really be required to substantiate fully any such results.

Consider the problem that much of the data comes from shadowing experiments, next. Shadowing is really a very complicated task. The listener receives at least three and possibly four inputs in a 'two-channel' situation. Through one ear comes the accepted message. Through the other comes the rejected message. In addition each ear receives a message which is the feedback of the spoken response, phenomenally fused to form a single sound image, highly correlated with the accepted message but delayed in time. The real point of shadowing, the reason for its effectiveness, is almost certainly that it keeps the listener so busy handling the accepted and feedback messages (we shall see in a subsequent chapter that there is reason to think that he must be sharing his attention between the accepted message and the response) that he has no time to handle the rejected message. The same effect should be obtainable with simple responses such as key pressing, provided that the presentation rate is high. The writer is at present in the middle of a programme of research of this kind (Moray, 1969a, b, c).

We are then left with a fairly impressive body of qualitative generalisations. Listeners can make use of such factors as pitch, voice quality, loudness, semantic continuity, spatial localisation and time of onset in order to select a message. The more similar in such respects the messages are the more likely they are to be confused by the listener and the less effective is attentional selection. It looks as though the heavier the load imposed on the listener by the accepted message the less likely he is to switch attention or be distracted by the rejected message, unless the rejected message signals are highly probable in the context of the accepted message or emotionally important. On the basis of the experiments so far reported it seems that the most common stimuli causing switching are 'linguistic' ones, or the sudden onset of a signal in an otherwise uniform message; but it may be that with linguistic messages the pitch, loudness and position characteristics allow the message to be identified, and that it is the message to which the listener is then tuned.

What are missing are any systematic, quantitative, parametric studies. The use of speech, although satisfactory as approximating to 'real life' stimulation, itself raises problems. What does a listener do when hearing a stream of prose? Does he listen to the whole of each word? Only to the first 50 milliseconds? To the transients or the distinctive features? When does a speech signal functionally start and stop? Most experiments have totalled scores over long runs, but we desperately need more experiments where the analysis is really signal by signal, and where moment to moment probabilities and latencies are analysed, rather than overall performance. We need experiments on the effects of the relative values of payoffs for responding to the different channels and different targets. Selection by lateralisation seems extremely powerful, and whenever experimenters have deliberately asked for monitoring of the second channel (Mowbray, 1964) they have invariably found a catastrophic decline in performance on the accepted channel. But perhaps with payoffs suitably adjusted, and above all with long practice (another field which needs investigating), this might not be true.

Norman, D. (1969, *Quart. J. Exp. Psychol.*, *21*, 85–94) found that if a listener shadows a message to one ear, he can accurately report on the content of the rejected message providing that he reports on the content of the rejected message within one or two seconds of its occurrence. With longer delays he confirmed Moray's work quoted on page 51 above.
Treisman (1967, *Quart. J. Exp. Psychol.*, *19*, 362–368) tested a prediction which Deutsch thought should distinguish between his and her models, and obtained evidence in favour of her model.
Moray and Fee (1969, in preparation) repeated Lawson's experiment (page 68, above) with more adequate controls, and found that there was poorer detection for pure tone bursts in the rejected message, contradicting her findings. This result is also relevant to the question of low level, pre-attenuator analysis of simple physical characteristics which is presumed in Treisman's model. For the relation between auditory attention and memory, see Norman, D., *Memory and Attention*, 1969, Wiley, N.Y.

5 VISUAL SELECTIVITY

Although work on visual selectivity has for some years been rather less popular than work on auditory selectivity, considerable progress has been made. The paucity of research may be related to the technical and conceptual difficulties involved, but even so it is rather surprising when one considers that probably the most common of all instruction in visual experiments is an attentional instruction such as: 'Fixate the dim red spot, and pay attention to the stimuli which will appear just to its left.' It is curious that there has been very little modern work, if any, on the importance and effect of this instruction. Obviously it ensures that the observer will at least be looking in the right direction when the signal is presented and, as we shall see from the work of Sanders (1963), this can be expected to have a marked effect. There are a number of studies on the effect upon the accuracy of perception of the angular distance from the fovea at which the stimuli are presented, but they are scattered and unsystematic. Only a few recent papers have attempted to investigate directly the effect of attentional factors (e.g. Grindley and Townsend, 1968) and they found quite substantial effects. Grindley and Townsend compared the accuracy of reports of the occurrence and orientation of a small geometrical figure in the periphery of the visual field by subjects who were with and without knowledge of which quadrant was to contain the signal.

It is rather difficult to know just what we are asking of a viewer when we require him to fixate one part of the visual field and pay attention to another. The subjects can apparently obey the instructions as in auditory selectivity although there is no physical action which one obviously performs when listening with one ear and rejecting another. Although there is a voluminious literature from early years on just this kind of experiment the judgment required of the viewers was usually to do with the 'attensity' or 'sensible clearness' of the stimuli under different conditions of stimulus properties and different degrees of attention (see for example, Friedline and Dallenbach, 1929) and it is rather difficult to interpret the results. There are very few recent experiments in which the viewer's attention has been directed to one area of the visual field and questions then asked about another region and the signals presented therein.

No attempt will be made to cover the work on integration of information near the visual threshold, where the probability of seeing seems to be dependent on the integration of luminous energy over time. All the studies reported will deal with stimuli which under all normal single channel presentation conditions may be expected to be well above threshold. Conveniently we may begin with a monograph by Sanders (1963) which provides a terminology useful for discussing other research. Unlike hearing it is obviously possible to 'turn off' in a most direct way a signal which appears in the visual field. The viewer may close his eyes, move his eyes so that the signal disappears from the edge of the visual field or move his entire head so that it likewise disappears. In hearing it may be that in animals with large and moveable ears the orientation of the ear may make a substantial difference (although because of the relative magnitudes of the wavelength of sound and the size of the ears, this will be less than the effect of moving the head in vision); but in man the most obvious effect of head movement is merely to alter the apparent direction of the source of the sound. In line with this Sanders distinguishes between three types or subdivisions of the visual field: the *headfield* (which is that part of the visual field which can be sampled by moving the head, and amounts to a circle of 360° in the horizontal plane and some 200° in the saggital plane); the *eyefield* (that part of the visual field which can be sampled by moving the eyes, but with the head held still); and the *stationary field* (that region which can be sampled while holding both head and eyes still, i.e. in a single glance). His own work is mainly to do with the way in which moving from the use of one of these fields to another influences behaviour. The work of Senders (1967) on reading instruments in the environment of an aircraft cockpit is mainly concerned with head and eye fields, while that of many early workers and more recently Sampson (1964) and Whelan (1968) is concerned with the eyefield. It is not at once apparent that there will only be one theory of attention needed to cover all three cases.

Sanders' experiments recorded judgments by his observers of the number of lights present in two rows of lighted dots. The observer sat in front of a table 70 cm from the displays. The two displays, one to the right and one to the left, each consisted of a vertical column of lights. In most of the experiments there could be either four or five spots of light in each column, and the observer was asked to press one of four keys to indicate whether the pattern was 4/4, 4/5, 5/4, 5/5. In some experiments, used to investigate the effects of target discriminability, the number was 2/2, 2/3, 3/2, 3/3. Sanders applied the measure devised by Crossman (1955) to measure the expected discriminability of these patterns and gives the value of 1·71 and 3·13 for the smaller and larger arrays respectively.

He remarks that earlier workers had discussed the relation of eye movements to attention. Karslake (1940) had reported that the rankings for parts of a display as to their 'attention value' were found to correlate highly with the number of fixations on those parts of the display, a kind of study to which Mackworth (1967) has recently given attention. On the other hand Guilford (1936) and McMillan (1941) had concluded that eye movements do not correlate with 'attensity' (sensory clearness). Sanders' initial experiment presented his columns of lights at either 20° or 94° separation. He measured the reaction time in noise and in quiet and found that there was an increase in variance due to the noise only at the greater separation. Relating this result to earlier work by Corbin et al. (1958) he suggested that the reason could be a change in strategy in the way in which signals are handled when the visual angle of the display becomes large. (Corbin et al. had found that the best detection was obtained when no eye movements occurred, even at large separation; but their signals were only presented for 0·1 seconds, so that there is reason to think that eye movements might be positively harmful, as will appear from the chapter on switching time.)

Sanders next turned to a more elaborate experiment. The two values of discriminability were used, and judgments were required at light separations of 31, 49, 62, 73, and 86 degrees. Subjects were tested either with their heads free to move or under conditions of restricted head movements. Eighty subjects were used. Each received some practice and was then tested on a preliminary setting with the lights 19° apart. The 80 subjects were then divided into groups of four, and each group performed in the experiment under one of the movement × separation × discriminability conditions. The run was self-paced; each time a response was made the lights changed to a new pattern, which was presented 0·5 seconds after the response. Reaction times and errors were scored. The data used in the analysis was the difference between the preliminary run at 19° and the score under the test condition, averaged for the four subjects in the group. The results are shown in Figure 10.

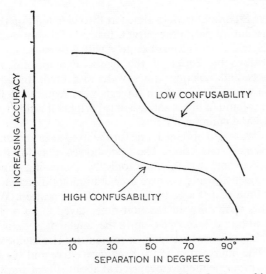

FIG. 10. Sanders experiment on the transition from one kind of visual attention to another

The visual angle and the discriminability factors both gave highly significant contributions to the variance, as did the interaction of the head movements with discriminability. Finally a test of the relationship between visual angle and performance showed marked departures from linearity, which were related to obvious discontinuities in the region of 40° (for the 1·71 lights) and 80° (for the 3·13 lights). In a further experiment in which the range of angular separations of the displays was increased Sanders was able to show that both the curves had two discontinuities, one in the region of 25–30° and one in the region of 80°, and suggested that these corresponded to the change from stationary field to eyefield and from eyefield to headfield respectively. He also found that in the later experiment his observers, who there is reason to think were more highly motivated than the observers in the earlier experiments, performed much better at large angles of separation without head movements. He concluded:

> . . . we must assume the existence of an area where head movements are preferred, but not strictly necessary in order to maintain performance.

Further experiments were aimed at throwing light on the nature of the discontinuities in the curves. Instead of a continuous series of signals, trials were given discretely, with a three second warning period before the onset of the lights. Eye movements, head movements and reaction times were measured. In addition a condition was added in which subjects were required to fixate the left hand column of lights and use only peripheral vision to observe the right hand column of lights.

Two curves were obtained, one for the fixed gaze and one for the free movement condition. The first showed that for fixed gaze the reaction time was a monotonically increasing function of display angle, showing positive acceleration and reaching a mean reaction time of 1·0 seconds at about 30° separation. When eye movements were allowed reaction time stayed more or less constant at about 0·7 seconds until the angle of separation was approaching 80°, whereupon it began to rise smoothly and rapidly. The intersection of the fixed gaze curve and the first part of the eye movement curve occurred at about 30° separation of the displays, and combining the two curves yielded a plot very similar to that seen in the earlier experiments. The discontinuities seemed to be caused by the change from observing the stationary field to observing the eyefield; and then at extreme separations from observing the eyefield to observing the headfield. The observers remarked that at extreme values of the stationary field, where the columns of lights were separated by about 25°, they were judging on an overall impression of the height of the column rather than observing the number of lights. This is not surprising, since acuity falls off very rapidly away from the fovea, and 25° is an extreme value at which to expect discrimination. The idea that the second discontinuity is due to the change from eyefield to headfield was confirmed by data comparing the response to a monocular display with that to a binocular display. In the latter the discontinuity appeared at a greater angle.

Since there was great individual variation among his observers Sanders concluded that often the change from stationary to eyefield to headfield might occur at separations where it was not absolutely necessary, but merely preferred. He therefore turned his attention to an analysis of the strategies which limited his observers' performances, and asked whether there was any information read in from the second stimulus even before the eye movement had begun, or during that movement. In a very extensive experiment he measured eye movements, head movements, movement time, reaction time, the compensation by eye movements for overshoot by the head and several other factors. Eye movement time was linearly related to angular separation with a slope of about 2·5 milliseconds per degree. The observers fixated the left hand column of lights until they were turned on, and then could move their eyes if they wished. For large separations the reaction time to the right hand lights was significantly longer than the reaction time to the left hand lights, but for separations of less than 25° there was no difference. To quote Sanders again:

> Only in the headfield would two successive selective acts be required; the stationary field would be covered by one selective act, while in the eyefield the intermediate process would occur.

It is interesting that an attempt to train observers to avoid shifting their gaze until they had finished the *response* to the first light proved extremely difficult. The natural strategy seems to be to group the responses to the two lights as a single response whenever possible, at least until the separation is so great that they are operating in the headfield mode.

Sanders further examined the way in which information was being taken in through the periphery of the visual field. Senders, Webb, and Baker (1955) had observed that when people view a series of dials, they appear to be able to take in more information than might be expected by means of peripheral vision, once they have formed a hypothesis of what is likely to happen there. It appears that they can confirm or reject such an hypothesis without direct vision of the instrument such as would be required for accurate quantitative readings, so that it would seem that some information can be usefully extracted even from the extreme periphery of the visual field. Sanders used the same displays as before, and again observers were required to fixate the left side of the field at the start of the trial. The two columns of lights came on together, but the right hand one was extinguished very shortly afterwards, the intervals ranging from less than the time required to start an eye movement to more than enough for one to be completed.

It appeared that some information could be obtained even during eye movements, providing that the stimulus occurred within the eyefield; but the confidence ratings given by the observers were very low, and performance was poor especially at extreme separations.

A number of other studies are reported in Sanders' monograph. They include vigilance, information content of the signals, visual search, and memory tasks. From them it appears that the nature of the task, and in particular the amount of information in the display, alters the points at which the change from one kind of field to another is made. For example, in a visual search task sequential redundancy may be unobserved if the two lists are so far separated that a 'two stage' intake of information is required. In the search experiment the stimulus array consisted of six columns of lights, five of which had four lights and one of which had five. The task was to detect the latter. Sanders found that observers began their search at the column where five appeared on the previous trial, and that the increase in search time as a function of visual angle was entirely due to the five lights being more than 35° from the previously successful column. That is,

> ... in the first (selective) act 35° is covered while the remainder must await the next intake of information.

Sanders' experiments provide a useful division of work on visual attention. The way in which attention may be 'switched' by moving the eyes or head is obviously different and more 'thorough' (including as it does the total prevention of visual input from some parts of the environment) than is the case of attention directed within the stationary field. Perhaps the stationary field is analogous to experiments on selective listening described in the previous chapter. But how close is the analogy? There are some grounds for regarding the auditory system as fundamentally a sequential system, and the visual system as fundamentally a parallel system as regards the initial coding of sensory input. Are the two eyes really comparable to the two ears? Or should the two sides of a single retina be thought of as the two channels? Should a person examining the visual field within an angle of 35° but without really trying to hold his eyes still (perhaps looking at the illustrations of Gestalten in a text book) be regarded as working within the stationary field or within the eyefield? Is binocular rivalry comparable to competition between two auditory messages? Such are some of the conceptual difficulties to which reference was made earlier. In fact there have been rather few studies within the stationary field properly so-called. On the other hand there is an extensive literature on binocular rivalry and other forms of ocular interaction, and also on searching the visual field either when reading sentences or lists or when scanning an array of instruments, and recently there has been renewed interest in eye movements as a means of measuring the distribution of attention when looking at pictorial scenes. In addition there is a large, older literature on the 'attention getting' characteristics of various dimensions of stimuli such as size, brightness, and so on, which might also find a parallel in the work of modern ethologists on the 'innate releasing mechanisms' (Tinbergen, 1951). It may prove possible to relate such results to the problem of whether messages can be selected on the basis of these regions of signal space, just as we investigated the role of pitch, loudness and so on in hearing.

The practical difficulties of experiments on vision are considerable but are beginning to be overcome. Just as the invention of the tape-recorder has made such a difference to the recording of auditory material, so too there have been great improvements in eye movement recording and in methods of presenting visual stimuli. Anyone who has tried to prepare a run of 100 visual stimuli of known duration, variable interstimulus intervals, etc., with the aim of presenting them at rates as fast as one per second (which is already the limit of automatic slide projection), and has spent weeks shooting ciné film frame by frame, will know how large is the ratio of time spent in preparation to useful run time. The biggest methodological breakthrough for a long time is thus seen in the development of character generating oscilloscope displays driven online by small computers, in which stimulus properties, duration, rate of presentation, etc., can be changed in a few moments by typing instruction on a console. We may hope for great advances in this area in the near future.

One of the most extensive investigations is that by Senders and others into the allocation of attention to a number of instruments whose readings must be continuously monitored. The current state of his research has recently been summarised in two papers (Senders, 1966a, and 1967). In the former he states:

> The various analyses which will be presented rest on the following assumptions:
> 1 Visual distribution of attention is the major indicator of operator workload.
> 2 The various signals which must be monitored demand attention in a way which is dependent on the characteristics of the signal and the required precision of readout of the signal by the human operator.
> 3 The human operator is effectively a single channel device capable of attending to only one signal at a time.
> 4 The probability of human failure at any time is equal to the probability that two or more signals will demand simultaneous attention.

The simplest form of his theory deals with the case where the observer confronts several instruments, which in a laboratory experiment might be four centre-zero ammeters. His task is to press a button whenever the needle on any one of the ammeters exceeds some criterion. The movements of the needles are caused by feeding them with mixtures of complex low frequency sinusoidal current variations, so that the movements appear effectively random to the observer. The movement of each instrument is independent of the others, and the bandwidth of the function driving the instruments varies from one instrument to another. How will the observer allocate his attention?

In the simple case a very good estimate of his allocation of attention can be made simply on the basis of the Sampling Theorem. This states that for a complete reconstruction of a signal by an ideal mechanism, samples should be taken at least at twice the frequency of the maximum frequency present in the waveform being sampled. Senders assumed that the eye movements of the observers could be used to measure the moments at which samples were taken of the instrument's readings, and was able to obtain a remarkably good fit of his predicted curves to his experimental curves relating frequency of fixations to signal bandwidth. Allowance had to be made for the cases where an observer took two successive samples from the same instrument (in which case there was no change in fixation), and at a very low frequency samples were taken rather too often. The latter point is related by Senders to the difficulty of obtaining velocity information from the display at very low frequencies.

Subsequently the model has been elaborated to incorporate more realistic characteristics of displays, and has continued to predict behaviour remarkably well. The modifications allow for the fact that in real life situations there is frequently an interrelation between members of a set of instruments, so that their readings are not statistically independent. An obvious example would be the relation between the air speed indicator and the climb and dive attitude indicator in an aircraft. The model has been applied to the behaviour of pilots flying both a simulator and real aircraft and, despite disagreeing with the pilots' own account of how they distributed their attention, matches records of their eye-movements extremely well (Senders, 1966b). Quoting Senders from that paper:

We suppose that the probability of being on instrument A is P_a and the probability of being on instrument B is P_b. What then is the probability that a transition will occur from instrument A to instrument B? Since we assume that the probabilities of a transition to any instrument is merely the probability of being on that instrument, the transition probability (in one direction) is the product of the two state probabilities, $P_{\bar{a}\bar{b}} = P_a P_b$, and the probability of a transition in either direction is $2P_a P_b$. However, since the eye may make a transition from any instrument to that same instrument, the number of transitions which can be recorded by the cameras is less than the total number of transitions which can take place ...

As a result the probability of observing a transition between instruments A and B will be greater than the calculated probability $2P_{\bar{a}\bar{b}}$. Since a pair of looks on any instrument i has probability $P_i{}^2$, the measured frequency of transitions between A and B will be:

$$P_{\bar{a}\bar{b}_{meas}} = \frac{2P_{\bar{a}\bar{b}}}{1 - \sum_i P_{(i)}^2}$$

D

This theory, when applied to laboratory and real life data (films taken in the cockpit of aircraft while in flight), has accounted on occasion for over 90% of the variance, a truly remarkable achievement.

We may notice two features of the model. The first is that it is to do with the direction of attention in what Sanders would call the eyefield or the headfield, or both. Secondly it is a model in which the distribution of attention is entirely determined by the properties of the stimuli, not by the voluntary paying attention of the observer. In the terminology of Chapter 2, the observer is being tuned by the display, not paying attention to it. This is emphasised by the fact that the pilots who took part in these experiments were quite certain that they could describe the way in which they distributed their attention over the instruments. Some of them were extremely surprised to discover the real pattern of their eye movements. Senders has gone so far (personal communication) as to maintain that attention is almost never voluntary; that it is always determined by the stimulus configuration. This is obviously too extreme a view, since an observer could decide simply to ignore the instruments on the left hand side, say, of the instrument panel, a decision both voluntary and perilous! But it may be that once the observer voluntarily decides what portion of the environment he is going to handle to the exclusion of others, then within that region he is in fact tuned by the display, and is not in full control of the allocation of his attention. There is no reason why this kind of analysis could not be extended to the stationary field, in which case the model might have interesting possibilities also for the auditory modality, and hence for a more generalised quantitative theory of attention. It should be noted that if this turns out to be so it implies a discontinuous, discrete sampling of different regions of signal space with the rejected regions being turned off completely and not merely attenuated, as current theories for auditory selection seem to suggest. We shall return to this point in the final chapter.

The interaction between the properties of the stimulus and the direction of gaze has recently been taken up by Mackworth (1968). Using an improved eye movement recording system he examined what part of a picture viewers fixated most frequently, and correlated the regions of maximum fixation with the amount of information, in an informal sense, which those regions contained. In general the more information present in a region, the greater the number of fixations it received. This result clearly relates in some way to the theory put forward by Senders. But in addition there must be a large effect due to the observer's interests. It would be interesting to have a comparative study of the fixation preferences of artists and art critics of differing inclination, when looking at a range of pictures structured to a greater or lesser degree. For example the quasi-random pattern of a Jackson Pollock and the almost unstructured canvasses of Rothko or Olitski must have very different amounts of 'information' in them, and yet may be equally accept   objects to view for long periods, although we may expec   between observers of different critical schools.

The boundary between w   and headfields and work on the stationary field seems to   dition where the extent to which peripheral vision is use   is upon the nature of the task. We have noticed that   et al. (1955) found that observers were able, once they had some idea of what to look for, to make more than usual use of the periphery of the visual field: and Sanders noted that under different conditions of motivation it seemed that the change from stationary field to eyefield behaviour might be delayed. Similar results come from two studies on the effect of changes in transitional probabilities between words on the eye-voice span in reading. As is well known, people when reading actually look ahead a considerable distance. Both Lawson (1961) and Morton (1964b) examined how such looking ahead was related to reading different orders of approximation to English (Taylor and Moray, 1960). Both workers found that the eye-voice span increases with increasing redundancy of the material read. It is also interesting that Morton found no change in the fixation time as a function of the order of approximation; for Senders, while finding that the frequency of fixations changed with the bandwidth of the signal, found that the duration of fixations did not. It appears that information can be used over a wider visual angle when it is predictable, suggesting that the visual system, although a limited channel, may approach parallel processing at low information rates, as would be expected theoretically.

If the size of the stationary field can thus alter, or at least the extent to which its periphery provides information can vary as a function of the task and of the subject's motivation, is it possible to pay attention to one part of the stationary field and ignore others? That is, can attention be voluntarily directed to one part of the field and another part ignored, within the visual angle which normally could be handled with a single fixation? To put the question another way, suppose that we are performing an experiment in which stimuli are presented in a monocular tachistoscope. We present a dim red light as a fixation point and stimulus patterns 1° to the left of the spot. Will it make any difference to the observer whether we ask him to fixate the spot and pay attention to the stimulus to the left of it or ask him simply to fixate the spot?

It is obvious that the position of a stimulus within the stationary field does make a difference. (From this point on, unless specifically noted, reference to 'the field' will be to Sanders' 'stationary field'— what is seen without eye or head movements.) The acuity of the eye falls off very rapidly as we move away from the centre of the fovea, a change related to the structure of the retina. Is it possible to alter the acuity of two regions of nominally equal acuity merely by 'paying attention' to one of them? Remember that here 'to pay attention' to one region is a rather curious instruction, since there is nothing obvious which the viewer can do; there are no peripheral adjustments to be made. (The same question arises, as we have noted, in hearing, but one gets a slight impression from talking to subjects that they feel it easier to carry out the instructions in hearing than in vision.)

It has been known since the time of Dallenbach (1923) at least that there are gradients of 'importance', as he called them, in the visual field, and that these seem to be learnt or in some way acquired, and are not directly dependent, so far as is known, on non-homogeneities in the retina itself. All else being equal, the left hand side and the top of the field seem to have priority and to lead to more efficient processing of information, at least in Western gentiles. Short term voluntary changes have frequently been claimed. For example Kohler and Adams (1958) report three experiments. In the first observers were presented with grids of dots. Either they were asked to move the pattern to the left or right according to whether they liked it or not, or they were asked specific questions about its structure. The threshold (separation of components) at which the grid broke up into rows and columns was smaller when the subjects' attention had been drawn to the pattern than when they merely judged it for pleasantness. In the second experiment mirror words were presented (see

Figure 11) and the separation needed for the two parts of the word to be seen was greater if a judgment about the length of lines beside the word was given than if the words themselves were being described. Finally the authors claim that the extent of a figural after effect depends upon the degree of attention paid to the inducing figure.

Now obviously such experiments leave something to be desired. In the last mentioned paying attention might very well

Fig. 11. Separation of mirror words

alter the amount of eye movement, and hence might very well alter the size of the figural after effect. Another experiment in which eye movements were not controlled, and which produced a very strange outcome, was one reported by Babington-Smith (1961a). He claimed that if while fixating a point in the visual field the observer tries to 'attend to one of the objects (in the periphery) and try to see or describe it in detail' the object on which the observer concentrates, but not the other peripherally viewed objects, tends to disappear. Further discussion of this has followed (Thomson, 1961; Babington-Smith, 1961b). The writer has also replicated this observation using a table on which a number of playing cards were dispersed, with a class of students as subjects. Almost all of them reported Babington-Smith's effect. This observation seems extremely puzzling. It may be that what happens is that fading due to the Troxler effect is noticed in the case of the object on which the observer concentrates, and in trying to change his concentration to another object he also changes his direction of gaze slightly so that the fading for the new object appears less.

Recently (Grindley and Townsend, 1968), more carefully controlled experiments have shown that voluntary attention can be directed to some extent within the field. If the observer does not know within which quadrant of the field a small stimulus is to be presented he does less well in reporting its properties than if he knows the quadrant, even though eye movements are not apparent.

Kolers (personal communication) reports that if a semi-silvered mirror is arranged in such a way that an observer can see both the world ahead *through* the mirror and the world behind *in* the mirror he can voluntarily determine which image to suppress, despite the fact that no change in accommodation, focus, or fixation is required.

Probably the class of experiments on visual attention with the longest history is that on the 'span of apprehension', or 'how many things can one take in at a glance'. Although traditionally such experiments have been regarded as experiments on attention recent work has tended to reclassify the effects as largely due to memory, with either storage or retrieval mechanisms being mainly responsible for the limits on performance. In particular the work of Sperling (1960) places heavy emphasis on the rate of read-out rather than attention at input. Similar results were found by Moray et al. (1965) in the auditory modality. But such modern work does none the less bear on the question of whether there is processing of information in parallel, and if so how far into the nervous system. The eye as a transducer has clearly evolved to handle information which arrives at its receptor surface as a spatial array; the input is parallel. At least for foveal vision the anatomical design suggests that transmission in parallel continues for some distance into the nervous system. If twelve stimuli are presented, and leave the retina as signals on twelve sets of active transmission lines, where does the convergence take place which makes it so difficult to read this input? The span of apprehension experiment is a very strong argument for Broadbent's (1958) parallel to serial conversion through a filter with storage early in the system. It is worth making the point that, as usually carried out, such experiments are not likely to optimise the system's performance. A number of stimuli are presented, and either the observer is asked to repeat them (as in Sperling's experiment) or to give a number which corresponds to the number of stimuli present (as in the classical experiments). The first of these modes of response is obviously very complex. If letters of the alphabet are being used the observer must select, say, nine letters out of twenty-six and repeat them. Confusions may arise either in the perception or in the response selection, and speaking, writing, etc. take several seconds. Even the simple counting response to 'how many spots were present?' involves a coded response, in which a single name is chosen for a number of different spots. It is clearly possible that with more highly compatible input-output relations the span might be much higher. The nearest experimental design to avoiding such difficulties is the 'probe' experiment, but this has not been applied extensively to the span of apprehension as such, since Sperling's paper.

It is obvious that under everyday conditions we get the impression that information enters the visual system in parallel. We do not usually find ourselves unable to report both the height of a person and also his colour. We do seem to see at least small visual objects as wholes. But normal perception equally obviously involves taking a number of small discrete samples of different parts of visual displays and integrating the results in memory. We may then enquire to what extent different kinds of information and information from different parts of the visual array may be handled simultaneously.

There is a large literature from the early years of attention research on the interaction of different aspects of visual stimuli. Thus Meads (1915), Curtis and Foster (1917), Bowman (1920), and Friedline and Dallenbach (1929) examined such factors as the size, intensity, and position of stimuli as determiners of attention. Unfortunately, these studies often leave something to be desired by modern standards of control and, more importantly, the question usually put to the observers was whether attention made the perception of the stimulus 'more clear'. The use of the word 'attensity' and the interest explicitly in subject clarity rather than in overt responses, makes the work difficult to integrate with modern approaches.

Recent work does suggest that there may be non-homogeneities in the way in which the visual field is processed which alter the relation between stimuli presented in different regions. For example Payne (1967) studied reaction times to stimuli presented at various points on a circle about the fovea and 15° out. He reported that reaction times appeared to be slower to lights presented in the region 40° and 220° from the vertical (reading clockwise), and fastest in the regions 90–180° and 300–20°. Also he found that there were faster average reaction times when the light was presented in the region corresponding to the blind spot of the opposite eye. If these results can be substantiated, and if stable regions of differing reaction times do exist, then clearly the priority of entry to the perceptual mechanisms may differ for stimuli presented in different parts of the visual field. (The alternative explanation would be that the response side of the system is differentially reactive.) Whether such regions are retinal or central is unclear, nor is there evidence as to whether they have a permanent anatomical basis or are 'functional' (such as the learnt reading gradient from left to right). Recently Latour (1966) has shown that there may be local fluctuations of retinal sensitivity extending over perhaps 15′ of arc, in addition to slow fluctuations of retinal sensitivity over much larger areas. The extent to which various dimensions of a visual signal are handled independently of one another has been investigated by several workers in the field of information theory, and the reader is referred to the relevant chapters of Garner (1962), and to the following chapter.

Two series of experiments have directly attacked the division of attention within the stationary field in a way analogous to the methods used in hearing. These are by Sampson and his group (Sampson and Spong, 1961a; 1961b; Sampson, 1964; Sampson and Horrocks, 1967) who have applied the 'split span' method of Broadbent (1954) to vision, and by Whelan (1967). In the Sampson experiments a slide projector is used to back-project stimuli on a screen down the middle of which is an opaque division so that the left eye cannot see the right side of the field and the right eye cannot see the left side of the field. In some of the experiments fixation points were provided so that by fusing them a standard direction of gaze was maintained, and also a standard degree of binocular fusion of the fields. It will be recalled that one of the characteristics of Broadbent's experiments was that listeners tended to recall all the stimuli from one ear followed by all those from the other ear. Sampson and his co-workers began by presenting one series of digits to one eye and another to the other eye simultaneously. Typically the sets consisted of four left + right pairs, followed by time for recall. In this condition viewers tended to recall them as simultaneous pairs of digits, not eye by eye. (In earlier experiments care was taken by means of the fixation points to ensure that the stimuli appeared side by side and did not overlap.) This result is not surprising, whatever one may think about the organisation of the visual and auditory systems respectively. If two digits appear side by side in the visual field, the natural tendency will be to read them as single two-digit numbers. To read them otherwise might be expected to require considerable practice, just as one needs practice in order to see the world as an array of patches of colour side by side and not as a world of objects. Sampson presented digits to one eye and coloured patches to the other. Although there were great individual differences at least some of the subjects tended to report all digits together and then all colours together, rather than alternating. Digits were recalled more efficiently than colours, and had a shorter response time. This might be thought to show that response factors were involved rather than attentional ones, since it is plausible that most people have had greater practice at naming numbers than colour patches in everyday life, and therefore would show a reduced latency for numbers. No controls for this sort of effect were made. Stimuli presented to the left eye were less well recalled than stimuli presented to the right eye by those subjects who alternated between colours and digits. Recall from left eye was slower. (These last two findings could be linked, slow recall causing less accurate performance.) There were complicated interactions between side of the visual field, type of material and eye, which do not form a coherent pattern.

In the most recent paper Sampson and Horrocks (1967) explore in more detail the importance of different regions of the visual field. The method of presentation was the same as in the earlier experiments, but the arrangements of the stimuli in the first of their experiments were as shown in Figure 12.

By far the most frequent pairing of responses was upper-lower; that is the upper of a pair was given before the lower. The only exception, for which the relation was strongly reversed, was the last condition, where the upper stimulus appeared on the right hand side of the right eye and the lower on the left hand side of the left eye. Subjects again spontaneously reported in pairs as in the first experiment. When monocular presentation was used there was no difference in the accuracy of recall between the eyes. To quote Sampson and Horrocks:

> . . . there is no suggestion from this experiment that such differences can be demonstrated without binocular stimulation.

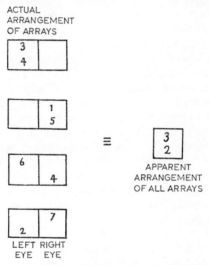

FIG. 12 Displays used by Sampson and Horrocks (1)

Under monocular viewing more information must be handled from one eye, because the same number of digits was presented on each trial, . . . Yet this additional information load had no effect, which indicates that simultaneous binocular stimulation has a significance other than that of simply adding to the number of stimuli which must be handled at once.

Unfortunately the paper does not give the scores in terms of relative or absolute per cent correct, nor as raw scores.

Finally the authors investigated the effect of overlapping the stimuli either binocularly or monocularly. Figure 13 shows the arrangements used.

Again unfortunately no scores are given, but only the significance of the relative differences. This severely reduces the value of the study. Recall was more accurate when viewing monocularly overlapped stimuli than when the overlapping was caused by binocular fusion. Again stimuli tended to be recalled pair by pair, giving the left hand digit first; and this tendency was

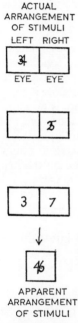

ACTUAL
ARRANGEMENT
OF STIMULI

APPARENT
ARRANGEMENT
OF STIMULI

FIG. 13. Displays used by Sampson and Horrocks (2)

more marked in the monocular recall condition. A further experiment was conducted to investigate the possible role of binocular rivalry. The slides of type C from the last experiment were presented one by one and viewers were asked to call out after *each* slide what they had seen. Again it is best to quote Sampson and Horrocks:

> The mean level of accuracy of report was 74·2% from the left eye and 85% from the right eye . . . this difference is statistically significant . . . this suggests that under these

conditions there is binocular rivalry . . . which is resolved in favour of the right eye. On the other hand when subjects are required to *fixate* binocularly . . . superimposing two points while digits are projected, there are no differences in accuracy of recall between the eyes.

Taken altogether these results suggest that providing fixation points binocularly results in an equal division of attention between the two eyes . . . which does not occur when the two eyes are left free.

It is difficult to follow the reasoning behind this argument. Even though the two monocular conditions with overlapping stimuli did not show any difference between the eyes it does not follow that a percentage difference score in the binocular condition shows that rivalry is present. There is no indication in the protocol that there was a fixation point used, and there was no control for eye movements. Hence it is quite possible that part of the difference is due to a tendency for fixation points to reduce somehow the efficiency with which stimuli on the left side are handled. Moreover even if binocular rivalry is present it cannot be occurring the whole time, since both eyes have a score of well over 50 %, implying that neither display was suppressed for more than about 20–25 % of the time.

These experiments are interesting and could be developed further, but they cannot be considered satisfactory as they are. It may be helpful to consider some of the difficulties inherent in this kind of display.

In the first place, it appears that no control was kept on eye movements. The duration of each of the stimuli was 0·3 seconds, and the interstimulus interval was 0·8 seconds. It is quite possible for there to be changes of fixation from moment to moment within a list, especially when fixation points were not provided. At any rate, since presumably the field was dark between presentations, there would be alternate moments when there were and were not fixation points, and mixed with these there might be after images of the display (no indication is given of the brightness of either ground or stimulus). There may have been loss of fixation during the dark period between stimuli, especially under the rather peculiar viewing conditions of a divided field. Since so few numerical data are given several points of this kind cannot be examined. The stimuli were of the order of 41′

of arc wide and 1°11′ high, and appear to have been presented at about 2° angular separation. However, there was no attempt to see whether acuity was symmetrical about the fixation point, and as Whelan (1968) has shown there are marked differences. It is also possible that 0·3 seconds, enormously long compared with the minimum time required to read in visual material, provides so certain a reading of the stimulus that relatively slight changes of performance due to differences between the left and right side, etc., would be swamped. Finally the optics of the situation leave a lot to be desired. Sampson and Horrocks themselves say that the eyes of the viewers probably 'over converged' for the display. The separation of the centres of the display was slightly greater than the average interpupillary distance, and was not adjusted for the individual subject; hence there would be an unknown degree of partial fusion, changes in convergence and accommodation, etc., which would introduce large individual variation in acuity from subject to subject. For all these reasons one might regard the experiments as interesting, but in need of repetition with better equipment and a more adequate account of the data obtained.

Related to this work, and including several of the required controls, is a series of recent studies by Whelan (1968). A diagram of his equipment is given in Chapter 8 (Figure 24). His study is remarkable for keeping one small group of observers right through the pilot, calibration and main experiment. The equipment could be adjusted for each observer, allowances made for their individual interocular distances, etc., and each tested against his own earlier calibration. The visual displays were basically similar to Sampson's, in that stimuli could be presented to either side of the visual field of either eye. Some experiments were done using ciné film; the later ones with a computer generated display with online control, so that onset and offset times, intersignal duration, etc., could be varied within a run and was accurate and reproducible to a millisecond. One part of the display could be altered while another could be left on, etc. Long runs were used, with the observers reading off the stimuli as they appeared. The optical train allowed control of convergence, brightness, etc., to suit the individual subject.

Before the main experiments Whelan mapped acuity for the detection of spots of light and of different letters of the alphabet of different sizes, different stimulus durations, and at three different degrees of eccentricity from the fixation point (2°, 4° and

6°) and obtained a confusion matrix for the stimulus material used. Viewers were tested both with a tachistoscope and with the binocular display system. In addition some flicker fusion experiments were included under binocular and monocular conditions. Eye movements were not continually monitored, but were sampled from time to time by direct observation of the edge of the pupil. Factors such as 'attention gradient' could be offset by staggering the onset times of the two sides of the display until they were equally efficient in report, so that the asymmetry in probability of report disappeared.

Whelan has not, at the time of writing, published the results of his experiments, but it is to be hoped that they will be soon made available. The following partial summary is based on a personal communication.

> I specifically attempted to eliminate attentional bias and took pains to select stimuli free from contamination of reading habits (directional coding, scanning, etc.). Use of fixation point (by the subject) . . . was checked by monitoring eye movements and analysis of confusion errors. This showed that the left of fixation recognition was *not* explicable solely in terms of left of fixation attention.

In his experiment the displays can be thought of as being arranged as in Figure 14.

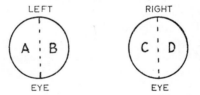

FIG. 14. Whelan's display in the stationary field

Whelan continues:

> . . . actual efficiency of recognition of a single number appearing in either A, B, C, or D with a letter in the other symmetrical position but with attention paid equally to both sides of the display was

A	B	C	D
25·10	24·10	28·03	25·27

A+C vs B+D shows left of fixation superior (p less than 0·05). A+B vs C+D shows right (dominant) eye superior (p less than 0·01). These are combining presentations at 2°, 4°, and 6° eccentricities of presentation from the fovea for each of the 4 hemifields; and for 10 subjects, all right eye dominant.

In one experiment the duration for which the stimulus was shown was decreased progressively during the run from 200 to 20 msecs. in 20 msec. steps. One stimulus was presented to region A and the other to D. Viewers were told which to report first. At short stimulus durations only (less than 80 msecs.) reporting D before A caused an increase in accuracy of reporting D, with no decline in the reporting of A. This underlines the point made earlier about the use of long stimuli by Sampson's group. Whelan comments:

> Heron, Mishkin, Forgays, Terrace, etc. have indicated that during central fixation reading habits cause attention to the left of a display presenting stimuli to both sides of fixation. Pre-exposure knowledge that right stimuli should be reported first would counteract the otherwise left of fixation bias due to the use of two stimuli simultaneously . . . Certain discontinuities in the curves of recognition scores as a function of duration and other data support [this] interpretation and show that the effect is not an artifact of the method of presentation (A goes to the left, non-dominant eye, and D to the right, dominant eye.)

When the onset of the stimuli was not simultaneous (A to the left eye before or after D to the right eye, or B before or after C) there was a greater tendency for subjects to accept a right-before-left order as simultaneous than a left-before-right. Whelan interprets this in terms of the right side of the brain being a centre for comparing information to the two sides of the visual field, and hence there being an added time for transcallosal transmission from the right field (left side of the retina) signals.

Evidence for asymmetries in the handling of non-alphanumeric signals came from his flicker fusion experiments. In-phase flicker delivered to regions A and C together gave a higher CFF than either A or C singly. Similarly in-phase flicker to B and D simultaneously gave higher CFF than B or D. And the increase in the first case was significantly greater than the increase in the second case.

Whelan thus provides evidence for a complicated interaction between eye dominance, position in the stationary eyefield at which the stimulus is presented, order of recall and type of stimulus; but he also shows that it is possible to sort out the different effects. For example, when a letter stimulus was used to 'mask' a number given to the same region of the opposite eye (like Sampson's last experiment but with total instead of partial overlap) and tachistoscopic presentation was used, the dominant eye received the higher recognition score, but both dominant and non-dominant eye showed superior performance when the stimulus was on the left of fixation. Many of the effects are small, though definite, and precise methods of presentation are required to detect them. The use of slide projectors is far too crude a method.

Finally, let us turn to a brief consideration of the question of binocular rivalry and similar binocular interactions. It is not intended to review the vast literature, but some studies are of special interest.

The most striking difference between hearing and vision, and one frequently remarked on, is that if a stimulus is presented to one eye only, and its duration and method of presentation precludes the use of cues such as closing the eye, etc., then the observer cannot say which eye has been stimulated, while listeners are in no doubt as to which ear has been stimulated in a monaural situation. In binocular rivalry situations there are few people who can decide with which eye they will see. In general, the viewer is tuned, rather than paying attention, in binocular conflict. First one eye and then the other, first one part of the display and then another, catches his attention.

It may be that stereoscopic displays will provide a powerful way of analysing the degree of independence of the dimensions of a visual stimulus. Thus Creed (1935) observed that if two postage stamps were placed in a stereoscope the design of one might appear in the colour of the other. Treisman (1962) reported several experiments in which there were disparities of brightness, position or colour between the eyes. The stimuli were annuli, which might be concentric or have nasal disparity of one pair of rings. Each eye saw an inner and an outer annulus. They might be either red or green, and were on a white background. There was enough nasal disparity to be seen as depth by all viewers. Therefore depth information was being combined from both eyes. But at the same time information about colour seemed to be acting independently.

It is rather rare for coloured fields presented stereoscopically to show a mixed colour, and no subjects reported yellow or brown circles. When the left eye received two red annuli and the right eye two green annuli most observers reported seeing only one colour at least part of the time, and yet depth was present. When the left eye received an outer red annulus and an inner green one, and the right eye the opposite, all observers saw depth, and all saw the annuli as patchy, part of the ring being in one colour and part in another. Seven out of nine subjects saw both annuli in the same colour at some time. Sometimes the displays were most striking, with the colours chasing one another round and round the ring, while the impression of depth stayed completely stable. In general the appearance of the displays was not under voluntary control. It was quite clear that to some extent different aspects of the display were being independently processed of one another, notably colour and position. Treisman said:

> There seem to be at least three kinds of perception: a random patchy network, suppression of one colour as a whole, and suppression of one retina as a whole.

Her conclusions have been confirmed by other workers. We have seen that Latour (1966) believes that there can be local fluctuations of threshold within a single retina. And Levelt (1965a, 1965b, 1966, 1967) has further quantified the relation between brightness and contour information. He advances the interesting hypothesis that a switch from one eye to the other in a rivalling situation is primarily dependent upon the state of the second eye. That is, it is not so much the fact that the left eye is brighter than the right eye which ensures that it dominates in the rivalry situation, as the fact that the other eye is less strongly stimulated.

The length of time for which a stimulus is visible is not determined by its own strength but by the strength of the contralateral stimulus. Figure 15 clarifies this point.

Levelt also provides a rationale for subsuming brightness, colour and amount of contour under the single concept of 'stimulus strength' and claims that the proportion of time that one eye dominates the other can be predicted on the basis of four principles: increase of stimulus strength in one eye will increase the predominance of that stimulus; increase of stimulus strength in one eye will not increase the mean duration for which that

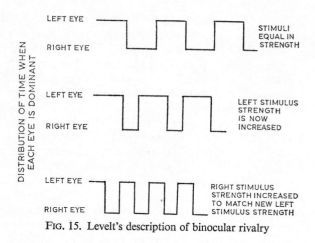

FIG. 15. Levelt's description of binocular rivalry

stimulus stays visible once it becomes visible (i.e. the average 'on period' before another switch); increase of stimulus strength in one eye will increase the alternation frequency. Levelt also investigated the range over which one contour can affect another so as to alter the time during which rivalry occurs, and found evidence that while local in its effect (which agrees with Treisman's observations), it is considerably bigger than Panum's area (6 minutes of arc), in which complete fusion occurs. Actually the degree to which Panum's area is the limiting factor depends to a considerable extent on how the experiment is carried out. It is well known that once the binocular fusion of a stereo pair has occurred, especially if the stimuli are photographs of the real world, the angular separation between the contours can be increased to a staggering amount before the images 'tear apart', while if initially presented at so large a separation they will not fuse. Fender and Julesz (1967) have recently provided some 'hysteresis curves' for this effect. A similar effect occurs in hearing. If the temporal disparity in time of arrival of a signal at the two ears is continuously increased beyond the point where complete lateralisation has occurred the messages eventually 'tear apart'. In general the tolerable delay depends on the meaningfulness of the signals, and is less when starting from the separated than from the fused condition. Julesz's work emphasises the degree to which the visual system is being tuned by the stimulus rather than being under the control of the observer when the eyes receive disparate input; for, as is well known, random patterns which have no observable monocular contours can produce stable three-dimensional displays when presented stereoscopically.

One study which reports that voluntary control can be exercised is that of Kaufmann and Pitblado (1965). The stimuli were arrays of typed letters, with position and brightness disparities, and the authors report that the perceived depth could be reversed by the observers at will. By contrast it is well known that if a stereo pair of pictures of the real world is arranged so that depth should be seen in reverse it will not be so seen, the observer's expectancies overriding what would be an absurd interpretation of the scene.

The discussion of the degree to which various aspects of a visual array may function independently, at least to some extent, reminds one of the large literature on the effects of perceptual set, and the degree to which such things as the organisation of ambiguous Gestalten, visual illusions and so on are under voluntary control. There is no doubt that there is valuable information about the way in which selective visual perception operates concealed in the vast amount of work on such topics. But apart from the laws, or rather descriptive generalisations, propounded by the Gestalt school, it is difficult to make a coherent picture. Perhaps the nearest recently is that of Neisser (1967) even though one may disagree with his conclusions. That there are selective processes available to viewers of the unified visual field which relate to the 'dissection' of information in rivalry is shown, for example, by Rabbitt's (1962) experiment, in which subjects performed a split span task, recalling by colour and shape instead of by ear and by ear. It is also possible that some of the phenomena connected with stabilised retinal images and their fading and re-appearance will, when we know more about them, be seen to be relevant to the control of visual attention (Evans and Piggins, 1963; Warrington, 1965, McFarland, 1965). Kolers (1968, personal communication) reports that it is possible to prevent selected parts of a stabilised image from fading as rapidly as non-selected parts.

Where, then, does this leave us? Apart from the obvious difference caused by the directivity of gaze, the fact that the eyes can be closed, and that head movements can 'switch off' visual input, it seems that the biggest difference is the degree to which voluntary control over attention can be exercised. However, this may turn out only to be an apparent difference. May there be bin-aural rivalry for certain classes of signals? The timing of events in the two modalities is certainly very different; perhaps a more fine grained analysis of hearing will reveal that there is auditory rivalry for very short signals.

Treisman (personal communication) has recently found that with computer synchronised dichotic pairs of digits there is considerable uncertainty as to which ear received which signal. It may be that with perfect auditory syn-chrony 'aural rivalry' occurs, although if so, it can be voluntarily controlled, as we will see in the final chapter on the psychophysics of pure tone dichotic presentation.

Comparatively little work has been done on cross-modal selection
using continuous tasks of the kind which are characteristic of
much of the auditory work. On the other hand there is an extensive
literature on the processing of multidimensional information,
particularly from psychophysical experiments designed to use
information theory or signal detection theory as the conceptual
framework to explain the results and using single signal presentation.

On the whole the psychophysics experiments imply that often
two dimensions of a stimulus, or two stimuli, may be better than
one. Whether the dimensions are completely independent, or
whether two modalities are used, there are a number of experiments which show that increasing dimensionality leads to
increasing information transmission. Extensive reviews of this
work are available in Attneave (1959) and Garner (1962). The
addition of an extra dimension to the stimulus once the limit of
information transmission has been reached frequently results in
at least a slight increase in performance. This is the opposite to
what one might expect from the work on selective attention
which we have already discussed in the previous chapters.
How it can happen is not well understood at present. But there
seem to be at least two pointers to an explanation. Firstly most of
the experiments which show that adding a dimension or a channel
can increase information transmission are 'one shot' experiments,
while most of the experiments which show only competition are
continuous tasks; and secondly there is often some way in which
the dimensions are correlated when they improve performance.

For example Howarth and Treisman (1958) found that a
simultaneous warning signal in one modality can lower the
threshold for the detection of a target presented in another modality. Tulving and Lindsay (1967) found that the simultaneous

presentation of a signal in one modality did not lower the accuracy of absolute identification in another. Taylor, Lindsay and Forbes (1967) investigated the sharing of capacity between several discrimination tasks, and found that requiring two tasks to be done reduced the apparent information capacity of the human observer by some 15%, but that, allowing for that reduction, two visual, two auditory, or one visual and one auditory task, or even two visual and two auditory tasks could be performed simultaneously. They write:

> The general result is consistent with Moray's position that the processor capacity is finite may be used for any of several tasks, and must be devoted partly to programming when complex problems arise. Processor capacity is less efficiently used for discrimination when it must be shared between two tasks than when it can all be devoted to one task, but it costs no more to share among four than among two. Sharing within a modality is as difficult as sharing between modalities.

On the other hand there are equally a number of studies which show that signals in two modalities interfere severely one with another. Broadbent (1956) found that there was a decrement in a visual task when an auditory task with much information was presented simultaneously. Mowbray (1952, 1953, 1954) in some of the earliest of the modern selective attention experiments found that in reading or 'Listen-and-Answer' tasks there was severe mutual interference to material presented simultaneously in two different modalities.

How is the difference to be resolved? It may be that memory is crucial. In 'one shot' experiments a warning is given, the stimulus occurs, the observer makes his response, there is a pause, and the next cycle begins. It is possible that in such experiments the observer, as Broadbent suggested in his Filter Theory, handles one of the inputs directly, and then reads out the remainder of the information from a short term memory store. Since there is plenty of time this stored material can be used for correlation with the earlier (directly processed) information, or processed (in a slightly degraded form) in its own right. At least it is available for use and there is time to use it. For independent stimuli, especially in more than one modality, the idea of the information being stored separately is straightforward; but for independent storage of the several dimensions of a single stimulus we would need to postulate that the passage of the information through the receptors and associated structures resulted in its being effectively separated along the different dimensions, with the subsequent storage and sequential scanning of the different dimensions as if they were independent signals, followed by the reintegration of the information. The fact that Howarth and Treisman (1958) found that the warning signal was effective even if presented *after* the target signal for which it was a warning strongly implicates memory in some way in the integration of such 'simultaneous' cross-modal stimuli.

Multiple or continuous presentations at high signal rates would alter the picture. If more than three or four signals in quick succession are presented the running memory span is exceeded, and it is well known that even within a running memory span the extent to which information is available from the memory trace is much reduced. In line with the ideas just presented we would expect that when a continuous task is presented there is no time for the observer to make use of the memory trace of the second channel, which is anyway less effective than in single shot conditions (Pollack, Johnson and Knaff, 1959; Moray and Reid, 1967). Hence there is competition and interference, rather than integration of information from the two sources. Throughout the literature there seems to be this discrepancy between continuous and one-shot tasks, and it is obviously an area in need of research.

Finally let us turn to the groups of experiments which raise the question of the range of selectivity, and also questions of memory and whether there may be several rather different selective mechanisms present. This work has recently been reviewed by Moray (1969a) and will not be extensively treated.

We have seen that sensory modality and various dimensions within a modality such as pitch, colour, position, etc., can all be the basis of selectivity. Just how far ranging are such categories? Most of the experiments in this field have been modifications of the 'split span' experiment of Broadbent (1954). In this, three simultaneous pairs of digits or other signals are presented to the listener, who is then required to recall them. In the original version one of each pair was presented to the left ear and one of each pair simultaneously to the right ear of a listener, and Broadbent found that recall ear by ear (LLLRRR) was much superior to alternating. Since then Moray and Barnett (1965) have found that selection could be similarly directed to male and female voices over a single loudspeaker, with similar results; and Moray and Jordan (1966) that practice and compatibility play a crucial part in the levels of performance reached. Gray and Wedderburn (1960) extended the classes used with the following paradigm,

Left ear: Poor 9 Jane
Right ear: 4 Aunt 6

and with two interleaved sentences. They found that recall was just as good along the sentence or category as ear by ear. Broadbent and Gregory (1964a) confirmed this for letters and numbers, but pointed out that such response modes seem more difficult than ear by ear. Broadbent (1958) had originally suggested that the filter in his theory might be tunable to a verbal class in addition to being tunable to physical characteristics of incoming signals; but Moray (1961) found that, if so, the classes which could be chosen were rather limited. Kolers has recently (1968) discussed switching between languages, and has suggested (personal communication) that those sets of stimuli which are denumerable by the subject may be usable as the basis of selection (so that, for example, the class 'all nouns' would probably not be a possible basis for selection). As we have seen, Treisman (1964a) found that languages could be the basis of selection except in true bilinguals.

It seems likely that selection on the basis of such 'high level' classifications as those just mentioned would necessitate us postulating a rather different kind of selective mechanism from that needed merely to select a sensory dimension. There is obviously a great need for work on the cataloguing of categories and properties which can be the basis of selection. It is interesting in this respect that the work of Sutherland (1964) and Mackintosh (1964, 1965) has led to the introduction of a concept very similar to attentional categories on discrimination learning in animals. Their theory postulates a two-stage learning process in which the animal must first learn what dimension of the stimulus is relevant, and then the discrimination along that dimension. This work, it is to be hoped, will provide the beginning of the inclusion of animal work into research on attention, a most important development both for behavioural theory and for the hope that some decent physiological work may follow.

For a systematic quantitative model of the learning of categories in discrimination experiments, see Trabasso, T., and Bower, G., *Attention in Learning*, 1969, Wiley, N.Y.

7 THE SHARING OF ATTENTION BETWEEN INPUT AND OUTPUT

The several theories which have been offered to explain the limits on our ability to handle information have essentially been concerned with the generation of responses to one or more incoming messages. Competition is between messages received in parallel. Thus Broadbent (1958) originally postulated selection by a filter which occurred fairly peripherally; Treisman (1966) placed selection somewhere along the input pathways but before the recognition system; and Deutsch and Deutsch (1963) in the recognition system itself but prior to conscious perception.

Common to all these is the idea that there must be a narrowing of the information channel somewhere between input and output, before which signals can be handled in parallel and after which a drastic reduction in the information rate occurs. Models of attention have been concerned with input. On the other hand, although there has been little theoretical discussion linking such experiments with attention, it is now well known that the availability of responses and stimulus-response compatibility relations may be a vital factor in determining the maximum rate at which information may be handled. The work of Pollack (1959), Crossman (1953), Rabbitt (1962) and others has shown that often it is response entropy rather than stimulus entropy which produces the characteristic slope relating uncertainty to response time. Fitts and Deininger (1954), Leonard (1959) and Davis et al. (1961) have shown cases where SR compatibility results in apparently parallel processing in reaction time studies; Moray and Jordan (1966) have shown the importance of such factors in split span tasks; and Taylor et al. (1967) have followed the suggestion of Moray that the narrowest part of the information channel is a function of the task, some of the capacity being taken up in organising the channels, and the rest shared.

In this chapter we shall examine the role of responses in limiting attention. Just as too heavy a load of incoming information may force time sharing between incoming messages to occur (with consequent loss of information due to overloading but with the possibility that the net transmission rate may be maintained by increasing the time spent on handling one message and decreasing it on the other), so may the same kind of relationship hold when we consider the two halves of a transmission task, input and output. Just as two incoming messages may compete for attention, so may input and output. If a person is trying to to write a letter he will not be able to report also on the content of an informative message which he overheard.

The most direct example of the interaction between input and output comes from an experiment by Baddeley (1966). Baddeley was concerned with the ability of a human being to act as a random generator. The task was to speak letters of the alphabet 'at random' at a rate paced by a metronome. Runs of 100 utterances were recorded and analysed on the basis of digram frequencies and of first order probability distributions over the letters. Subjects proved surprisingly good randomisers, but showed more redundancy as the rate of generation was increased by speeding up the metronome. In addition Baddeley investigated the interaction of the generation task with a secondary distracting task, card sorting. The effect of adding the secondary task was that the redundancy of the generated sequence increased with the logarithm of the number of categories into which the cards had to be sorted. Furthermore the redundancy of the generated sequence increased with the logarithm of the size of the ensemble which the subject was generating, up to eight alternatives.

Baddeley concluded that his people were acting like limited capacity systems involved in a search task, and related his results to choice reaction times and naming tasks (absolute identification). However, a detail of his second experiment is particularly interesting in the light of other later work. In the card sorting task his subjects made almost no errors, although the sorting was paced. The random generation became more redundant. Harrison and Moray performed a very similar experiment (unpublished) and found the opposite result. In this the subjects were asked to type random numbers on a typewriter in time to a metronome and without seeing their output. The secondary task was to listen for spoken numbers which from time to time were heard over a loudspeaker. On hearing a number the listener was required to add or subtract a constant and speak his answer without ceasing to type out his response. Over the range of constants (zero to plus or minus seven) the accuracy of addition was inversely related to the size of the constant, but the redundancy of the typed sequence of digits did not alter.

The two experiments will fit neatly into a single explanatory scheme if we make the simple assumption that the information processing capacity of the system is common to both the input and the output aspects of the tasks. Consequently if the instructions, tone of voice and manner of the experimenter leads the subject to expect that the generator task is more important than the secondary one, enough capacity will be provided for the former, while the secondary task will suffer. If, on the other hand, the subject receives the impression that what we are calling the secondary task is actually the one at which he should try to maintain perfect performance, then the performance on the primary task will suffer. The allocation of capacity within the overall outlines of the experimental instructions may be carried out on a kind of game-theoretic planning of behaviour (Miller et al., 1960). The competition for 'processing space' can be seen in several other experiments covering different fields. Murdock (1965), for example, found that short term recall suffered if a card sorting task were carried out, and vice versa. Moray and Beck, (see Moray, 1969a) investigated the direction of attention to different aspects of a split span task. Following the suggestion by Moray and Barnett (1965) that errors in recall in split span tasks were primarily linked to output mechanisms, and omission errors to input mechanisms, they were able to abolish one or other kind of errors by paying subjects to avoid them. Again, Broadbent and Gregory (1963) found evidence that performing a storage task and a detection task simultaneously resulted in a decrement of performance on each, and Broadbent and Heron (1962) concluded that:

> immediate memory involves continuous action on the part of some mechanism which is also needed for perception, and that this mechanism cannot handle both tasks simultaneously.

Norman and Lindsey (1967) have found that performing a detection and recall task together affects the memory task but not the detection task. An apparent exception to the generalisation that output competes with input for capacity and vice versa comes from an experiment by Lawson (1966b). She found that the rate of spontaneous speech was not affected by having to monitor a message for the occurrence of clicks and to respond by tapping the microphone. She related her results to the observations by Cherry, Treisman and Moray that nonverbal messages do not suffer attenuation in shadowing tasks. However there are not fully adequate controls in Lawson's experiment to establish the influence of the secondary task, and it cannot be considered a strong argument against the thesis being put forward here: that is, if we pay attention to input space, our capacity to handle output space suffers, and vice versa.

Confirmation of this idea of the relation of input to output from very different kinds of experiments can be found in some modern work with a Gestalt psychological flavour. Gardner and Lohrenz (1961) and Adamthwaite and Schaffer (1965) investigated the degree of 'assimilation' of one form to another as a function of an interfering task. A pair of abstract geometrical forms was presented and a few seconds later the subject was required to reproduce the forms by drawing. The drawings were then rated by judges on assimilation. (Assimilation means that each had become similar to the other member of the pair.) Correlation between the judges was better than $+0.8$. In both experiments the distracting task was to count backwards by twos during the initial presentation. In both it was found that assimilation was greater if there had been such counting backwards. Unfortunately the methods of scoring are not sufficiently accurate to give much quantitative information. More unfortunately still no measure of performance on the secondary task was made; but in their account Gardner and Lohrenz remark that they had to ask their subjects to count loudly since some of them lowered their voices 'as if to reduce distraction', which suggests that they were indeed trying to reduce their generator load while taking in information about the stimuli.

This phenomenon of talking quietly or whispering or responding *sotto voce* recurs throughout the literature on selective listening. It is not obvious why talking less loudly should reduce the load on the central processor. Intuitively it might be thought that the selection and organisation of output rather than the actual wiggling of the tongue and activation of the laryngeal muscles would be the major source of the load. It may be that it is not the output of the response that is causing the trouble, however, but its monitoring by the speaker. As is well known from studies on delayed auditory feedback (see Yates, 1964, for a review) and also from studies on the masking of speech output with noise, a speaker usually monitors his output. We shall see when we come to consider the measuring of switching time that the result of this is to add one extra task to the load on selective sharing of attention which confronts the subject. If we use the notation developed in chapter 2 we may say that any task which uses a continuous spoken (or written) response, and perhaps more generally any non-ballistic output, is not a single task which may be described by

$$\overset{a}{\underset{\uparrow}{}} : (r_a) | I\{a\}$$

but rather by

$$\overset{a}{\underset{\uparrow}{}} : (r_a) | I\{a_t\} + J\{f_a\}_{t + \Delta t}$$

where f is the feedback from r_a. That is, if we are right in suggesting that there is competition for attention between input and output, then all tasks with non-ballistic (and hence monitored) or servo-controlled responses are actually attention-competitive tasks.

We may now interpret the tendency to become quiet in spoken response tasks as an attempt to reduce the extra burden of secondary incoming information. The exact nature of *sotto voce* responses has not received much attention since the attempts of the behaviourists to establish that all thought was represented by muscular activity too slight to be observed. In some cases a *sotto voce* response may disappear, output ceasing completely as a reception task proceeds (Haydeck et al., 1966). It would seem at least that if the feedback from spoken responses is not monitored, signals which occupy some of the same regions of input space as the original signals (and hence require a share of the processor) would be omitted, and so the information load would be reduced. There is some evidence that adopting *sotto voce* achieves more than this, and may in some sense actually avoid output altogether, at least to the extent of the subject not having to control output musculature. In an early shadowing experiment Poulton (1953) found that his subjects responded with jargon, although thinking that they were producing correct speech. In a personal communication to the writer Poulton said that one possible reason for this was that the subjects were whispering their responses into microphones very close to their mouths. It is also worth observing that the speech rates used by Poulton were considerably faster than those later used for the greater part of the shadowing work, which would also encourage his subjects to find some way of reducing the load. Poulton compared shadowing performance with responding in the gaps between groups of seven to ten words. The messages were presented over headphones, and in the condition where responses were made between presentations subjects said 'Ah—ah—ah . . .' while listening, as a control for masking.

To quote Poulton, his subjects remained unaware that they 'were speaking drivel'. Two more quotations are in order from Poulton's paper. The first is to do with the 'Ah—ah' response used to control self masking:

> During practice the production of this sound became pretty automatic and from then on required little attention.

The second is:

> It is to be concluded that the subject cannot give the necessary attention simultaneously both to an incoming message and to what he is saying,

which antedates the suggestion of the present writer by over a decade!

Unfortunately we cannot make use of the difference in accuracy between Poulton's subjects and those of later workers, since the drop in errors in shadowing which we might expect due to the elimination of feedback reception is of course offset by the increase due to the utterance of jargon. Poulton's subjects seem to have thought that their utterances were coherent speech, and it is interesting in connection with this to turn to a paper by Moray and Taylor (1958). They asked listeners to shadow statistical approximations to English (Miller and Selfridge, 1950; Taylor and Moray, 1960; Moray, 1966). The competing message to be rejected was continuous English prose. The initial expectation was that where the accepted message became nonsense, at low orders of approximation, there would be a greater number of importations of words from the rejected message. What was observed, however, was a rise in both omission and commission errors in the shadowing, and also, at low orders of approximation, a kind of transient dysphasia. For example, where the listener was shadowing a second order approximation that went

'the boy went to eat fish on plates is only washed up on Sunday. . . .'

the response might be:

'the boy went to . . . ah . . . ah . . . and then is washed up . . . ah . . . ah . . . Sunday . . .'

and so on. The majority of the subjects maintained that they 'could hear the message correctly but could not get it out'.

Now in a shadowing situation where the message being received is unusually low in redundancy, and indeed actually conflicts with the learnt transitional probabilities of English speech, it becomes essential in order correctly to repeat the message to hear all the incoming words, for the loss of the usual digram and trigram associations means that few mistakes can be offset by using the learnt store of linguistic relations. Various estimates of the redundancy of written and spoken speech are available, and the lessons from them and from such experiments as the speech switching experiments of Cherry and Taylor (1954) and Schubert and Parker (1955) are clear. At speech rates of around 150 words per minute a listener can spend a large proportion of his time in monitoring and controlling his output, and still be able to cash in on redundancy and make correct identifications of incoming signals. With non-redundant signals, however, he must pay attention to each incoming word as it arrives, since only by accurate reception can he possibly carry out his instructions to repeat the message. Hence, in terms of our present suggestions, he has less capacity available to generate responses, and hence the 'dysphasia'.

Further evidence comes from some recent experiments by Salter (personal communication to the writer). The present writer interprets his work to show that, at least under some conditions where delayed auditory feedback is interfering with speech, the presence of a secondary task may reduce the interference caused by the delay. The secondary task prevents the speaker from hearing the delayed feedback, which will have less effect on him. Lawson (1966b) found that the different composition of secondary messages used as distractions made no difference to the rate of spontaneous speech generation; but since in this case no control condition was used without any distraction, and since the spontaneous speech rate was 170 words per minute (which may be high enough almost to fully occupy the processor) it seems doubtful whether any distracting effect was being produced at all. The failure to find differential effects is not surprising.

Many other studies can be found in the literature which might be used to strengthen the case here being presented. For example Tune (1964) provides an example of a visually orientated generating task with secondary auditory distraction. And much of the relevant literature has already been summarised in Broadbent's *Perception and Communication*. As he noted in that monograph (p. 31):

> The more complex the response, the more the interference with the reception of information.

There is, then, little doubt about the facts. But none of the models which we reviewed in Chapter 3 explicitly deals with this aspect of attention. Broadbent's and Treisman's models were created essentially to deal with competition among inputs, Deutsch and Deutsch's as a revision of Treisman's, and neither Reynolds nor Egeth's reviews really offer a coherent theory. The nearest to a theory dealing with both input, output and transmission features of competition for capacity is Neisser's. But, as we saw earlier, he has excluded most of our kind of experiments as 'preattentional', and does not really offer a discussion of how more than one analysis-by-synthesis might be carried out at the same time, although not ruling out the possibility. The emphasis hitherto has always been upon what might be called the classical idea of attention, in which more than one signal from the external world competes for attention. However, the extension of this competition between different aspects of a task in the way proposed here is not entirely new, for the usual way in which people ask about research in attention when they hear about it is, 'Can a person *do* two things at once?' and all we are doing here is to underline the importance of all aspects of a task as determining the maximum rate at which it may be carried out.

Before trying to suggest some theoretical ideas which may serve to draw the work together we may do well to consider some rather distantly related work which seems relevant. For example one theory of the psychological refractory period (see for a summary, Welford, 1967) says that following a response the central processor is occupied by some activity to do with the response (perhaps the monitoring of feedback) so that the later incoming information can only get as far as a temporary store and cannot occupy the central processor contemporaneously with the activity representing the response. This could be taken as an example of one kind of experiment where response and reception compete for capacity. It would, if one were to adopt such an interpretation, lead to the suggestion that the locking out of the incoming information was at least as complete as is the rejection of the unwanted message in shadowing, although one study (Bertleson, 1967) has suggested that in some cases partial processing of the second signal may be happening during the refractory period, even though another (Davis, 1967) came to the opposite conclusion.

Perhaps even closer conceptually is the body of data on stimulus-response compatibility. This term was introduced by Fitts and Deininger (1954) to describe the important departures from information theoretical relationships between stimulus ensemble and reaction time where there is a specially close relationship, often in a straightforward geometrical sense, between receptors and response. Perhaps the clearest example of this is the study by Leonard (1959) in which people rested their fingers upon relays which were energised by alternating current. The subjects were asked to press down the finger which was stimulated, a highly 'compatible' response, and Leonard found no difference between two, four and eight alternatives. Recently Broadbent and Gregory (1965) have found that if in Leonard's task incompatible responses are demanded there is an increase in reaction time. The effect of distraction is greater the larger the number of alternatives and the less the compatibility, which the idea being put forward in this chapter would predict.

It is also known that with prolonged practice of an incompatible reaction time task (Mowbray and Rhoades, 1959) or with rather shorter practice of a compatible task (Davis et al., 1961) the reaction time becomes independent of the number of alternatives, at least up to an ensemble of eight. Practice clearly allows subjects to learn a more efficient way of processing the data, and hence reducing the amount of processing required. An interesting example of what may be a similar reduction of

E

the load by dropping non-essential features of the initial mode of information processing is the finding by Haydeck et al. (1966) that during silent reading the activity of the speech muscles extinguished rapidly. As was mentioned earlier, this may relate to the apparent 'expansion' of the channel in *sotto voce* shadowing.

Now it is well known that in many cases the selection of responses is what is taking the time in a reaction time experiment. Bearing in mind the findings on stimulus-response compatibility, and assuming that the central nervous system constantly tries to raise the rate of information flow to follow the instructions given, what is it that is reduced by practice, and what is the nature of the set of alternatives, selection among which takes so much time?

In an earlier chapter we referred to Broadbent's suggestion that stimuli should be specified as points in a multidimensional space. Could we plausibly suggest that there is similarly a response space within which responses can be identified as points specifiable by a series of co-ordinates? If so we might think of the transmission of signals in, for example, a reaction time experiment as the mapping of points in the input space on to points of the output space (Moray, 1967). The exact number, and indeed the nature, of the points in the input space is unclear, since there is the well known discrepancy between the number of discriminable differences in sensory space and the achievements of subjects in absolute identification tasks (see the series of papers by Pollack, 1952–1955; and Garner, 1962). Whatever the nature of the input and output spaces it is clear that the mapping functions which we require of people acting as subjects are extremely variable. Four lights in different positions, four sounds of differing loudnesses, four touches to different fingers might each be linked, by experimental instructions, to the same output, 'Press key 1 for stimulus 1, key 2 for stimulus 2, and so on.' Since we commonly use a rather small set of responses for many different experimental stimulus situations the reaction time situation as such (though not necessarily within a given experiment) is a many-to-one mapping of stimulus on to response. In experiments where there are fewer responses than stimuli there is a many-to-one mapping within an experiment, and there is no reason to think that a particular one-to-one mapping is equivalent to another (say four lights and four sounds). This question of the convergence or divergence of information flow has been discussed by Posner (1964) in an interesting paper on the taxonomy of information processing tasks.

We may thus think of a set of 'sensory co-ordinates' and a set of 'motor co-ordinates'. The initiating of a response begins with the selection of a subset of motor co-ordinates in the motor space, which define an overt response in the sense of determining which muscles shall be activated, and to what extent. If there is an arbitrary allocation of stimulus to response, or vice versa, involving many-to-one or one-to-many mapping, or even complex or 'crowded' one-to-one mapping, we may expect such mapping to take extensive computation by the nervous system and hence to require more time and 'hardware' than a direct one-to-one mapping. In other words incompatible S–R relationships will produce longer reaction times than compatible ones. It is note-worthy that in Leonard's experiment the mapping was particularly direct. In fact in that experiment the spinal cord motoneurones for the muscle groups involved are at the same level as the sensory roots of the dermatomes of the fingers involved. The flexor digitorum sublimis, flexor digitorum profundus and flexor digiti V muscles are innervated from C7, C8, and T1 roots, and the skin of the hand feeds into dorsal roots of C7, C8, and T1. It is a common adage of motor physiology that what is represented at the cortex are movements rather than muscle groups; but it can hardly be a mere accident that such a striking concordance be-tween sensory and motor innervation, providing an obvious and direct mapping of skin to finger movement, also provides a situation where there is no difference between two, four, and eight choice reaction times. Likewise, the other situation where little practice was required to abolish the difference due to ensemble size was that of echoic responses to spoken signals (Davis et al., 1961). As Cherry has observed (1957), speech is almost the only case where we emit the same signals that we receive, and we might therefore expect the input-output mapping functions to be of a particularly simple and direct kind. (Recently Rabbitt (personal communication to the writer) has found evidence that confusions occur more between the same finger of opposite hands than between adjacent fingers of the same hand, which suggests that the ideas outlined in the above paragraph need considerable refinements.)

Returning to the mainstream of the discussion, the point is that, taken all in all, the evidence suggests that just as a person in an experiment may select one input rather than another, so he may select one output rather than another, or output rather than input, or vice versa, as the aspect of the task to which he will pay attention. Just as his attention may be caught by one message rather than another, so it may be caught by output rather than input, or vice versa, depending upon the amount of processing which is required to identify the signal received and to determine the value of the co-ordinates of the desired response in the output space.

The possible nature of this hypothetical output space remains to be considered. It is clearly to do with the moment-to-moment control of motor output. If we were to think of it as selection among cortical motoneurones we would have to predict very slow reaction times for speech and thumb responses compared with the little finger, since the cortical representation of lips, tongue, etc., and the thumb, are very large compared with that of the little finger. In fact, reaction times with the latter are slower than with either of the former. On the other hand, as has been said, it seems to be in some sense true that movements, not muscles, are represented at the cortex. Movements, even so-called 'ballistic' ones, involve many muscles, the interaction of flexors, extensors, synergists and antagonists, and usually some kind of control through the kinaesthetic afferent system which monitors position and force. It is not easy, therefore, to say within what set selection may be occurring. A very large number of motoneurones in the cortex may have a more direct relation to a complex response than may relatively few motoneurones controlling movement of a clumsily synthesised 'analogue' kind. The large population might represent a small population of discrete movements. Very complex sets of alternatives may be called upon in tasks such as simultaneous translation or even in straightforward speech shadowing. Cramer (1965) found that affective stimuli called up more associations than neutral words, and tried to estimate the relative sizes of the response sets available. (Her use of 'entropy' to describe her results is, incidentally, misleading, since she gives a direct measure not a metric based on log (probability of occurrence).) Goldmann-Eisler (1958a, 1958b) has shown that pauses in speech relate to parts of sentences where there is an unusually heavy information load imposed by the large number of possible alternative words available due to the grammatical and syntactical structure of the sentence, a clear case of response selection. Morton (1964a) has discussed response selection in speech operation. A more direct example of response selection can be seen in the experiments which show that people can be trained to activate single motor units rather than entire muscles (Basmajian, 1963). This must be regarded as the most refined response selection task which can be envisaged, and it would be interesting to see how learning time and performance in what might be called 'Reaction Twitch Studies' vary with the size of the innervation to particular muscles. It is to be hoped that the recent upsurge of interest in motor behaviour will lead to studies of the selectivity and control of responses, parallel to our now quite extensive knowledge of the sensory side of information flow.

Finally we may consider two further possibilities. Firstly is there competition between outputs at the behavioural level? At an anecdotal level this would seem to be true to anyone who has tried to pat their head while rubbing their stomach with a circular motion at the same time. Indeed the early stages of any complex sensory-motor skill give a strong impression of competition between responses, although the analysis here is complicated by the presence of both a display and a feedback component. There seems to be little work on the simultaneous performance of two generator tasks, at least in recent papers, but there is little doubt that two such tasks would compete. An interesting anecdote in this connection was told the writer by a stenographer who had for some time been working for an employer in the north of England. When later taking dictation from a southern employer with a different accent, she found her fingers 'locking up' on the keyboard because, although she knew what word to expect next, it came in a different phonetic form. (Stenotyping is essentially a phonetic transcription.)

Secondly let us try to generalise the idea of competition between the different aspects of a task one stage further, and say that, just as competition may occur between inputs, outputs and between either, so the performing of complex transformations upon a message being transmitted between input and output may compete for the subject's attention either actively or passively (attention being caught). Thus tasks involving reordering, parallel to serial conversion, or vice versa, translation, arithmetic operations ('add three to each number and speak the sum') etc., will all reduce the apparent rate of handling the input-output transmission proportionately to the complexity of the transform. Figure 16 shows examples schematically.

FIG. 16. The reorganisation of the central processor for different tasks

In this chapter we turn to what is one of the two central problems of attention, the other being to what extent attention may be shared between two tasks. Their importance lies in the fact that an adequate knowledge of the answers is required before any model of attention can be constructed. The problem of the switching of attention has been tackled by several workers in the last few years, but with the exception of visually switching attention by fixating different regions of visual space we have at present no completely satisfactory information about it. Until we know more we cannot rule out a 'flip-flop' model of selective attention, unlikely though the latter may be intuitively. If we ask the question 'How exactly does paying attention alter the way in which a subject performs a task?' it is obvious that two essential features of the answer will be how often he can switch his attention from one aspect of the task to another, and how long it may take him to do so.

There is one source of ambiguity which is often not made apparent in the research literature on this topic. In asking the question, 'How quickly can one switch attention?' either of two answers may be required. On the one hand, we may wish to know how many times per second an attentional switch can be made; on the other hand how long it takes, on a particular switch, to get from one message to the other—that is, whether there is any 'dead time' such as exists in a relay change-over while the common contact is travelling from one fixed contact to the other, and if so, what is the duration of this dead time. The relation between the two, which will be called the *switching rate* and *switching time* problems respectively, is complicated. Obviously a long switching time must produce a low switching rate. It is however by no means true that a low switching time must produce a high switching rate, since it is quite possible that a system may have a 'minimum dwell time' which entails its staying in the state which it has recently entered for some minimum time. One source of such a minimum dwell time in a mechanical system might be inertia. Neurologically several possible causes can be envisaged, although there is not enough evidence to support any of them at present. Basically, the minimum dwell time would be limited by neuro-chemical processes at inhibitory and excitatory synapses.

The relation between switching time and switching rate, and the way in which they interact to produce a limit on the rate at which the information processing capacities of an organism can be shared, may be illustrated by Figure 17.

The first four diagrams show how performance would be limited when the selective mechanism was switching as rapidly as possible in an attempt to monitor both messages at once. The final diagram shows a momentary lapse of attention when the task is to select one message continuously. It is assumed for the moment that the mechanism is a flip-flop switch, not an attenuation mechanism as suggested by Treisman. If one were to assume an attenuation mechanism, then much the same diagrams could be drawn, but they would plot the probability of message transmission as a continuous function of time rather than simply which message is being selected. That is to say that the diagrams could either be read to mean that the reject message is completely switched off, or that it merely has a reduced chance of being further processed accurately. The properties of the four types will, however, be discussed in the first instance as though the switch were on/off, not an attenuator. The discussion is simpler, and, as was outlined earlier, we have not enough evidence firmly to reject the possibility as a real alternative model for selective attention. Throughout the following discussion 'short' means of the order of 10 milliseconds, and 'long' greater than 100 milliseconds.

Type 1 is a mechanism with a very short minimum dwell time, but a long switching time. The time-sharing performance will be extremely poor. The long switching time will mean that there will be long periods of dead time during which no information is entering the system, and if the subject samples only for the minimum dwell time before switching back, there will be little time in which to acquire incoming information in either state. Hence we would expect that such a mechanism will perform poorly when signals are presented on two inputs at once, even if

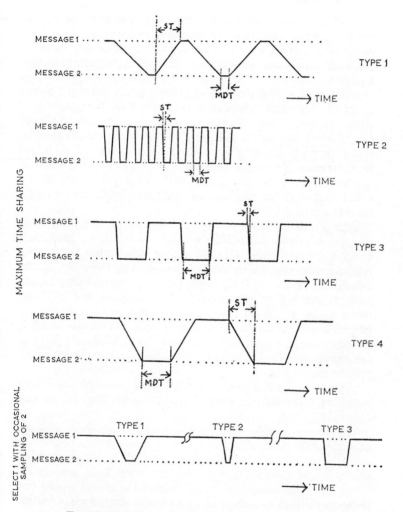

FIG. 17. The relation of switching time to switching rate

the signals are relatively long, such as speech signals. In the case of short signals it is clear that the chance of being on the right message at the right time will be extremely small. Such a mechanism will perform very poorly under all conditions when presented with simultaneous inputs.

Type 2 has both a short minimum dwell time and a very short switching time. Therefore the switching rate can be high. As a result time sharing may be expected to be reasonably efficient. For long signals several samples of each will be obtained, so that a fairly high level of performance will be obtainable, approaching 50% on each channel for non-redundant signals and much higher levels for redundant signals such as speech. Even for rather short signals the large number of samples per second taken and the short dead time should on the average give a good chance of detecting signals on both channels. Certainly this mechanism will do better for both kinds of signals than Type 1. The only exception will be if the incoming signals are time-locked to the periodicity of the switch and 180° out of phase, in which case performance could drop to zero.

Type 3 is the opposite of Type 1. It has a high switching speed (short dead time) but a long minimum dwell time, producing again a low switching rate. In such a mechanism the timing relations between the incoming message and the state of the switch will be critical. If the signals are in phase and time locked performance will be extremely good. If they are out of phase performance will be extremely bad. Simultaneous signals, even if of considerable duration, will always produce a response which is either one or the other signal but not both, whereas a Type 2 mechanism will tend to produce two responses even though they may be inaccurate.

Type 4 has both a long minimum dwell time and also a long switching time. Its performance when time sharing will be well below 50%.

The above considerations might lead one to think that an experiment to distinguish between the types would not be difficult to devise, and should embody signals of varying durations, in or out of phase by various amounts, etc. Such ideas are clearly in the right direction, but the analysis of the results would not immediately lead to a clear distinction between the mechanisms. If it were possible independently to have some measure of the phase relations between incoming signals and the switching mechanism analysis would be straightforward. Such information is not available, and it is not even certain that it exists. It is quite possible that there is a distribution of switching times (see below, Kristofferson, 1967a), and also that the minimum dwell time and dead time might vary as a function of the kind of signal presented, payoff, etc. For example, consider Figure 17 again, and suppose that a train of signals each 20 msecs. in duration were presented on each channel, with a 50 msec. gap between signals, and the signals were synchronised on both channels. It would be quite possible for a Type 1 mechanism to show a zero score if out of phase with the incoming signal; at best it would show a performance of some 50% since if the switching time were such as to allow it to reach the opposite channel 70 msecs after the onset of the signal it would pick up alternate signals first from one and then from the other input. Similarly Type 3 could also show 50%, depending on the exact phase locking of the incoming signals and the sampling time. For very short signals (shorter than the minimum dwell time), a Type 3 system would necessarily approach 50% performance when receiving simultaneous signals. Type 2, on the other hand, would only show a decrement for very short signals, and would otherwise be expected to show little effect at all from time sharing, since for relatively long signals each channel would receive several samples of each signal.

All these arguments would be far less clear cut, and might indeed prove impossible to use for the purpose of distinguishing between the four types of mechanism, if the phase of the switching mechanism were not time locked to the signal; if there were a distribution of switching time with a significant variance compared with the minimum dwell time; or if multiples of the minimum dwell time were used before switching, as is to be expected. Finally there is the possibility, which will be discussed again later in interpreting Kristofferson's results, that the detection of a signal on a channel which was being sampled might result in the channel locking on to that signal until it ended, thus altering drastically the timing of the sampling.

It has already been mentioned that these difficulties in relating the observed results in so-called 'switching time' experiments apply equally to a flip-flop model and to an attenuation model such as that suggested by Treisman. The difference would be that the probability of detecting a signal on the switched-off message in an attenuator theory would not fall to zero. Switching in an attenuation model would mean resetting the balance between inhibition and transmission. Intuitively it would seem likely that any system which can alter its properties will require time to do so.

The last statement holds true except for one possibility which does not seem to have been seriously considered in discussions of switching, although at the level of speculative neurophysiology it has a certain plausibility. If true, it would render experimental analysis of switching time even more difficult. The usual model for these hypothetical switches is that of a relay change-over. All the remarks made above, and the models in the literature, have usually assumed that switching is rather like a real relay, with infinite resistance to the passage of information, except when the contact is actually made with the input line carrying one or other message. It is quite possible that switching is not like that, but rather that, as the changeover occurs, the probability of a message being passed on further into the nervous system falls on one transmission line and rises on the other as a continuous function of time, so that switching, like Treisman's selective mechanism, is analogue rather than digital. There is nothing in the literature to rule this out.

The absolute need for more information about switching time can be made explicit by considering a radical alternative to Treisman's attenuation model. Deutsch and Deutsch suggested (see Chapter 3) that there was no attenuation of incoming signals before the level at which they were analysed for meaning. So we might for the sake of argument propose that the selection is in fact really flip-flop in nature. The switch is a digital switch after all. We observed in reviewing the experiments on speech shadowing that the chances of the subject reporting the content of a rejected message is drastically reduced although his ability to report crude overall features of the wave form remains reasonably good. This is just what would be expected from a digital switch, providing both the minimum dwell time were short and the dead time while switching were short; that is, that we were dealing with a Type 2 mechanism. If such a mechanism were spending most of its time locked on to one of the two incoming messages it would get only occasional, and very inadequate, samples from which to reconstruct the rejected message; but this relatively short sample would suffice to establish the overall pitch, rhythm and suchlike characteristics. The amount of information gained would be directly related to the sampling time. Speech signals have a large bandwidth in which much of the information is contained in the high frequency components (Miller, 1951). From the Sampling Theorem we would predict that a high sampling rate would be needed to extract such information. But to extract only a rough indication of, say, the first formant would require a much less frequent sampling. It is possible that an experiment could be devised to test this suggestion, using pulses of short duration and requiring the absolute identification of the frequency of such pulses when presented in simultaneous pairs. A digital switching model should break down quite sharply when the bandwidth of the signals and the switching time interact so as to lower the maximum achievable sampling rate below that defined as necessary by the Sampling Theorem. As we shall see, Kristoffer-son has begun experiments aimed in this direction for bimodal stimulation.

We will assume for the time being that switching is digital and contains at least a short dead time. The reader should consider throughout the following discussion two questions: whether there is evidence for the intake of information during switching; and if so, whether there is evidence as to the effectiveness of such information as the basis of perceptual judgments.

One of the most direct attacks on the question of switching time was made by Cherry and Taylor (1954). They switched a speech message rapidly between the ears while listeners tried to listen to it. The switching was time locked, not synchronised to the structure of the speech, so that some words were cut into sections by the switching. They found clear evidence for a sharp drop in intelligi-bility at a rate of about three cycles per second. It appeared that subjectively the listeners felt that at slow speeds they were following the message and at high speeds listening to both ears as a single source. Either strategy produced reasonable intelligi-bility. Cherry and Taylor suggested that the loss in intelligi-bility at six cycles per second was due to the message switching at a rate just on the borderline of the rate at which the attention switching mechanism could follow. Huggins (1964), however, reported that exactly the drop in intelligibility could be accounted for on the basis of the loss in intelligibility found in observers who listened to interrupted, monaural speech. Moreover, since the effect is related to speech rate it seems likely that it is due to the destruction of critical parts of speech signals, possibly phoneme boundaries, rather than to switching. Although the actual estimated value for switching time agrees with some other estimates it seems likely that this is fortuitous. Broadbent (1958) interpreted their result as evidence for a periodicity in information intake (Ladefoged and Broadbent, 1960), but the present writer inclines to the phoneme distortion explanation. (For other relevant studies, see Schubert and Parker, 1955; and Miller and Licklider, 1950.) It has also been reported (in a paper which unfortunately the writer has been unable to trace) that wives listening to the interrupted speech of their own husbands do not show loss in intelligibility. In this case it may be that constant exposure to the intonation patterns of a particular speaker allows an unusually great reduction in redundancy to be tolerated. On the other hand the finding might relate to the fact that emotionally evocative signals such as one's own name are more detectable than other signals. Although no further work has been done on this curious finding it might well repay effort.

Simultaneously with Cherry and Taylor's attack on the problem, Broadbent (1954) published the first of the experiments which have come to be called 'split span experiments' and which have been followed by several groups of workers, including those with interests not primarily concerned with attention (e.g. Bryden, 1964; Inglis, 1960; Kimura, 1964). This experiment is particularly important since it is one of the cornerstones of Broadbent's Filter Theory of the human information processor.

Broadbent presented spoken digits to his listeners. The digits were presented in the form of simultaneous pairs. One member of each pair was presented to the listener's left ear, the other member to the right ear, at the same moment. Three pairs were presented, and the listener was then asked to recall the whole message, sometimes in any order he liked, sometimes in a specified order. In the original experiment recall was by writing down the lists; later experiments by other workers have used spoken recall (e.g. Moray, 1960b) and have found substantially the same results. Rates of presentation varied from one pair every two seconds to two pairs per second (1 digit/ear/2 seconds to 2 digits/ear/second). The subjects were naval ratings. They each received ten trials under free recall conditions, and ten trials under each of the specified recall conditions, at each speed. (A trial is one set of three pairs.) The score was the number of trials totally correct. (This detailed description is given because there are some passages in the original paper which have frequently been mis-interpreted. For the purpose of the following discussion the important thing to note is that the signals are presented in *simultaneous* pairs.)

Broadbent found that if the rate of presentation were faster than about one pair every 1·5 seconds (a very slow rate), and listeners were required to recall in the order left ear-right ear left ear-right ear-left ear-right ear or vice versa, they found it extremely difficult. The average level of performance, measured in trials completely free from errors, was about 20 %. If, on the other hand, listeners recalled all the signals from one ear followed by all those from the other, then they achieved almost perfect performance; very high levels of performance were seen even at presentation rates of two pairs per second. The latter strategy (hereafter called sequential to distinguish it from the former, alternating strategy) is used spontaneously by most subjects. Broadbent concluded:

> Failures to record digits in the actual order of arrival are no less frequent at a 1-sec. rate than at a 1/2-sec. rate, but 11 of the 12 S's show a considerable improvement between a 1-sec. and a 2-sec. rate . . . This seems to imply that when attention is shifted away from one channel to another and then back to the first a time interval of between 1 and 2 sec. will be required.

Before criticising this attempt to measure switching time and reviewing later work performed in its context it should be said that the experiment and its results are among the most readily reproducible in the whole of psychology. With unpractised subjects, at the rates mentioned, and with the materials used by Broadbent, it is impossible to avoid replicating it. Even the most tenacious critics of Broadbent's conclusions accept the facts. For instance Moray and Barnett (1965) found exactly the same effect and almost the same level of performance using pairs of digits presented over a loudspeaker and coded by means of one male and one female voice speaking the members of each pair. There are, however, problems of interpretation of Broadbent's experiment.

In the first place notice that the method of scoring used indicates that, contrary to Broadbent's conclusion, some subjects can switch at faster rates at least some of the time. About 20 % of the trials are *totally correct* which implies that on those trials switching was taking place sufficiently fast. At least the tail of the distribution of switching times must extend into significantly more rapid regions. To find the limit we must look for the region where subjects get no correct results, and we should at least enquire into the sources of variability which result in listeners doing so much worse overall than they do on 20% of trials.

Next we may ask what sense can be given to a phrase such as 'the time taken for a perception', for it is by subtracting perception time that the switching time is estimated by Broadbent. A normally spoken digit may be expected to last somewhere in the region of 200 msecs. But it has been shown (Moray, 1960a, quoted in Davis et al., 1961) that digits can be correctly identified on the basis of rather less than the first 50 milliseconds of the waveform, to take a conservative estimate. Moray presented digits one by one and asked listeners to identify them. An electronic timing circuit cut off the later parts of the signals progressively and, even allowing for the difference in sensitivity which may have existed between the voice keys used in the apparatus and the human ear, the above estimate stands. Furthermore Moray (1960b) found almost perfect recall of six digit lists presented at rates of four per second as a single binaural message. Experiments have also been performed using computer generated digits at presentation rates of up to 10 digits per second, and even there the limit of a listener's ability to identify signals has not been reached (Yntema et al., 1964). It is not, of course, possible to argue that because the perception of an auditorily presented digit need only take a small fraction of a second (less than 100 msecs. seems a reasonable value) only that amount of time is taken on any particular occasion. But it does make it difficult to use estimates of perception time as the basis for an estimate of switching time.

Finally we may notice that it was in fact impossible for the subjects to carry out their instructions. They were asked to recall 'in the correct order of arrival'. But left-right-left-right-left-right is no more the correct order of arrival than is left-left-left-right-right-right. In either sequential or alternating recall there must be parallel to serial recoding before output, since subjects can usually neither write nor speak two digits at once. (Broadbent generally has used written, Moray spoken, responses.) The difficulty might be due not to the fact that attention cannot be switched between the messages at the time of their reception, but that three serial to parallel recodings followed by storage followed by retrieval is a less efficient method of processing the signals than is storage followed by one serial to parallel recoding. The efficiency of the transformation, not the rate of switching, is the limiting factor.

This experiment by Broadbent was followed by a number of studies, designed to clarifiy the points at issue. It must be confessed that 13 years after the initial report the picture is if anything more confused rather than clearer, due to the range over which later workers have extended the initial findings. Moray (1960b) attacked the experiment on a number of grounds. He pointed out that the absolute number of errors observed in a replication of the experiment was too small for the time constants proposed by Broadbent, and argued that the distribution of errors among the items of the list was not in accordance with Broadbent's suggestions. He suggested that the difficulty lay in the retrieval mechanism, and that the incoming messages were in fact handled in parallel. Broadbent and Gregory (1961) showed, however, that the crucial point was whether subjects knew in advance in which order they would have to recall when using the sequential strategy, and they suggested that it was at the time of the initial input that messages were recoded. Sampson and Spong (1961a) used vision and hearing as the two input dimensions, finding slightly different results. The work of this group will be discussed under visual switching time. Of particular interest was the finding by Gray and Wedderburn (1960) that if the incoming material contains some features which allow it to be coded efficiently other than ear by ear, then alternative strategies of recall are open to the subject. For example mixed sentences like

> *Left ear:*   4   aunt   7
> *Right ear:* poor   3   Jane

can be recalled phrase by phrase as well as ear by ear. Broadbent has pointed out that in this case the ear by ear recall is relatively poor, so it is a reduction in ear by ear efficiency, not the use of the new strategy, which is reducing the difference.

Recently Savin (1967) presented two pairs of digits, all spoken by the same voice, over a single loudspeaker, taking care that there was no particular carry over of characteristics such as intonation or stress patterns from the first to the second pairs during recording. He found that in this situation, where there was no reason to recall sequentially rather than pair by pair, the listeners seldom used the pair-by-simultaneous-pair recall order, preferring to recall sequential pairs instead. He argues for an inherent tendency of the auditory system to process material sequentially rather than in parallel, a reasonable suggestion bearing in mind the sequential nature of speech and most natural sound signals. But his result does not really contradict Broadbent's finding. And Gray and Wedderburn's results could be interpreted in exactly the same way as Savin's. We could then say that, when there is no way of sorting signals except into classes based on temporal contiguity, sequential contiguity is preferred to simultaneous contiguity. For Broadbent's effect to require extra explanations over and above that offered by Savin we would need to find that his subjects do worse than Savin's when forced to recall in simultaneous pairs. Unfortunately this comparison cannot be made. In the first place the number of pairs is different, and secondly Savin's subjects were faced with a very much harder task in that all the signals came over a single loudspeaker, so that there was a considerable amount of masking of one signal by the other. Moray and Reid (1967) investigated two-channel memory span in the traditional way by presenting increasingly long lists of simultaneous pairs, but their subjects had a special keyboard which allowed them to type their responses simultaneously, left hand for left ear, right hand for right ear. Moray and Reid included a case where the subjects received two pairs, and obtained very much higher scores on simultaneous pair recall than did Savin. Savin's subjects gave only 58 totally correct simultaneous pair recalls out of 319 totally correct quartets from 525 trials, which means that only 10% of the trials were recalled correctly when 'simultaneous' recall was used (this might have been higher had he asked the subjects to perform that way). Moray and Reid found 80% correct, but again the experiments are not strictly comparable because of the different amounts of peripheral masking and also because of the special response keyboard used by Moray and Reid.

At the opposite extreme from that of Savin is an experiment by Day (1967). She gave her listeners material which could be readily coded either serially or simultaneously. Pairs of items such as PODUCT and RODUCT, COSET and LOSET were presented dichotically, and the subjects were asked to say what they heard. The vast majority reported words such as PRODUCT and CLOSET. When asked to identify only one of the signals identification was correct (PODUCT, not PRODUCT, when PODUCT was presented), suggesting that there was neither conscious nor unconscious guessing on the basis of one or other of the channels. Moreover in a personal communication to the writer Day said that most of her subjects reported hearing the single word centrally and sometimes externally, suggesting that full fusion of the information was occurring and producing the classical binaural lateralisation effects. This seems to be similar to Broadbent's findings (1955) on filtered signals.

It begins to look as though the decision by a research worker as to whether the auditory system is primarily one which condenses information by sequential or by parallel integration depends largely upon the material which he uses and the way in which he conducts the experiment. In general one may say that discrete, uncorrelated signals arriving over different regions of auditory space will be kept separate and encoded sequentially while highly correlated messages will often be handled in parallel, at least in so far as both inputs will reach a level where the information common to both, or highly probable in the context each of the other, will be fused into a single message; a conclusion which was suggested by Treisman's studies on simultaneous messages one of which was a translation of the other.

Returning to the original split span experiment, it would seem important to investigate what happens when there is a completely compatible output available to the subjects, for, as we saw, neither sequential nor alternating recall is in fact recall in the correct order arrival. A full understanding of the phenomena clearly presupposes an analysis of the relative roles of input and output factors. Moray and Barnett (1965), using voice quality to distinguish two messages, investigated the relative importance of rate of presentation, strategy of recall and signal ensemble size on split span performance. They also used four different error scores in an attempt to resolve some of the differences in the earlier studies: number of lists totally correct, number of digits omitted, number of lists with items correct but in the wrong order, and number of commission (intrusion) errors. Their analysis of variance suggested that omissions were largely related to presentation rate, and order errors and lists-with-at-least-one-error (the criterion used by Broadbent) to recall strategy. Strategy of recall, then, would seem to be affecting lists which have been received correctly. This brings us back to the criticism of Broadbent made earlier on the grounds of the relative number of errors. Subsequently Moray and Beck (in Moray, 1969a) found that either order or omission errors could be abolished by suitably paying subjects to avoid the appropriate error. Unpaid subjects perform like those paid to avoid omissions, making errors predominantly affected by recall, not presentation factors.

Further work on the importance of the response side of parallel processing comes in a paper by Moray and Jordan (1966). As in the experiment by Moray and Reid (1967) subjects used a stenographer's keyboard to make their responses. They were thus able to use a different set of response keys for each hand and to press them simultaneously to print out signals that had been presented simultaneously. Although precise timing of the responses was not obtained the subjects were urged to type the two responses at once, and, at least to the writer, appeared to do so. Moray and Reid found a marked reduction in two-channel scores from the equivalent total one-channel presentation. 2×4 signals produced a lesser span than 1×8 signals. But they were deliberately working with unpractised subjects because of the findings of Moray and Jordan. The latter found extremely good performance in a split span task with a signal presentation rate of two pairs per second. This is almost four times the rate at which Broadbent found his subjects beginning to fail. But as can be seen from Table 3, several subjects were within reach of 90%, a level at which one is inclined to attribute the residual errors to unfamiliarity with the keyboard.

It is also noteworthy that these subjects, who were scored for lists totally correct on the last 50 trials of 100 trials on the traditional vocal LRLRLR recall condition; on the last 50 of these latter trials some subjects achieved performances better than 80% correct, an almost incredible level to anyone who has worked with shorter runs in such experiments. (The writer managed to reach over 90% correct on LRLRLR, LLLRRR, or simultaneous typing responses, motivated no doubt by an intense interest in the outcome!) Since the average performance, taken subject by subject, was considerably higher on the manual keyboard condition than in the vocal alternating condition, we may assume that both stimulus response compatibility and practice are important in setting limits on split span performance.

What is it that alters with practice? Can people learn to switch more rapidly? Are they learning more efficiently to encode parallel inputs? Or is a more effective transformation from parallel to serial representation learnt? At present we do not have answers to these questions. More work deserves to be done on practice and compatibility, since preliminary work by Jordan

TABLE 3 *Scores by listeners responding to split span lists when using a two-hand response and a well practised vocal response*

Keyboard L+R L+R L+R		Vocal LRLRLR
S 1	44	37
S 2	46	46
S 3	33	21
S 4	18	21
S 5	32	13
S 6	31	20
S 7	44	34
S 8	42	44
S 9	45	41
S 10	25	14
S 11	33	34
Mean	35·7	29·5
S.D.	8·8	11·5

Number of lists completely correct
Maximum possible lists correct = 50

(now discontinued and reported briefly in Moray and Reid) suggests that two handed *shadowing,* as distinct from short split spans, is not possible at rates of one pair per second even with practice, and that subjects appear to spend roughly half their time on each channel.

It will be apparent from the above that it is difficult, if not impossible, to use this kind of experiment as an estimate of switching time. If we take the best performance so far obtained the switching time would seem to be nearer to 50–100 msecs. than to the 300 msecs. or more which was originally estimated. But little confidence can be placed in such calculations. To use this way of computing switching time really presupposes acceptance of Broadbent's Filter Model in its 1958 version, and there are considerable reasons for feeling that there are alternatives to this.

Broadbent has, in fact, modified his original model in several details. The relation between selection and analysis is now rather more closely related to Treisman's suggestions, and accommodates the findings of Treisman, Gray and Wedderburn, and Moray which suggests that word continuity, language differences, etc., can be 'channels'. Indeed a prediction by Broadbent himself in 1958 has obviously come true:

> It may be desirable to think of the stimuli used in any experiment as having dimensions in an 'information space' made up of all the dimensions discriminable by the sense organs.

and also:

> By 'channel' we may mean 'sense organ', but not always so, since some of the best illustrations of the effect come from the role of auditory localisation. Sounds reaching the two ears are of course often perceived as coming from different directions, although the sense organs affected are the same; and such sounds we shall regard as arriving by different 'channels'.

There have so far been no attempts to measure switching time between 'channels' other than ears, or between sensory modalities using split span methods; and a noticeable omission from the research literature is work on the effect on split span performance of the distance by which the messages are separated in signal space. Does it make any difference whether the messages are only 20° apart instead of dichotic? Is the difference between tenor and bass less effective than the difference between the male and female voices? This would seem a fertile ground for research.

Quite a different approach to the problem of switching time has recently been offered by Kristofferson. Unfortunately, with the exception of a summary in *Attention and Performance* (Kristofferson, 1967) all the detailed papers are at present only available as NASA and other research reports (but see Kristofferson, 1967b, also). His line of attack is absolutely direct, and, if valid, provides a clear cut answer to the question of the minimum dwell time. In his first experiment he presented two signals, a light and a tone, to his subjects. The signals began simultaneously and after a short interval one or other ceased. The task of the subject was to press a single response key when the appropriate signal ceased, the one requiring a response appropriate to the way indicated in advance by the experimenter. Kristofferson looked for lengthened reaction times when the subject did not know which signal was to cease compared with when he did. He argued as follows:

Suppose that there is a minimum dwell time dt. If the subject is in one selective state and a signal arrives in another input region the brain will detect its presence and send a request for attention to the selective switch. This will not, however, respond until the end of the minimum dwell time, when it will switch to the new message. Having arrived in any state the mechanism will stay in that state for one minimum dwell time or integral multiples of that time. The mechanism changes state in relation to discrete quanta of time. Allowing for a slight variability in this quantum, Kristofferson postulated a gaussian distribution of quantal intervals. He could then relate performance to reaction time. If a signal is presented to the subject in a two input task, at a chance moment in time, the probability that he will be in the correct state is 0·5. As time passes the probability that he reaches the end of one minimum dwell will rise, and at the end of that quantum he will switch to deal with the new signal. Therefore the probability of being in the correct state to handle the signal will grow as time passes from 0·5 at the moment of signal presentation to 1·0 at the end of one minimum dwell time. Reaction time is presumed to be linearly related to the delay so produced.

The shorter the period until the end of the quantum, the shorter the reaction time. Hence the function relating time to the probability of being on the correct channel can be thought of as directly related to the delay in reaction time. A study of the distribution of such delays is in effect a way of sampling the distribution of delays due to the time uncertainty of the signal with respect to the state of the sampling mechanism, and hence can be used to estimate the time which it takes to switch, or to be more accurate, the length of time which the subject must remain in a given state, since Kristofferson postulates that the actual switching time, i.e. the dead time while changing state, is negligible. This is perhaps the biggest conceptual weakness of his scheme.

After allowing for the known difference between visual and auditory reaction times Kristofferson failed in his first experiment to find any lengthening in reaction time such as he had predicted. He concluded that when the signals were simply a light and a tone, and the responses simply to press one key to the 'offset' of the signal, the signals could apparently be processed in parallel. In fact there is a simpler theoretical analysis of such a result which does not entail the idea of parallel processing in quite the sense implied by Kristofferson. If we suppose that at some point in the nervous system the total incoming sensory stimulation produces a distribution of activity which is the sum of the excitations produced by the inputs to a single sensory modality, the problem becomes a simple reaction time, unusual only in the fact that the signal is a reduction in signal strength, whereas it is more usual to use increments in such experiments. The detection problem for the subject may be alternatively represented by either of Figures 18. Since reaction times to the ending of signals are not very

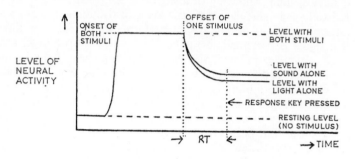

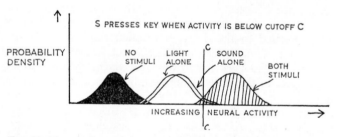

FIG. 18. Two versions of the 'simple RT' analysis of Kristofferson's experiment

frequent in the literature it is not possible to find a case where the results can be compared directly with simple offset reaction times, but the order of magnitude which Kristofferson obtained would not be unreasonable, 173 msecs. for tone ending and 204 msecs. for light ending.

Having failed to find reaction time lengthening which he could relate to the minimum dwell time Kristofferson turned to a more complex task, reasoning that if a discrimination were required in each modality, it would no longer be possible for the subjects merely to analyse the input as a whole. He therefore presented four signals—a light on the left hand side, a light on the right hand side, a high pitched tone, and a low pitched tone. A warning signal was given and a second later all four signals came on. Shortly afterwards one of them ceased. The subject was required to press a response key if either the right hand light had gone out, or the high pitched tone had ended. If the left hand light had gone out or the low pitched tone had ended he was to make no response. Under these conditions Kristofferson found the lengthening of reaction time for which he was looking. Arguing in two different ways, and repeating the experiment with some differences in technique, he concluded that the minimum dwell time was of the order of 60 msecs., or that a complete cycle of one sample on one channel followed by a sample on the other channel occupied some 120 msecs.

It is again possible to think of an alternative explanation in terms of reaction times, but in this case the explanation is less likely. We might define the condition of all signals 'on' by the tetrad (LL, RL, HT, LT) for the left light, right light, high tone and low tone respectively. The condition with no signals present would be the empty set (O, O, O, O). The signals among which the subjects were required to discriminate would then be the set of tetrads (LL, RL, HT, O), (LL, RL, O, LT), (LL, O, HT, LT) or (O, RL, HT, LT). Hence by analogy with the first experiment, we could argue that the subjects, having learned to identify each of the tetrads, were performing an absolute identification experiment on one channel, and that the experiment is actually a rather unusual single channel four choice reaction time. Again, it would be nice to be able to refer to data on four choice offset reaction times but it does not, to the writer's knowledge, exist. On the whole it seems that the simple reaction time model for the first of Kristofferson's experiments is rather likely, and that the four choice reaction time explanation for the second is not ruled out, since the actual reaction times observed were of the order of 280 msecs. for sound, and 250 msecs. for light offsets, which are plausible for a complex four choice offset reaction.

It will be seen that Kristofferson's model is an extreme form of the Type 3 mechanism, with a long minimum dwell time as the limiting factor and a very low (negligible) switching time. It also bears some relation to the postulates put forward by Broadbent in his Filter Theory. The value given by Kristofferson seems intuitively reasonable and bears a fairly close similarity to various other estimates of periodicity found in the literature (sequential reaction times, threshold fluctuation, etc.). Any curious features of the experiment may be at least partly ascribed to the use of offsets of signals, not onsets, so as to reduce the time uncertainty as to when the signal would come. (It is at first a little disconcerting to read about the offset of a tone and a light, since this phrase is usually used by workers to refer to an asynchrony in time or space between some aspects of a signal. Kristofferson uses it throughout to mean 'end'.) He found, for example, that the reaction time to the end of a tone was rather longer than the reaction time to the end of a light. Usually reaction times to sounds are assumed

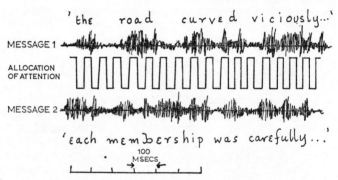

FIG. 19. Time-sharing in shadowing and Kristofferson's estimate

to be shorter than reaction times to lights, but Plomp (1964) has found that the time taken for a sound to decay to threshold is approximately 200–300 msecs. irrespective of its initial intensity, and that the intensity of sensation is inversely related to the logarithm of time. Thus there may well be differences between the situation used by Kristofferson and onset reaction times, with respect to the time taken for observable change in signal level to be produced, and offset sound RTs maybe slower than offset light RTs.

All in all his estimate seems the most promising to date. How then does it fit with other experiments? We may usefully consider its relation to two sets of experiments, the first the shadowing experiments of Treisman, Moray, Mowbray and others, the second some recent 'pure selective listening' experiments by Moray and his co-workers. It is notorious that in shadowing experiments it is impossible to shadow one channel and also to report or to shadow the other. Mowbray (1964) found very strong evidence that the price of detecting and recalling the signals on the second channel was a complete failure to shadow the primary message at the point where the secondary message occurred. Now most shadowing experiments are performed at around 120–150 words per minute per message. Frequently experimenters deliberately reduce the silent period between words and try to maintain a constant word rate rather than a constant syllabic rate. Let us say, then, that each word occupies around 350 msecs. The two messages are not usually synchronised word for word, but are at least spoken

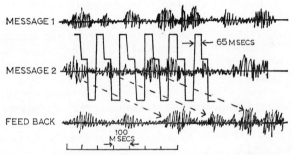

FIG. 20. Time-sharing in shadowing: allowance for feedback

at the same rate. If now it is possible for listeners to switch from one channel to the other every 60 msecs., Figure 19 represents what they could optimally achieve by way of analysing the incoming messages if they were trying deliberately to time share between the two messages.

It will be readily seen that 50% sampling of each signal at intervals of 60 msecs. should be expected to give rather good information about such redundant signals as speech. Even allowing for the fact that in the case of the shorter monosyllable perhaps the last 60 msecs. does not give a good enough sample to reconstruct the signal, we would expect very much better performance in a time sharing mode than is ever observed; and this at first sight suggests that the combination of minimum dwell time and switching time must be very much longer than Kristofferson's work indicates. For the sake of discussion we will adopt his contention that the dead time during switching is negligible.

The application of his suggested switching rate constant to shadowing experiments shows how difficult the latter are to use for quantitative predications. It seems likely that Treisman has used them with great skill to allow a considerable degree of qualitative insight into the mechanism, but some new approach is needed to go beyond the point now reached, at least with regard explicitly to work on attention as such. For consider the following. It was mentioned elsewhere that Poulton (1953) found that his subjects could not shadow coherently, apparently because they did not hear their own output. In the experiments of the last decade the subjects shadowed extremely well. This suggests that they were listening to their own responses as well as to the incoming stimuli. Consequently the time sharing diagram should more accurately be drawn as Figure 20. (We will assume conservatively that despite the fact that some of the speech feedback enters each ear it is perceived as a single message: possibly even it is the tactile or kinaesthetic component which constitutes the feedback.)

Now only 33 % can be given to each of the three messages in a time sharing situation. And there must necessarily be very great difficulties at the response side. If we ask a person to shadow at a rate of even 100 words per minute, a rate much lower than that generally used in such experiments, and require him to report on both channels, then we are asking him to output speech at a rate of 200 words per minute, a really rather rapid speech rate. Moreover the signals which he receives are made up of sequential samples of one message interleaved with samples from the other message. Broadbent (1952) showed many years ago how difficult it was to disentangle two messages when they were interleaved word by word. It is much harder for a listener to recall either of the sentences from

> the A cat CAR eats NEEDS fish FUEL

than from

> the cat eats fish—A CAR NEEDS FUEL

despite the fact that in neither case is there any masking, and indeed, word for word the first sentence in the second pair must be stored longer before recall. It seems not unreasonable to think that a similar reconstitution of signals from a shattered set of phonemes will be even harder. It may therefore be that the limits on the handling of simultaneously presented messages is largely due to factors other than the maximum rate at which attention can be switched. There is one other slightly different shadowing experiment which deserves mention, because it is not open to this objection to quite the same extent. Moray (1959) asked subjects to shadow short sentences some of which ended with sets of digits, of the form:

> This is sentence number alpha 5 4 2 9
> This is sentence number beta   7 1 3 0

Some of his subjects were told that there would be numbers on both channels, that their task was to shadow only one of the two messages, but to repeat all the numbers they could at the end of each message. There were very few recalls of numbers from the non-shadowed messages, despite the fact that the numbers on each channel were separated by one second, and that in another experiment (Moray, 1960) subjects performing a 'split span' recall task could accept interleaved digits at a rate of two per ear per second. It appears here again that the making of the response itself interferes with the time sharing in some way. We shall return to this point in the next chapter. (Norman has recently shown that there is good memory for the rejected message if recall is very rapid.)

A few experiments have appeared which did not require shadowing. The first of these was by Broadbent and Gregory (1963) and involved a simple signal detection task on one ear and a digit monitoring task on the other. The second was more closely akin to the usual way of doing a shadowing experiment. Moray and O'Brien (1967) presented messages dichotically to their listeners. In each ear the listener received 900 digits, among which were quasi-randomly dispersed 100 letters. Of the 100 letters 25 occurred at the moment that a different letter occurred in the other message. Moray and O'Brien were primarily concerned with the question of whether signal detection theory might usefully be applied to the changes in performance which were observed when subjects were asked to time share attention between the two messages, or to listen to one and reject the other. But they also looked at the special case of the targets which occurred in simultaneous pairs. Table 4 is taken from their paper, and shows the relative probabilities of detecting one member, both members, or no member of a pair of simultaneous targets which occur one in one ear and the other in the other.

It will be observed that for most subjects the chances of detecting at least one of a pair are extremely good, while the changes of detecting both members of a pair are extremely poor. The 1967 paper argued against a discrete switching time model, but the writer is now less impressed by the arguments for an attenuation model of the kind suggested by Treisman than at the time the paper was

TABLE 4   *Simultaneous dichotic signals: probability of responding to one or both*

	S_1	S_2	S_3	S_4	S_5	S_6	S_7	S_8
Probability of giving one response	1·000	1·000	0·500	0·720	0·840	0·680	0·880	0·880
Probability of giving two responses	0·000	0·000	0·500	0·240	0·120	0·240	0·120	0·120
Probability of missing both	0·000	0·000	0·000	0·040	0·040	0·080	0·000	0·000

published. It is difficult, however, to fit Kristofferson's estimate of switching time to this data. The response which Moray and O'Brien's subjects had to make was simply to press a key with the right hand when they heard a letter in the right ear, and a different key with the left hand when they heard a signal in the left ear. When they heard two simultaneous signals they were to press both keys. It is unlikely that as much interference as shadowing undoubtedly produces was present in this experiment. Nor is monitoring of the response needed to the degree in which it is required in spoken responses. On the other hand the spoken signals had durations of the order of 200 msecs. upwards, and were only presented at a rate of 100 per minute on each channel. Since an attempt was made during recording to ensure that silent periods between signals were as short as possible, it is likely that the duration of the signals (which sounded slow but not distorted) was nearer to 400 or even 500 msecs. It is extremely hard to relate the attention sampling cycle time of 120 msecs. to the fact that it is so very difficult to detect both of a simultaneous pair of speech signals.

More recent experiments (Moray, 1969b, c, d) have confirmed this finding about the difficulty of detecting simultaneous targets in the case of 100 msec. pure tone bursts, using increments in intensity and in frequency. Once more the performance does not agree with Kristofferson's estimate. This work will be discussed in the final chapter of this book.

Once again the question forces itself on us. If a listener can sample one channel for about 60 msecs., and then switch with negligible loss of time to the other so that he receives the later part of the other signal, why does he not detect both of a simultaneous pair, when he must have at worst a 60 msec. sample of one and a 40 msec. sample of the other on average? These results cannot be made consistent with Kristofferson's estimate of switching time. It is, of course, true that his estimate was for the time taken to switch from one modality to another, and may not be a general constant applicable to all within modality switching. But another possibility might also be borne in mind.

Looking over the experiments (and both being a subject oneself on occasion and also discussing experiences with other subjects) it seems just possible that what happens is that a listener can switch very rapidly unless he detects a signal. It may be that when a switch is called for by an incoming signal, as Kristofferson suggests can happen, or when in the course of time sharing a signal arrives while the listener is sampling the message of which it is a constituent part, the switch as it were locks up, and cannot again switch until the end of the signal plus the remainder of minimum dwell time quantum during which the signal ends. Perhaps more likely is that the presence of a signal locks the mechanism on to it not until the end of the signal but at least until the signal has been processed to the point of identification, when enough information has been received to allow the decisions concerning a response to be made. Were this indeed the case then we might expect pairs of short simple signals and pairs of long complex ones to be equally difficult to handle. The short signal could be identified in a minimum of time, but a switch could not be made until the end of a minimum dwell time period, at which time the contralateral signal would already have ceased. A long complex signal would lock up the switch until so far into the signal duration that the eventual switch would not leave enough of the contralateral signal to be identified. The preliminary results referred to above suggest that when two simultaneous signals, each being a pure tone and separated by about an octave, are presented one to each ear, then if their duration is 100 msecs. it is extremely difficult for subjects to detect both of them. This would not be expected on the basis of the earlier work on speech shadowing, which led us to think that 'simple' signals could be handled in parallel.

There is no strong reason for adopting these hypotheses, but they might go far towards fitting Kristofferson's estimate to the other experiments, if the reader is disposed to think that Kristofferson has in fact provided an estimate of switching rate which is applicable to intramodal auditory time sharing tasks.

Visual switching

The case of visual switching raises quite different problems. In fact experiments can be divided into two quite distinct classes: fixation experiments, and experiments on information intake with steady fixation but from different regions of the visual display. The most characteristic way of directing visual attention is, of course, by changing the direction of gaze so that the region of the visual world which it is desired to sample falls on the fovea. This response seems to have the status of a built-in reflex, and is certainly the primary means used in everyday life to direct attention to different regions of the visual field. The effect of fixation is to align the stimulus with that part of the retina where acuity is greatest, where colour vision is most acute, and where there is probably a direct one-to-one connection between the receptors and fibres in the optic nerve. There is a very large literature on eye movements now available, and a comprehensive bibliography has recently been prepared (Itek Corp., 1967).

The maximum rate at which fixations can be made seems definitely to be in the region of four per second, and just over two more usual. Young and Stark (1963) show that the power spectrum is 6 db down at 3 cps when tracking complex sinusoids. This switching rate seems to be true of widely different tasks, and largely independent of the angular separation of the stimuli, since the eye-ball is relatively overpowered for its inertia. The rate may be influenced within these limits by the nature of the task and by other factors internal to the subject. Thus White and Ford (1960) found that the mean duration of a fixation in a simulated radar watching task was about 100 msecs. longer than in a free search of an unstructured field. (The structure in such a task is the search path imposed by the sweep line moving round the display.) Williams (1967) provides data from a quite different and much more complex task which agree well with the values given by White and Ford. Williams asked his subjects to search a large array of coloured shapes of different sizes, each of which contained a two digit number. The task was to find a particular two digit number, and Williams compared performance with different kinds of cueing. The number of fixations and time to solution was measured as a function of the different kinds of cue the subjects received. But perhaps the most successful example of a quantitative model of attention comes from the work of Senders (1967). Not only has this work provided a highly successful predictive theory to account for visual scanning but it has proved sufficiently robust to be used for decisions concerned with instrument panel layouts in real life situations.

Senders has investigated the behaviour of both amateur and professional airline pilots scanning instruments while flying, but the particular experiment to be discussed here was a laboratory simulation of such a task. Subjects were required to monitor the position of a needle on each of six instruments. These were centrezero microammeters and they were fed with a quasi-random mixture of sinusoidal voltages which had been band-passed filtered at different cutoff points. The bandwidths of the signals varied from 0·08 to 0·8 cycles per second. Senders assumed that a viewer distributed his scanning time over the instruments in such a way that the time spent sampling an instrument was proportional to its information content, and that the jumps from one instrument to another could be described by a Markov process. Specifically, if a signal has a bandwidth of W cycles per second, then Shannon has shown (Shannon and Weaver, 1949) that to extract the maximum amount of information from it requires sampling at a rate of 2W samples per second. An ideal observer confronted with an array of instruments generating signals of different bandwidths would be expected to distribute his attention proportionally to the bandwidths of the signals, and theoretically should sample each at a rate of $2W_i$ samples per second where W_i is the bandwidth of the *ith* signal. Taking the frequency of sampling to be the same as the frequency of fixation, and correcting for the possibility that some jumps may be to the same instrument which has just been sampled, Senders found that fixation frequency was indeed related in the predicted way to the bandwidth, except for signals of extremely low frequency, and was constant at around one fixation every 350 msecs. It seems likely that the departure from constancy for the instrument with extremely low signal frequency is due to the difficulty of extracting velocity information from the display.

White (1967) has suggested that the minimum time needed to

F

read in visual information in a task involving successive fixations is somewhere around 250 msecs. or at least that there is some kind of definite discontinuity of performance at that point. He reports (see White, 1967, for several references) that the estimated numerosity of a train of flashes is halved for presentations longer that 250 msecs. and has provided some evidence of differences in the evoked potential linked to that periodicity. If we were to combine that suggestion with the estimate of Senders and others for fixation duration we would come up with a mechanism which has a minimum dwell time of about 250 msecs. and a dead time,

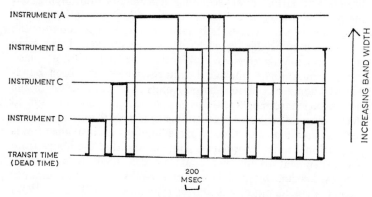

Fig. 21. Allocation of sampling in visual attention

the actual switching time, of about 100+msecs. which agrees quite well with the work on the duration of eye movements by other workers (see Itek Corp., 1967). We again find evidence for a Type 3 mechanism, and definite evidence in this case for dead time, suggesting that we describe a typical Senders experiment by Figure 21.

Note that we allow successive samples to be taken from the same source.

Evidence suggests that there is indeed a dead time in such switching. Several studies have shown evidence that very little information is taken in while the eye is in motion. And Ditchburn (1959) and Latour (1966) have provided evidence that there is actually a considerable rise in threshold prior to and during the early part of an eye movement. Recent physiological evidence suggests that there may be specific signals indicating the end of

eye movement (Schiller and Chorover, 1968), and there is evidence
that information as to where to fixate has been read in from peripheral vision before the movement starts. If a target towards which
a subject is glancing is extinguished, fixation may nonetheless be
accurately completed. The relative inefficiency of sampling with
scanning, due to the dead time which occurs during the movement of the eyes, is confirmed by an experiment of Baker's (1967)
in which he obtained a stationary radar plan-position-indicator

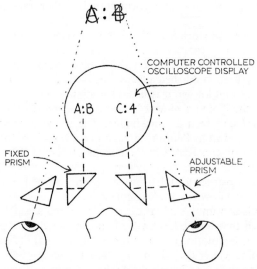

Fig. 22. Whelan's apparatus for multichannel vision

display by rotating the entire display tube in synchrony with the
sweep of the beam but in the opposite direction. The percentage of
targets detected was approximately doubled compared with a con-
ventional display in which an observer followed the path of the
scan around the tube as it rotated.

As regards attentional switching without eye movements,
there is rather less data. Although it seems intuitively that it
might be possible to use the two eyes as separate channels, or
different spatial locations on the retina as two channels, most of
the work done in this field is extremely difficult to interpret. Is
one eye one channel and the other another? Are the two halves of

a retina, projecting as they do to opposite hemispheres of the brain, separate input lines? Are two visual signals presented side by side, or one to one eye and the other to the other eye, equivalent to two messages presented one to one ear and the other to the other ear? Recent work on split-brain preparations shows that under abnormal conditions the two halves of the visual system can indeed become dissociated, and Gazzaniga (1967) has recently confirmed this in humans who have undergone callosal section for epilepsy. But most of the evidence suggests that such dissociation of information is rather rare in normal humans.

Much classical work is available on the relation of the two eyes in the field of stereopsis, eye dominance and binocular rivalry. A good recent monograph on the subject, some material from which has been published elsewhere, is that by Levelt (1965b, 1966). As is well known it is usual for stimuli with approximately the same shape and size and location presented to the two eyes to be fused and seen as one image. The range over which this happens is known as Panum's area, and for lines is of the order of six minutes of arc. Recently Fender and Julesz (1967) have produced some very interesting 'hysteresis curves', relating fusion and splitting of abstract visual forms in the region of Panum's area. Equally well known is the extreme reluctance to fuse of certain other kinds of stimuli such as different coloured areas. It is generally agreed that binocular rivalry is not under the control of the viewer. The fluctuations come and go, and there is little he can do to determine which shall dominate. The system appears to be one that is tunable but to which the subject cannot pay attention (see Chapter 2). The rate of fluctuation appears to be determined by several factors such as the relative brightnesses of the fields in the two eyes, the presence or absence of contours in one or other field and their relative positions, and so on. On Levelt's theory of how the periodicity of rivalry is determined it is not possible to give a value for the shortest time for which an image is observed before rivalry sets in. There probably is a fundamental lower limit, but the periodicity is clearly influenced by a very large number of factors. There is in theory no reason why it should not be measured if a series of stimuli were presented to subjects, the stimuli being designed to rival at a maximum rate. According to Levelt we should expect this to happen when there are big differences in the distribution of contours in the two eyes, for example a horizontal grid in one eye and a vertical grid in the other, and the overall brightness of the display is high. Looking at what information is available a guess may be made that the minimum time is of the order of a second; but from the literature there is no strong reason to believe that any workers have attained the maximum rate of fluctuations. (Levelt (1967) gives 0·8 seconds as the mode.)

Continuing on the subject of involuntary fluctuations, Latour (1966) claims to have found that there are threshold fluctuations in the retina which are the result of efferent, possibly cortical, control. These are local to patches within a retina, and do not, according to him, involve fluctuations of the threshold of the eye as a whole. They show a periodicity of about 25 msecs., and may alter the probability of seeing a flash by up to nearly 20%.

Concerning voluntary direction of attention within the visual field, two recent sets of experiments mark the beginning of what promises to be a fruitful field to explore. Sampson and his co-workers (Sampson and Spong, 1961a, 1961b; Sampson, 1964; Sampson and Horrocks, 1967) have reported several experiments which are analogous, they claim, to the Broadbent 'split span' hearing work. Since their work has been more directly aimed at the organisation of visual memory, comparing it with hearing, and with the relation of their results to dominance, and because they have not used a very large range of rates of presentation and interstimulus intervals, and bearing in mind also the arguments earlier advanced about the difficulties inherent in arguing from these kinds of experiments to switching times, we will not add anything to the account of their work which was given in Chapter 5. Whelan's (1967) work, on the other hand, provides an extensive body of information. He used both cinematographic projection and also on-line computer generated alphanumeric symbols to provide arrays of stimuli as shown in Figure 22.

Whelan used an optical train of prisms to ensure that there were no difficulties involved in convergence, and that the stimuli would appear symmetrically on either side of the fixation point and at a comfortable viewing distance. The optical system could be adjusted for each subject. He performed a series of calibration tests using spots, flicker and alphanumeric symbols of varying sizes, and presented them at different eccentricities from the fovea and at various exposures, so that he was able to establish comparable measures of acuity for his various stimuli. These calibration runs were performed both monocularly and binocularly, and measures both of errors and of latencies were used. Keeping the same subjects throughout, he was able to pick suitable angular separation for his stimuli, and to measure for each individual how the stereoscopic presentation affected performance. The particular part of his work which is of interest here is that in which the subject

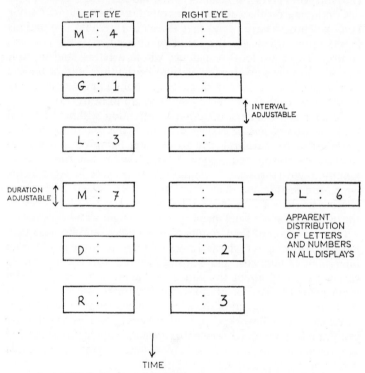

FIG. 23. Typical stimulus sequence from Whelan's experiments

was asked, say, to read out aloud the stimulus which appeared to the right of fixation. It is obvious that such a stimulus may enter either the left or the right eye, but the viewer will not be able to say which because of his inability to say which eye is being stimulated in a stereoscopic situation. Whelan was able to present a series such as that shown in Figure 23.

The critical question is whether there is any difference in the accuracy or latency of response to the target signal following the switch. The subjects' responses were recorded, and timing was from the onset of the display to the closure of a voice key. Various interstimulus durations and target durations were used, and in some cases progressive runs, during which the mark/space ratio of signal/dark period was gradually increased or decreased under computer control with the measurement of response latency being

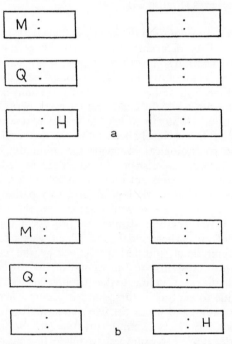

FIG. 24. Visual switching time in the stationary field (a) is faster than (b)

possible signal by signal, in order to see up to what rate-subjects could follow. It was possible to balance out the tendency of signals on the left side of the array to be read first (attention gradient in reading) by arranging for the right side signals to start a few milliseconds earlier under computer control. The experiments show, incidentally, the great power and flexibility of on-line experiments, and, since almost the whole of the experimental work was completed within 12 months, the considerable increase in the rate of work possible using such installations.

With regard to switching time, the following results of Whelan are pertinent. Firstly, there seems to be some asymmetry, since for short differences in onset time, a right-before-left presentation was more frequently accepted as simultaneous than a left-before-right presentation. Secondly, switching from the right to the left side of the visual field took about 35 msecs. less within an eye than between eyes (Figure 24).

Although a consideration of the physiological basis of attention mechanism will be deferred until the next chapter it may be in order here to mention some of the attempts which have been made to relate this kind of work to the various periodicities which have from time to time been discovered in human performance. Probably the most widely cited reference on periodicity is the paper by Stroud (1956) to which the reader is referred. But the search for what has variously been called the temporal integration interval, the psychological moment, the minimum dwell time, etc., is continuous. There seems to be a deep rooted belief that there must be such a constant underlying behaviour. There is the work on the so-called psychological refractory period, which has been taken by many workers to suggest that there is a period during which information cannot be processed following the acceptance of an earlier signal, and which seems to be of the order of magnitude of, and perhaps defined by, the reaction time. The delay in the response to the second of two signals, when it occurs within the reaction time to the first, appears well established, and to be due to central factors, since it occurs where there are two response keys, and where the two signals arrive over different sensory modalities. It is common practice (see Bertleson, 1966, and Welford, 1967, for example) to relate this apparent intermittency to the work by Craik (1948) and Vince (1950) in which it is generally accepted that not more than two or three corrections per second are possible in pursuit tracking tasks. An interesting example of an experiment which deliberately attempts to bridge the gap between tracking and key pressing tasks is described by Gottsdanker (1967). A pointer is moved towards a fixed target on the occurrence of the first stimulus. At the occurrence of the second stimulus the motion must either be continued or reversed, depending on the stimulus. While such an experiment shows one conceptual framework within which the two kinds of studies may be related, it must be said that there are alternative explanations for the limitation of tracking responses which do not include the usual model which postulated a servo-loop monitoring the progress of the response. While such monitoring is in progress the main information channel is occupied and so there is only an intermittent intake of information. One is struck, however, by the very close resemblance between the maximum of two or three fixations which can be made per second and the limit of the number of responses (two or three) which can be made. It is possible that the intermittency is due to the fact that the subject detects where the target has gone to, and then makes a response designed to end at that position. As soon as the visual system is ready for another fixation, another response can be made. Since little information can be taken in during the eye movement, since the threshold is raised prior to the beginning of the eye movement, and since there is evidence that even if a stimulus disappears before the eye movement is complete the fixation may still be accurate, such a limitation on pursuit tracking correction movements must certainly be considered before any central intermittency need be postulated. This is not to deny the existence of servo-loop monitoring of response, since the correction of overshoot seems to imply its existence; but merely to make the point that it may very well not be that aspect of the situation which limits the rate of responding, but rather eye movements *per se*. On the basis of the tracking limitations alone it does not seem right to infer a lengthy central intermittency.

Although the psychological refractory period appears to have a continuous distribution linked to the reaction time with respect to which it is being measured, Welford (1967) has deduced that underlying this there may be a sampling period of the order of 80 msecs. It will be recalled that Kristofferson argued for a quantum of about 60 msecs., while Latour has found fluctuations of the visual threshold at about 25 msecs., and eye movements run at about 300 msecs. Broadbent has on several occasions argued for a periodicity in the region of one tenth of a second. For example (Ladefoged and Broadbent, 1960) the way in which a click is placed among other signals which are being presented concurrently was interpreted by Broadbent to be a function of a discrete sampling interval and, as we saw earlier, he interpreted Cherry and Taylor's supposed 'switching' experiment in a similar way. Over all the literature broods the spectre of the alpha rhythm, which as long ago as the 1940's was suggested as an

F*

internal clock. In particular McCulloch (1949) argued that the alpha rhythm might be the scanning frequency at which the intake of information was sampled, the alpha representing the natural frequency with which the data field inside the brain was swept. As is well known, alpha has a dominant frequency of about 10 cycles per second.

On the basis of the evidence at present available it is impossible to decide that any of these periodicities in any way reflect a basic periodicity or sampling period in the processing of information, at least in the sense that we are absolutely certain that they represent limits. The most popular periodicity to which writers return again and again is without doubt the alpha rhythm. But it seems extremely unlikely that it represents an important, universal, fundamental mechanism on which the normal functioning of the system is based. Apart from arguments concerned with the nature of complex interconnected networks, to which we shall return in the next chapter, there is the almost conclusive fact that some people do not show any alpha rhythm. It is not just that the amplitude is rather low, or that the frequency is not exactly 10 cps (the literature seems to accept a major periodicity between about 7 and 14 cps as alpha). Several cases have been reported where even autocorrelograms of the EEG did not show any marked periodicities in this range. An example is to be seen in Latour (1966). These people nonetheless appear to show normal behaviour, give reaction times in the usual range and can pay attention adequately. Were alpha so important such a thing would be inconceivable.

In summary, it seems at the moment that there is not enough evidence to argue for a fundamental periodicity, or to give a firm estimate concerning switching time in attention, except for the fixation changes accompanying the overt switching of visual attention. Otherwise we do not know the value either of switching time or of switching rate. On the other hand there is the promise of new techniques which may allow estimates to be made in the not too distant future. One methodological point should perhaps be made again. Most people who have worked in the field of selective attention seem uncertain about the relation between estimates of performance made in experiments such as Kristofferson's and estimates in continuous tasks such as Treisman's and Whelan's. A subject in continuous experiments where responses are required to a long stream of signals often has the feeling that it takes some time to get 'locked on' to the message. (It will be recalled that various workers have remarked that the biggest difficulty in selective attention is to identify the message to be received at the beginning, and that staying on the message once this has been achieved is relatively easy.) It is possible that single stimulus pair estimates do not measure the same state of the system as do estimates where a long stream of signals is received. It is to be hoped that the future will see experiments comparable to Kristofferson's but which use continuous heavy load presentation, while at the same time monitoring performance signal by signal. On-line computing would seem to offer the necessary technology to match the sophistication and flexibility of the system whose performance characteristics we are trying to establish.

There has been no recent work which throws new light on switching time in heaving. With regard to vision, the important series of papers by Bekey's group should be consulted, for example Bekey, G., and Caswell, N., 1968, Identification of sampling intervals in sampled-data models of Human Operators, *IEEE Trans. Man-machine systems, MSS–9,* No. 4, 138–142. An attempt to generalise the application of sampled-data models seems desirable.

9 PHYSIOLOGICAL RESEARCH ON
ATTENTION MECHANISMS

We now turn to consider the extent to which it is possible to relate the behavioural experiments which we have discussed to the findings of neurophysiological research into attention. Three extensive reviews have recently appeared, by Horn (1965), Hernandez-Peon (1966) and Worden (1967). Worden is concerned with a particular problem: whether there is 'gating' of information at the cochlear nucleus. Hernandez-Peon's review is entirely concerned with the work of his group. Horn provides the most wide-ranging collection of physiological data of the three.

The main problem in identifying the physiological basis of selective attention is perhaps that we do not yet know what needs to be explained. Out of the large amount of work which we have reviewed in the earlier parts of this book, what is so certain that we can reasonably ask a neurophysiologist to search for its embodiment? We do not yet know the details of the range of attentional phenomena and therefore we do not know what to seek in the nervous system. Several of the experiments to be described in this chapter seem to be to do with attention, and yet in the end one is left with an uncomfortable feeling that the operational definitions adopted may not have a close relevance to the mechanisms sought. It is as well to remember that the relation between operational definitions and psychological experiments involving hypothetical construct models is rather different from that between such definitions and the actual hardware of the brain. It is quite possible to postulate a set of mechanisms which, taken as a whole, will give the requisite transfer function for describing a particular kind of behaviour, and yet have the hardware of the brain organised in quite a different way in order to compute the same function. In such a case a strong, consistent, well formed model based on behavioural experiments and hypothetical constructs may actually hinder rather than help physiological research by suggesting to the neurophysiologist that he look for quite different arrangements of nerve networks than are actually present.

Consider, for example, the differences which would be found in the hardware and circuitry of a multiplier, depending upon whether it was organised as a repetitive binary adder which kept a tally of the number of additions, or as a 'quarter square' amplifier, or for adding signals which had been translated into the logarithmic domain. In the present discussion, suppose that we talk of a 'switch'. We have no idea what the embodiment of such a function might be in terms of nerve cells, not even (as we saw in an earlier chapter) whether we should look for a step function or not in the plot of transmission against time, or whether perhaps desynchronisation with no decrease in the rate of firing might not be the way in which switching is done. Worden (1967, p. 75) emphasised this:

> It is instructive to note that throughout our experiments a prominent relationship between amplitude of auditory potentials (cochlear nucleus) and position of ears in space was persistently attributed to behavioural variables . . . as the animal oriented to the overhead speaker, the accompanying change in amplitude would be interpreted to reflect the shift of attention to the auditory signal. Similarly, during acoustic habituation, as the animal moved progressively through positions of standing alert, sitting with drooping head, and finally lying down and curling up, the concomitant amplitude changes were assumed to relate variously to levels of arousal and direction of attention. Some of the difficulties presented by these changes in auditory potentials could be resolved by behavioural speculation . . . Recognition of the significance of ear position in terms of acoustic variations within the sound field was finally forced upon us by observations which defied even imaginative behavioural interpretation.

The point is here that precisely those features of the behaviour which turned out to be irrelevant with respect to the neural correlates of attention are those which would naturally be taken to be operational definitions of attention-paying behaviour. The changes were actually being brought about by factors which were only accidentally related to that behaviour, and yet were just what might have been expected of an attention paying mechanism!

We must, therefore, regard neurophysiological work as parallel to, usually independent of, but capable of supplying ideas for, the behavioural work on attention which we have elsewhere been reviewing.

Physiological studies may conveniently be divided into six fields, although the boundaries are necessarily blurred because of the uncertainty just referred to about the definitions of attention. The divisions are: (a) the waning of sustained attention, or habituation; (b) the catching of attention by new stimuli, or dishabituation; (c) the selection of a neural 'channel'; (d) inter-action between stimuli; (e) indices of arousal level and correlates with overall performance; and (f) the question of the physical embodiment of overall strategies of paying attention, correspond-ing to one aspect of the 'Plans' of Miller et al. (1960).

The waning of attention: habituation

It has been known for many years that both behavioural and physiological indices of response alter when the same stimulus is repeatedly presented to an animal or man. An animal will show marked orientation responses to a stimulus, whether a click, flash or mild tactile stimulation, when it is first presented. Search-ing behaviour is frequently observed, from slight changes in ear position or degree of dilatation of the pupil to gross movements around the environment. When the stimulus is repeated at regular intervals this behaviour slowly and steadily declines until no observable response is seen to the occurrence of the stimulus. Parallel changes in the neural response may at times be recorded at several levels of the afferent pathways, suggesting that neural changes may be a reflection of the declining behavioural attention. There are, however, a number of problems. Typically the disappear-ance of the behavioural orientating responses is very rapid. With-in a few dozen presentations of the stimulus at most the animal ceases to respond, and often more quickly than that (Guzman-Flores, 1961). Sometimes there is a correspondingly rapid decline also in the neural responses. Horn and Hill (1964) show a record in which the number of spikes from a unit in the brain stem of a rabbit declined from 18 to four per stimulus in a series of about two dozen presentations. The stimulus was a pure tone burst. On the other hand some workers have found that it may take days or even weeks of presentations for the neural response to habituate, even though the behavioural response has long since disappeared (Galambos, 1960). In sense modalities such as smell the decline in behavioural response may be due not so much to central habituation as to the peripheral adaptation of the receptor system itself, which alters the sensitivity of the afferent system to stimulation. This would hardly count as an attention mechanism in the sense with which we are concerned, but it does however draw attention to an interesting conceptual problem. Worden (1967) remarks that it is almost inevitable to think that a decline in the amplitude of the evoked potential recorded from some part of an afferent pathway means that the signal strength has been decreased, but that this is by no means the case necessarily. Such an interpretation presupposes a great deal of knowledge about the coding rules used by the nervous system. Perhaps the reduction of the evoked potential actually means that there has been desynchronisation of the discharge pattern, and signals an increase in the rate of the transmission of the specific information. (For a very rough analogy compare the waking EEG with the large, synchronised delta waves of deep sleep.) Or consider how in bright light the pupillary diameter is reduced, lowering the amount of energy reaching the receptors during the first few seconds of stimulation and so reducing the amplitude of the response from the retina. Again the acoustic reflex lowers the sensitivity of the auditory pathway in response to violent sensory input.

But in both cases it is possible to imagine a situation where such a reduction might actually increase rather than decrease the efficiency with which information was extracted from the incoming signals. It is obvious that if stimulation is so intense that the system is overloaded all discrimination will be lost, since the system is saturated and gives the same output for all variations of input. Reducing the sensitivity of the system so that the overall level of stimulation comes back within its dynamic range will actually improve discrimination. Because most signals from the real world are highly redundant there is no reason to think *a priori* that such a reduction in overall signal magnitude as can be recorded from nervous pathways necessarily corresponds to an effective loss of information. It is apparent, for example, that if the intensity of stimulation received by an individual nerve cell is signalled as a frequency of firing which is proportional to the logarithm of the stimulus strength, and if the output of a particular nucleus where such a transform occurs is compared with the input then there will be an overall decrease in the number of spike potentials recorded, because of the arithmetic to logarithmic transformation. Summing over the entire pathway we would record an apparent decrease in signal strength, but there would be no loss in information, merely a recoding. Again, it seems rather likely that mechanisms of lateral inhibition (Ratliff, 1965; Békésy, 1966), although usually talked of as being for the enhancement of contours and suchlike, are actually more important as rapid adaptation mechanisms, which pull down the response of a system to keep it within the useful dynamic range; incidentally they also throw away redundant information and enhance contours, so that again a reduction in the size of the output of such a net with respect to its input does not necessarily correspond to a dangerous reduction of information. Rather a net gain in discrimination may be possible (Stockham, 1967; Moray, 1969e).

It is, then, not obvious just what we should expect to find happening in the nervous system when we observe a decline in behavioural attention. This conclusion is underlined by the fact that Sharpless and Jasper (1956) actually reported that the cortical response *increased* in some of their animals at the same time as the behavioural response showed complete habituation. It seems likely that this is because the usual emphasis on correlating the arrival of impulses at the cortex with perception is wrong. Cortical activity by itself is not sufficient to ensure that the owner of the cortex is aware of the stimulus; perception requires the interaction of many different areas of the nervous system, certainly including both the primary cortex and the reticular system (Oswald et al., 1960; Adrian et al., 1953; Samuels, 1959).

Finally the picture is complicated by some methodological problems to which Worden draws attention. For example, during habituation changes in amplitude of opposite sign may be observed under certain conditions of stimulation when the two cochlear nuclei of a cat are examined at the same time. It seems very likely that some of the changes which are observed in the neural responses relate somehow to the mechanisms of habituation or the loss of attention to the stimuli, but it is not clear which, and it is not clear how. It seems quite likely that no one has yet looked at the correct part or parts of the nervous system to find the relevant changes; and even more probable that it will be necessary to look at several at the same time rather than only in one place, a kind of experiment which is still rare. Arousal mechanisms

are certainly implicated. Horn and Hill (1964) reported habituation of units in the brain stem, but it is rather uncommon to find
rapid habituation of units in a specific afferent pathway, although
not unknown.

Dishabituation

The sudden reappearance of a response, both behavioural and
neural, is equally well known. Usually even a slight change in
some quality of the stimulus, such as pitch, loudness, wavelength,
etc., is sufficient to arouse an organism and restore the response.
This is a strong argument against the wholesale blocking of an
afferent pathway; or, at least, should a blockade be invoked, it
would have also to be postulated that the arrival of an 'unusual'
signal could call the sampling mechanism to switch. Typical
results which again underline the danger of identifying stimulus
strength with amplitude come from Voronin and Sokolov (1960)
who found that *reducing* the intensity of a signal was sufficient to
dishabituate the animal. Horn and Hill (1964) found that changing
the frequency of the signals by half an octave was sufficient to
cause a recovery in function of a midbrain unit in a rabbit as
great as that caused by several minutes' silence following a train of
1000 Hz tone bursts presented once every 1·5 seconds. Similar
results for evoked potentials from the cortex are reported by
Sharpless and Jasper (1956).

The recovery of function is very rapid, but not instantaneous.
Oswald et al. (1960) found when playing recordings of names to
sleeping subjects while recording the EEG that response was
greater if the names were repeated twice; and Horn and Hill
(1964) observed that in some of the units from which they recorded
there was an increase in response over the first two or three presentations of the new stimulus. This would be in agreement with an
interpretation in which the arousal system played an important
role, increasing the sensitivity of the organism and itself being
further aroused in its turn in a positive feedback loop.

The marked specificity of habituation and the remarkably
slight changes required to remove it clearly relate to findings at
the behavioural level that novel stimuli are important elicitors of
attention, as was stated by Titchener (1903), and included as one of
his postulates by Broadbent (1958). Once again, such specificity
argues for habituation taking place at a relatively high level in

the nervous system, although in the case of hearing such specificity could in principle be a property of the fibres leaving the cochlea itself or of the spiral ganglion, and certainly of the cochlear nucleus, since at all these levels there is some degree of tonotopic localisation.

The selection of neural 'channel'

We come now to a more controversial matter. By far the best known experiments on the physiology of attention are the long series by Hernandez-Peon and his associates (Hernandez-Peon, 1966). They are at first sight extremely attractive because, on the face of it, they seem to show changes in neural activity which have a striking connection with attention. Thus the response of the auditory pathway is reduced when a cat views a mouse in a glass bowl, or when fish odour is blown into the chamber which contains the cat. A description of three such experiments will serve both to show their attractive features and also the kind of problems which they raise.

Hernandez-Peon and Scherrer (1955), and Hernandez-Peon, Scherrer and Jouvet (1965) recorded the response of the dorsal cochlear nucleus unilaterally in an unanaesthetised cat, using chronically implanted electrodes. The stimuli were clicks delivered over a loudspeaker, responses were not averaged. The evoked responses to the clicks were recorded in the presence of a mouse in a glass jar, and when the cat was alone in a state of relaxed wakefulness. Two representative recordings are reproduced under each condition in the original papers, before, during and after the cat had been exposed to the mouse. Similarly Hernandez-Peon and Donoso (1959) recorded the evoked response to light using implanted electrodes in a human subject while the subject was relaxed and inactive, and also while she was talking about her daughter. They claimed that there was a marked decrease in the light-evoked potentials during the conversation. In a third experiment, using averaging by means of an oscilloscope trace, Hernandez-Peon also claimed that responses to tactile stimulation were reduced during intellectual conversation.

This group of workers has emphasised throughout its reports that its evidence is to be interpreted in terms of blocking or reduction of sensory input at rather peripheral levels of the afferent sensory pathways.

Thus the experiments with response to clicks in the cats have been interpreted as showing blocking at the site of the cochlear nuclei themselves, presumably under the control of efferent pathways from higher centres. Reticular system pathways are thought to be important in the operation of these 'switching' functions.

> The ... effect, observed at the lowest level of the auditory pathway during distraction ... similar results were obtained at the first synapse of the visual pathway ... reflex inhibition of the first sensory synapse can explain, at least partially, the suppression of a mild pain produced by another more painful stimulus arising in any other region of the body. (Hernandez-Peon, 1966)

Unfortunately there are a number of very important methodological criticisms which vitiate the value of these experiments. In the first place the changes which are shown in the records published are frequently rather small. One must assume, knowing human nature, that these are probably the most convincing records that were obtained. There is no indication that the records were scored 'blind', that is by people who did not know where in the record the expected change would take place. If averaging is not used blind scoring is absolutely essential when the changes are only small. Even averaging has its hazards (Perry, 1966), especially when there are rather large spontaneous fluctuations in the noise. Horn (1960) has recorded spontaneous variation in the photic response in cats which is at least as great as the changes recorded by Hernandez-Peon.

Moreover there is an inherent implausibility about turning off an entire receptor or modality. It would be biologically extremely dangerous for an organism, in what is usually a hostile environment, completely to abandon an entire sense modality as a source of information. Admittedly there might be a rapid sampling across modalities, and there does seem to be transient suppression of visual input during a saccade. But equally the behavioural evidence suggests that even when a message is strongly rejected there is continuous monitoring of it up to a very high level, probably including the cortex. That there are descending pathways which reach the cochlear nucleus and even beyond cannot be denied (Galambos, 1955; Worden, 1967) and it seems only logical that they are some kind of control system. But what kind of control do they exercise, and over what structures? The experiments of Treisman (1964) on listening to one out of three auditory messages dispersed in space, and of Moray et al. (1965) on listening to four—to mention but two—clearly show that you do not turn off both ears in order to listen to a third source of sound which is located in the middle of the head.

Now it might be argued that at least in many of Hernandez-Peon's experiments selection was between modalities, and that therefore the total switching off of one modality is not so implausible. There does seem to be a very strong interaction between modalities, which can be thought of as 'distracting'. One example is the 'auditory analgesia' effect which is sometimes used to dull the pain during dentistry and which has been discussed in some detail by Licklider (1961); and casual everyday experience suggests that at least at some times one almost totally ignores the input to one modality in order to concentrate on another. It does not, however, mean that blocking must be at the periphery.

Close inspection of Hernandez-Peon's methodology has shown that there are very strong reasons for thinking that many of the reported results are artifacts, in the sense that what causes changes in neural response are differences in the environment, not changes in neural command operations implemented by efferent neural impulses from higher centres. A large part of Worden's (1967) review is taken up with an examination in detail of such effects, with special reference to the cochlear nucleus response.

One of the main objections to Hernandez-Peon's methodology is that there was no control exercised for the effect of the middle ear muscles. Carmel and Starr (1963) have shown that the acoustic reflex can cause a reduction of up to 15 dB in the input to the cochlea, and that the response can be triggered by other than acoustic stimuli, so that stimuli in other modalities might be expected to initiate it. The time course of habituation is sometimes mirrored by a build up in the acoustic reflex, and it also shows dishabituation to a new stimulus. The evidence does not warrant the conclusion that all such changes in the cochlear nucleus response are due to the cochlear reflex, but it certainly plays a large part. This would cast doubt on the interpretation which Hernandez-Peon proposes as to the mechanisms involved. There are, however, more serious objections. Worden emphasises the importance of the acoustic field in which the animal is placed while hearing the stimuli. It is apparent from the photographs which Hernandez-Peon has published of the experiments in progress that they were not conducted in anechoic surroundings. Indeed the boxes appear to have been of perspex or glass. In such conditions there will be very marked variations in the sound field from point to point, due to the presence of standing waves. Even quite small variations in position can lead to very marked changes in the observer's relationship to the sound field. (This may be noticed if a human listener sits beside a television set and listens to the very high pitched whistle that the set emits; by turning the head the intensity of the whistle will be heard to change very markedly.) Even when an anechoic chamber is used there will usually be some standing waves present, and their position and form will alter with the frequency of the signal. The shape of the animal's head will, therefore, interfere with such standing wave patterns, and the degree of interference may be expected to vary as the animal moves around in the sound field. Such effects can cause the effective signal strength to vary with orientation, and so will cause changes in neural response when the animal turns its head, moves about, and in other ways responds to a 'distracting' signal. In fact one ear may be more strongly stimulated than another, which explains Worden's observation that during habituation the cochlear nucleus response may increase at one ear while decreasing at the other ear. Combinations of variations in the acoustic field and changes in the acoustic reflex will account for many, if not all, of the effects observed by Hernandez-Peon, and Worden and his group have found it impossible to replicate the earlier results with adequate controls included. It is especially noteworthy that when the animals are trained to wear headphones so as to minimise the role of head position the changes in the cochlear nucleus response when distracting stimuli are present or habituation takes place are very much smaller than when the animal is free to move in the sound field. Finally, Galambos (1960) claims that no consistent changes are found in response to visual, auditory or other stimuli when the middle ear muscles have been cut.

Similar criticisms can be made of the work of Hernandez-Peon in other sense modalities. In connection with his claimed reduction in the photic response Horn and Blundell (1959) and Horn (1960) found that the response to light was sometimes actually reduced when an animal paid attention to a visual stimulus by comparison with when it did not. Controls were run on the importance of pupillary size and head position, and Horn concludes (1965) that the visual searching behaviour is responsible for the changes. Some changes in the physiological response changes may be due to changes in fixation and accommodation which occur when visual searching ceases, causing blurring and other changes in the visual system. It is known that relaxing from visual search in humans can lead to loss of accommodation and convergence, thus reducing the correlation between corresponding points on the retinae and thus, perhaps, the efficacy of the binocular display for evoking strong cortical responses, since, as Hubel and Weisel (1962) have shown, there are many units which respond only to binocular stimulation. Thus there are a number of factors which might cause a change in the output of the visual system without invoking efferent suppression of the input.

Criticisms may also be made about the experiments on changes in tactile sensitivity. It is notoriously difficult to maintain a given strength of electrical stimulation in, for example, shock escape situations. Factors such as the dryness or dampness of the skin, the way in which an animal stands, whether the paws are flat on the shock grid or not, whether the muscles are tensed, all tend to alter the effective impedance of the tissues through which the current passes, and therefore both the effective strength of the shock and the sensitivity of the tissues stimulated. It seems likely that if a strong shock is given from time to time to one part of the animal, and a weak one to another part, the effect of the strong shock may be to alter the tenseness of the animal, to activate the autonomic system, and in many ways to alter the effective strength of the shock; so it is not surprising to find variations in the response to the mild shock. But whether it is necessary to invoke attentional mechanisms to explain these changes is doubtful in the absence of proper controls. Oswald (1962) has shown the human subjects who receive strong periodic shocks will learn to adapt to the rhythm at which the shocks come, even to the extent of going to sleep momentarily to avoid the shock; and it seems only reasonable to suppose that people or animals receiving shocks will tense themselves, move, or in other ways behave so as to reduce the intensity of the shock. Gross movements may well produce changes in the evoked response merely by altering the properties of the electrode-body interface. And, just as Horn found that the evoked response to light was reduced during attention, and Sharpless and Jasper (1956) that the cortical response to clicks increased during habituation, so Satterfield

(1965) found that in humans, when shocks were presented to the wrist and evoked response, the recorded response decreased in the wrist to which attention was being paid, while it stayed constant at the other side.

All in all, despite the very large body of experimental work which has come from the laboratory of Hernandez-Peon and his co-workers, we must agree with Horn (1965) when he says:

> It seems reasonable to conclude, on the basis of the evidence so far reviewed, that there is little to support the view that the evoked potential to a stimulus is consistently reduced when there is reason to suppose that the stimulus is not being perceived. Nor is there any incontrovertible evidence that, in the main sensory pathways, the evoked potential to a stimulus is increased in size when the stimulus is being perceived.

The position is that one can show the signal certainly does not reach the conscious awareness of the observer, but must be reaching the cortex. Oswald et al. (1960) investigated the ability of listeners to discriminate patterns while asleep. Sleep-deprived subjects visited the laboratory and went to sleep with EEG electrodes attached to the scalp. While they slept the EEG was monitored and tape-recordings of names were played to them. Before going to sleep they had been asked to respond whenever they heard their own name by clenching their fist. They were also asked to nominate a name which had no emotional significance for them, and clench their fist if they heard that name. Fist clenching produced a readily observable muscle potential in the EEG record. The recordings were scored blind, that is, without the scorers knowing at which moments the stimuli had been presented, and were examined for fist clenchings (evidence that the sleeper had heard the name), K-complexes (indices of cortical response) and GSR (indices of emotional arousal). Sleepers woke more frequently to their own names than to the neutral name, and also gave more K-complexes and GSRs without waking to their own name than to the other name. There is general agreement (Neff and Diamond, 1958; Cowey and Weiskrantz, 1963) that the cortex is needed for complex pattern discrimination such as must have been occurring in these responses. Furthermore, as we saw in Chapter 4, it is likely that GSRs can be conditioned to appear in the rejected channel when a listener is shadowing another message, even though the word is not heard, and it is thought that conditioned GSRs in humans require the participation of the cortex. Finally it is difficult to see how the experiment by Treisman (1964a), in which several of her subjects noticed that the meaning of a rejected message was identical to an accepted message when the latter was a translation of the former, could show that result if the message was completely blocked at a low level in the afferent pathway.

On the other hand there is such a thing as being aware of one stimulus but not of another, and there are large numbers of efferents known to exist from the cortex all the way down to the extreme periphery in most of the sensory modalities. In some cases these can be stimulated and produce a change in the response of nuclei in the classical afferent pathways. Galambos (1955) found that stimulating the olivo-cochlear bundle appeared to alter the response even of the cochlea; and Latour (1966) interprets his own results to mean that there are efferent effects detectable at the retina. The sensitivity of the kinaesthetic sense has been known for a number of years to be under efferent control of the gamma fibre system (Granit, 1953), and there is evidence for efferent activity in other cases also. The problem remains, what is the use and purpose of these mechanisms? For kinaesthesis the answer is clear—the efferent system allows the retuning of sensitivity of receptor organs to keep the system maximally sensitive, and is a special kind of adaptation mechanism, comparable to the light and dark adaptation mechanisms in vision, for ensuring that the dynamic range of the measuring devices present is not exceeded. But in general it is difficult to convince ourselves that we know what to look for at the level of physiology in other cases. We have already seen that it is not obvious, for example, that a decrease in attention should be represented by a decrease in the size of the evoked potential. Samuels (1959) made some of the most relevant remarks on this problem when reviewing the function of the reticular system; and that review is still a particularly clear statement of the problem in this kind of research of the rich interactions which occur between parts of the brain. For example, the discovery of collaterals given off by the ascending afferent pathways to all levels of the reticular formation, with reticulo-fugal paths running in the opposite direction to end on the synaptic junctions of sensory paths (Magoun, 1954), shows that there are ample pathways for the reticular formation to influence the auditory system in the way required. Samuels (op. cit.) remarks:

> ... the functional value of a more differentiated arousal system capable of localised control of the specific projection areas is unquestionable. Through selective facilitation or inhibition of various sensory inputs in the cortex, such an anatomical arrangement would provide for discriminative control over the elaboration of the specific sensory potentials at a cortical level and thus permit greater flexibility and a more finely graded regulation of processes involving selective awareness, perception, and memory than is possible through peripheral sensory control alone.

This is the more likely since, as she observes:

> The latency of the specific evoked potential in the sensorimotor cortex following stimulation of the sciatic nerve was 9–10 milliseconds. In the mid-brain reticular formation, the conduction times ranged from 13 to 23 milliseconds (French et. al., 1953). This difference of 4–14 milliseconds when compared to the 6–12 millisecond latencies of potentials from cortical areas to the reticular formation (French and Hernandez-Peon, 1955) suggests that there is time for a stimulus to reach the cortex via the specific paths and then relay down to the reticular formation in time to affect its own arousal properties.

This clearly refers to a system which begins to approach in sophistication the design required to show behaviour such as is observed in experiments on selective attention with human subjects. Lastly, she refers to the fact that:

'In the cortex the cue value of stimuli may be affected.'

And here she draws attention to the crucial point to which we keep returning. Attention seems to be often a function of cue *value*, not merely cue strength (see Deutsch and Deutsch's model in Chapter 3 for an explicit use of this idea). We have at present no idea at all how value is represented in the nervous system. Perhaps we might guess that looking at the size of evoked potentials is of no relevance at all in this respect, since such a dimension is more likely to be represented in time coincidences of activity, perhaps widely scattered throughout different regions of the brain. The recent work of Sprague (1966) demonstrates the extreme complexity of the mechanisms which we are studying. He found that following cortical ablations of the visual area in a cat visually guided reaching behaviour was lost, but that if the contralateral superior colliculus was also ablated the behaviour returned. This would seem to indicate (if confirmed) that cortical ablation does not result in loss of information, merely to its becoming inaccessible. Is this a paradigm of failure of attention? One is reminded of the cases in humans where a right-sided parietal lesion results in an apparent loss of awareness of the left side of the body. Denny-Brown and Chambers (1958), for example, report a case of a woman who seemed to ignore the left side of the body completely. When tested she could detect single, but not multiple, stimuli in the left visual field. Her two point tactile threshold seemed infinitely large. But information was not completely lost because, while it took ten pins pricking the left hand to equal the sensation of one pricking the right, when she concentrated this ratio dropped to seven to one. One wishes that there were some well-controlled psychophysical data available from such patients.

It seems clear that the mechanism which handles 'gating', 'switching', or call it what you will, is not something which only involves the afferent pathways of the sensory modality in question, but rather complex interactions between large numbers of neurons in widely dispersed circuits throughout the brain at many levels. Worden (1967) quotes Teuber (1959) as saying:

> This association (of specific and non-specific defects) is consistent with the view that specific cerebral systems mediate not only their own, but other activity, and that the highest levels of neural control require the interaction of both.

And himself adds:

> ... lesions in the classical afferent pathways produce not just 'specific sensory defects' but far flung behavioural disturbance reflecting spatial summation and other synthetic processes in the integration of perception.

Interaction between two or more stimuli

There are at least two quite different ways in which an incoming signal may be expected to interact with another present in the sensory pathways at the same time. Firstly there may be convergence of the signals on to a single neurone which is part of a nucleus in the afferent pathway concerned. Such convergence may lead either to facilitation or inhibition. Secondly, it is possible for one signal to influence the arousal system via collaterals from the afferent pathways, and thus indirectly influence the responses to the other signal by altering the state in which the cortex is when it arrives.

There is ample evidence in different parts of the nervous system for interference between stimuli. For example, several workers (Rosensweig and Sutton, 1958; Rosensweig and Wyers, 1955; Moushegian et al., 1964) have found that the response to a click may be altered by the presentation of a second, contralateral click, at most of the levels of the auditory pathway. The earlier click tends to reduce or delay the response to the second click unless the interval is either extremely short (in which case there is summation) or extremely long. The maximum duration of the inhibition set up by the first click seems to be of the order of 100 msecs. or more. Moushegian et al. reported that the effects are extremely complex, being both excitatory and inhibitory to both ipsilateral and contralateral pathways at the level of the olives. We have already mentioned the work of Galambos on the efferent fibres to the cochlea, and Allanson and Whitfield (1956) at the level of the cochlear nucleus. Kiang and his co-workers (1965) have found that a pure tone can inhibit the response to another, and that this may happen even as far peripherally as the cochlea itself.

Again, there is plenty of evidence for the masking of one visual stimulus by another, and even for the unmasking of such masking; and a start has been made on the identification of some of the mechanisms involved.

The work of Hubel and Weisel (1962) has shown that there are units in the visual system which fire only to monocular stimulation and others which fire only to binocular stimulation. We may assume that the latter are coincidence detectors, or are fed by coincidence detectors, and may be involved in gating inputs when there is a lack of coincidence between the input to the two eyes. Thus we may wonder about the relation of such signals to the switching of binocular rivalry. Coincidence of stimulation at corresponding points of the two retinae can lead to the summation of excitation in the visual system. Horn (1965) has suggested that it is the reduction of such coincidence due to loss of accommodation and convergence which may affect the response of the visual system when a subject listens rather than looking.

Wall and Sweet (1967) have shown that electrical stimulation of the dorsal roots can abolish pain, and suggest a model in terms of the blocking of input. Landgren (1959) has reported on the convergence of information from the tongue. He found units that were sensitive to as many as three or four different kinds of stimulation applied to the tongue, such as stretch, cooling, warmth, and taste, and estimated that some 25% of the cortical units he investigated responded to more than one modality. Wall (1961) discussed interaction and control of the skin sensation pathway, and Melzack and Carey (1968) the organisation of the pain system and the way in which such factors as motivation may be thought to control the flow of information. Hill and Horn (1968) have similarly reported units in the rabbit which respond to several kinds of stimuli. They found that six out of 87 units tested responded to auditory, visual and tactile stimulation; 14 to two of these classes of stimuli; and 39 to only one.

There is, therefore, no doubt as to the existence of interactions, sometimes inhibitory, sometimes facilitatory. But once again we are faced with the problem of how to interpret these mechanisms. If we knew for certain that the size of the evoked response was an indicator of the effectiveness of stimuli we could move fairly directly to an interpretation. But we have seen ample reason to doubt that such a straightforward interpretation is open to us. Dawson (1956) found that the size of the primary wave of the human evoked potential followed the intensity of the stimulus applied to the median nerve, over the range of intensities which he studied. But Tunturi (1960) found in the dog that the auditory evoked potential only followed the increase in intensity of sound up to about 20 db above threshold, after which there was no further increase. And van Hof (1960) has reported conditions in which the human evoked potential in response to light may be greater to a train of weak flashes than to a train of strong flashes.

Indices of arousal level and correlates of overall performance

The last mentioned experiments bring us naturally to a discussion of the more global electrical responses seen in EEG recording of evoked potentials and such studies. Since the discovery of the alpha rhythm there has been a series of attempts to relate it to behavioural phenomena. We have already seen that there are reasons for thinking that the correlations between alpha and periodicities round 10 cps in man are probably accidental; and that there are many people who show no alpha even in an auto-correlogram and yet show the behavioural periodicities. It is not therefore intended to discuss the alpha rhythm here.

More recently, however, a number of other features of the evoked response in the human EEG have become of interest. The most sensational is perhaps the so-called 'expectancy wave' which Walter (1964) has reported. He found that if a flash and a click are paired in conditions requiring a response to the click, when the click follows the flash by a short interval a negative-going wave appears just before the onset of the click. If after this the light is presented without the click the 'expectancy wave' disappears after a number of clickless presentations. The wave is intermediate in size if the click is only presented on some trials. This work requires to be repeated and developed. The wave is small and requires computer averaging for its detection. If its existence is confirmed it will be of great interest, although its interpretation will be difficult.

Several studies have recently appeared relating the human evoked response to attention and performance. Satterfield (1964), Wilkinson (1967) and Wilkinson and Morlock (1965) have all reported changes in the response to clicks as a function of different conditions of attention. Wilkinson found a correlation between the response and the reaction time to clicks, but that this only held when the testing session was long, suggesting that it may be related to vigilance rather than to the kind of attention with which this book has been concerned.

Ever since the symposium *Brain Mechanisms and Consciousness* (Adrian et al., 1953), it has been realised that the activity of the arousal system is crucial for behaviour. As we have seen, it may well be that for the physiological correlates of conscious perception we should look at the arousal system and its functional relations rather than at the cortex. The problem is that if the arousal system is in fact the controller of attention and selectivity, and acts not merely to alter the gross overall level of responsiveness of the entire central nervous system but also to control the flow of information over quite specific paths, we are going to have to find the anatomical locus of the 'gates' before we can begin to account for particular phenomena in the behaviour of an observer who is attending to one source of stimuli and ignoring another. There is not, to the writer's knowledge, even the beginning of such work available; nor, yet again, do we know what to look for. It seems likely that if we wish to deduce whether or not a particular stimulus has been consciously perceived we should look neither at the reticular system, nor at the cortical activity, but at the relationship between the electrical activity in those two parts of the brain at least, and perhaps also at the simultaneous activity in yet other parts of the brain. That is, the selective process may appear not as the activity of some particular part of the brain, even of some particular synapse, but as the relation between different parts. If so, we are a long way from having adequate physiological data either to confirm, deny, or even clarify ideas of selective attention which are based on behavioural experiments. It is possible that we do not as yet even have the necessary technological facility for uncovering the mechanisms.

Recently three papers have appeared by Wicklegren (1968a, b, c) which are the first signs of a breakthrough since Hernandez–Peon's work which turned out to be such a disappointment. In very well controlled experiments, Wicklegren found that whether habituation, distraction, or spontaneous activity was used to alter the attentional state of an animal no systematic changes were observable in recordings at any level of the auditory pathway below the level of the medial geniculate body. At the medial geniculate body and at the auditory cortex there were systematic changes in pattern, not merely in amplitude, of the evoked potentials as attention altered behaviourally. His work suggests that modulation of neural activity, rather than blocking, is the way in which attentional states are represented, and that all information enters the nervous system at least as far as the geniculate nucleus (a level at which we know pitch discrimination can be performed (Neff & Diamond, 1958)).

Physiological mechanisms of strategies

In an earlier chapter we saw that perhaps a compromise would be needed between the view that the allocation of attention was entirely stimulus-determined and the view that it was entirely voluntary. To take a specific instance, consider the experiment by Treisman (1960). Listeners were asked to shadow the message presented to their right ear, but during the passage the location of the left and right messages was reversed, so that in mid-sentence the selected message became the rejected one and vice versa. The listeners characteristically repeated about two words from what was now the rejected message and then returned to the accepted *ear*, despite the fact that the sense had changed. It seems clear that the transient change to the wrong ear for a couple of words was caused, as Treisman suggested, by the high probability of the words in the context of the preceding selected passage, and hence the switch was stimulus-determined. On the other hand the fact that the listeners then returned to the designated ear, together with the fact that they believed they had been on that ear the whole time, can be taken as evidence of a higher strategy voluntarily adopted.

What kind of physiological mechanisms might we expect to be involved? Firstly there is clearly activity in both the auditory pathways (left and right auditory nerves) which represents sounds as such. Since there is considerable cross over from one side of the auditory pathway to the other both messages will be represented on each side of the brain. In some way the signals seem to be labelled in respect of which region of auditory space they originated from. At least the signals from the accepted message, and probably also those of the rejected message, must reach the unilaterally localised language analysing centres of the brain, and also there is interaction between the cortex and lower centres such as the reticular system. Even if we were to adopt the hypothesis that rejection consists of the attenuation of the rejected message, to discover signs of this in the physiological responses if the rejection did not occur until high up in the auditory pathway would at present be an impossibly difficult task; we would have to be able to distinguish the accepted message evoked response from that caused by the rejected message, and show that one was smaller than the other. Since it seems likely that these two sets of evoked responses would be occurring in the same part of the brain this could not be done with present techniques; and we have seen that the evidence is overwhelmingly against blocking at an early stage in the pathway.

The concept of 'strategy' as used here is meant to be similar to the 'plans' spoken of by Miller et al. (1960). The problem of discovering the physiological basis of such plans is comparable, following the writer's analogy to that of discovering the embodiment of a particular programme in a computer. Since the programme consists not so much of a particular set of electrical states but more importantly as the relations between them, and since the events are often being distributed over a widely scattered collection of circuits, and on occasion over different pieces of hardware, it is hard to see how to look for functions at the level of structure. It has been suggested (Moray, 1967) that the central processor of the brain may indeed be quite closely related to a general purpose computer in that the same neural circuitry may be used for several different computations, and this would, if true, make it even harder to analyse its wiring diagram. To the question, 'What is this part of the brain for?' the answer may be, 'It depends upon what you are doing.' At least it seems clear that at present we cannot expect physiology to help our understanding of selective attention at complex levels of analysis such as these, although the use of autonomic indices of 'involvement' may turn out to be useful to tell *when* a task is being performed. (Hess, (1965) used pupil dilation as an index of affect, and Bradshaw (1967) found that pupil diameter varied with involvement in solving anagrams or trying to understand jokes.)

Summary and conclusions

Reading over the physiological work of the last few years which has either deliberately or accidentally been relevant to attention, one cannot help but be disappointed. The truth of the matter seems to be that we know almost nothing. The blame for this cannot be laid at the door of the physiologists alone; equally it is true that at present, despite the large amount of behavioural research, we have not produced a sufficiently clear picture of what to look for at a neural level. Until such a picture exists, until we are fairly sure of what functions we think the nervous system is computing when it controls the flow of information, we are unlikely to find the physiological basis of attention, even if the coding rules were to turn out to be quite simple and direct. The first stage in finding the physiological basis of attention is for the psychologists to give a much clearer picture of what needs to be explained.

No mention has been made here of work on the 'split brain' preparation by Sperry and his group (1964). Such studies would seem to be of great relevance to our understanding of attention, particularly the result showing spontaneous alteration when one eye has been trained to one solution and the other to another, incompatible solution. But once again it is difficult to know how to relate such studies to the function of the normal nervous system. Gazzaniga has recently reported 'parallel processing' in commissurectomised humans and monkeys (Gazzaniga and Sperry, 1966; Gazzaniga and Young, 1967). In the study using human patients two choice reaction times were obtained, one from the left half and one from the right half of the brain. These did not differ from a simple RT. Although the reaction times were very long compared with the best results from normal subjects (of the order of 700 + msecs.), after the operation the 'parallel' RT decreased to the level of the simple, rather than the opposite happening.

Other tantalising hints come from the symposium edited by Mountcastle (1962). For example, Teuber reports in it that following traumatic lesions to the human brain a single stimulus frequently fails to show deficits in performance, but that performance on simultaneous tasks is severely reduced. (An obvious exception is of course commisurotomy; and the two results together underline the point that the crucial feature of central processing is the changes in organisation rather than the function of a particular part.) Perhaps the point is also made by Pribram in the same symposium, when he reports that an animal which appears blind in the Wisconsin Test Apparatus may still catch gnats in real life; and a quotation from Pribram's paper will serve to end this chapter:

> We really have many brains; i.e. multiple possible cerebral organisations, each of which is activated in its own special circumstances, dominant for the moment, only to be dominated in turn by others more appropriate to now changed conditions.

But as to the embodiment of those mechanisms, we remain sadly ignorant.

G

In Chapter 3 several theories of attention were reviewed. How do they stand up in the light of the succeeding chapters?

To begin, it is unlikely that we can at present expect to construct a unified theory of attention. We have seen that there are many different kinds of behaviour which are included under the concept, and that there are strong reasons for thinking that several of them bear little real relation to one another, other than in name. Even when we restrict attention to the experiments on selection between simultaneously presented messages, or between input and output, there is evidence of selectivity occurring at several different levels of complexity, from loudness to language. It would be naive to expect such different types of classifying necessarily to be controlled by a single mechanism. Moreover there is no obvious reason to expect hearing and vision to be controlled in the same way. Visual signals tend to be spatially extended but of short duration, while characteristically auditory signals take a long time and consist of information presented sequentially. The estimated sampling times which we have seen in visual work seem to be much longer than in hearing. Even if there were a single control system sharing capacity between hearing and vision there might be a whole hierarchy of sampling times and switching times which would differ from sense to sense and perhaps even within senses.

We do not have enough information available to know what a unified theory would be like, and no attempt will be made to construct one. No attempt will even be made to unify the work within vision, despite the similarity of the mathematics used by Senders and Levelt to describe their findings. Once more, the information necessary to show that these systems are linked, let alone how they are linked, does not yet exist. The visual theories will therefore be left to stand alone. However, it may be significant that both of them postulate a discrete, discontinuous time sampling as the basis for handling simultaneous messages. None of the recent models for auditory selectivity have used a discontinuous sampling mechanism as their basis, although Broadbent did postulate such a system in his original statement on the Filter Theory model. The emphasis of Treisman on the partial attenuation of the rejected message, and Deutsch's rejection of any attenuation of the message before the recognisers have put discontinuous sampling out of fashion. It is certainly true that listening to simultaneous messages does not give an observer so clear a feeling of discontinuity of imput as does the experience of binocular rivalry or directing the glance in different directions; but then neither does the picture at the cinema seem discontinuous, because the nervous system smoothes over the discontinuities in input. In fact there has been very little attempt to find 'binaural rivalry', if it in fact exists. All the results which have been interpreted in terms of attenuation could be interpreted in terms of discontinuities in sampling, given the appropriate choice of sample duration, for all they show is that some, but not all, the information that reaches the periphery is available to consciousness. For example (we shall return to this in more detail later) suppose that the duration of a speech message were divided up into 50 millisecond segments, and 10% of those were chosen at random, all the rest of the message being turned off; it is highly probable that while the content of the message was not heard its pitch, the sex of the speaker, and perhaps even the language would be identifiable. This chapter will mainly be concerned to rehabilitate a version of discontinuous sequential sampling as the basis of all selective attention; to put forward, in other words, a modified version of Broadbent's original hypothesis.

Despite the emphasis on discontinuous sampling in the visual system, we may notice that there are some apparent exceptions. It will be recalled that it is possible for colours to rival in a stereoscopic display while depth is still seen, suggesting that when two separate sources of sensory information are available to the observer some features of the message may be treated as a single input (if they are highly correlated) while others compete for selective attention. Uncorrelated features compete, correlated features are handled as a single message.

This suggests that we might begin to build up a model by assuming that the passage of a complex signal through the receptors and associated structures results in its analysis and recoding into a set of signals occupying different loci in input space (colour, brightness, loudness, pitch, contour density, etc.). This recoding produces a set of signals which are now in the internal language of the nervous system, and so, despite representing very different aspects of the external world, they may be cross-correlated for similarity. Exactly what counts as similar is difficult to say; perhaps time of onset, rate of onset, duration, etc., may be some of the criteria. At any rate, cross-correlation means that those which are similar may be subsequently recoded into a single message, thus reducing the number of loci in input space which are carrying information and the load on the subsequent analysing systems.

Selection, competition, and integration will be among this reduced set of loci, allowing for partial fusion and partial dissociation of the stimulus dimensions of the incoming signals. This cross-correlation is assumed to take place well below the level of conscious perception, to be not under voluntary control and to act on the products of only rather simple analysis by the peripheral structures of the afferent pathways. It appears phenomenally as binocular fusion, binaural fusion, breakdown of separation in lead-lag shadowing, etc. It seems that in general cross-correlation of messages is a powerful and ubiquitous function in the nervous system, and is a particularly powerful way of overcoming selectivity. It probably also occurs at high levels in the brain, where what are correlated are very complex time and space transforms of the original messages. For the purposes of the suggested model only the simplest level will be invoked.

The functions thus far postulated (reception, encoding and allocation to loci in input space, and cross-correlation) seem to the writer to be necessary to any model of selective attention; essentially they are to do with how information reaches the selective mechanisms in the first place. Likewise, at the highest level of analysis we know from single channel experiments on the detection and intelligibility of speech signals in noise that there is some kind of pattern recogniser whose components ('dictionary units', 'recognisers') have different thresholds, and variable thresholds, which vary as a function of signal probability, emotional value of signals, and so on. This again seems necessary for *any* model of selective perception although the connection between the firing of a recogniser and the conscious awareness of the occurrence of the stimulus is not clear. On the whole the evidence seems to favour Deutsch's theory that conscious awareness is a response to the output of the recognisers, not identified with them. Probably conscious awareness is a global property of the interaction of activity of many parts of the brain, but a solution to this problem is not necessary, fortunately, to a discussion of the nature of selectivity. But experiments like those of Oswald et el. on recognition of names by sleeping subjects without their being aware, together with the arguments of Howarth and Ellis, are strong indications in this direction.

The remaining questions are those where controversy rages. Are incoming messages attenuated, or are responses selected? The evidence reviewed up to now is indecisive, a conclusion which is borne out by the fact that both sides in the controversy invoke the same experiments to support their rival views. Bearing this in mind it may be useful to summarise briefly what a theory needs to explain.

Item 1 In shadowing, complex (meaningful, verbal) information is not available from the rejected message.

Item 2 In shadowing, 'crude physical characteristics' from the rejected message are available.

Item 3 When one message is a translation of the other, bilinguals often show a breakdown of selection, and monolinguals who know something of the second language often realise what language it is in, at least.

Item 4 Highly probable verbal stimuli catch attention when they occur in the rejected message.

Item 5 Emotionally important stimuli switch attention.

Item 6 The sudden occurrence of a signal on an otherwise quiet channel, or more generally a sudden change in a channel which has been approximately in a steady state, will almost always be detected even though the channel is not one which is currently being selected (Broadbent, 1958).

Item 7 A lagging copy of a selected message is recognised as identical with it at a greater separation than a leading copy.

Item 8 It appears that selection and rejection are paralleled by changes in the d' parameter of signal detection theory.

Item 9   Simultaneous targets cannot readily be detected when the observer is time sharing equally between the two messages. (Moray and O'Brien, 1967; Moray, 1969b, c, d.)

Item 10   Trying to tap to targets in two messages while shadowing one seems impossible when the targets are words but possible when the targets are 'pips'. (But this finding is in dispute.)

To the above, we must add the results of some very recent experiments by the writer (Moray, 1969b, c, d) which mark the beginning of a programme of research designed to use much more simple and better controlled stimuli to establish the base line performance in selective and competitive tasks. Tone bursts of 3000 Hz were delivered to one ear and tone bursts of 2111 Hz to the other ear of observers. The onset and offset of the tone bursts were exactly simultaneous on the two ears, and controlled through a two-channel electronic switch. There was a 25 msec. ramp up and a 25 msec. ramp down at the start and finish of the tone bursts, so that transients were eliminated. The duration of the tone bursts was 100 msecs. from the beginning of the ramp up to the end of the ramp down. There was 400 msecs. of silence between each pair of tone bursts. The majority of the tone bursts were at a peak to peak level of about 35 dB above 0·0002 dynes/cm², 10% of them in each message were incremented. These were the targets, 50 of them throughout a run of 500 signals per channel. Three sizes of increments were used, 2 dB, 4 dB, and 6 dB. The timing, the injection of the increments, their value and the frequency of the tone bursts could all be controlled by programme on-line from a computer. Subjects were required to press a left hand button when they heard an increment in their left ear, a right hand button when they heard an increment in their right ear, and a central button when they heard an increment in both ears. Four conditions of presentation were used. These were Single Mode (in which only one ear was used, the other being silent throughout); Select Mode (in which both ears received tone bursts, but the listener was to ignore one ear completely and only respond to the other); XOR Mode (in which both ears received tone bursts, but targets never occurred simultaneously); and IOR Mode (in which targets could occur either on the left ear or on the right ear, or simultaneously on both, the last condition being a logical AND Mode). In addition a control was run using IOR presentation Mode but requiring the listener to ignore the single targets and respond only to the simultaneous pairs with the AND response.

It is rather curious that so little attention has been paid to the AND mode of presentation (simultaneous targets). Most of the experiments have been either Select Mode in which the listener accepts one message and rejects the other or, more rarely, XOR in which responses are made to targets in two messages, but targets are never simultaneous (Treisman and Geffen, 1967, for example). Indeed, while Deutsch and Deutsch's model clearly predicts that the AND condition will show severe interference between the messages, Treisman's model makes no explicit prediction about AND signals. Treisman says that in the XOR condition and the Select Mode the listener can attenuate an unwanted message (but there is no indication how rapidly such attenuation could be redirected in the XOR Mode). However, for the AND case, it is not clear that a listener should attenuate one and reject the other rather than rejecting both, or for that matter accepting both, since the theory only says that the Select Mode *can* result in the attenuation of one message, not that in all competitive situations attenuation of all except one message must occur.

It will be recalled that Moray and O'Brien using a key pressing response to verbal (alphanumeric) signals found that the AND condition was very difficult for all subjects and apparently impossible for some. In Moray's pure tone experiments this also appeared to be the case (for full details the original paper should be consulted. Here only selected results will be given). Figures 25 and 26 show the results, averaged over both ears and all subjects and Table 5 gives the graphical data in numerical form. Very similar results were found using frequency increments instead of intensity increments.

The table shows that Treisman's model will not fit the facts. Notice the last three rows of data. AND is the percentage of ANDs (simultaneous targets) which were correctly detected in the IOR presentation mode. AND* is where IOR presentation was used with AND response only (other targets being ignored). Here again responses to ANDs are extremely poor. (One subject detected *no* ANDs at 2 dB). NAND is the percentage of single responses made either to a left target, or a right target, or to what was really an AND.

Now, if Treisman's model says that an observer sharing his

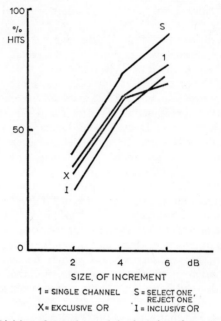

FIG. 25. Division of attention and the detection of pure tone signals

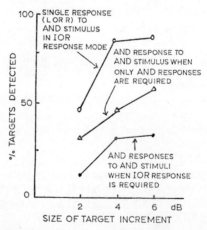

FIG. 26. Analysis of the logical AND mode of stimulus presentation

attention equally between two messages attenuates neither, ANDs should equal Singles. They do not. If he attenuates both messages when sharing equally between the two, NAND responses should be no better than AND responses, but they are. If the listener attenuates one channel and listens only to the other, given that attention wandered from side to side the observed results could be obtained; on the basis of the shadowing work Treisman maintains that information about crude physical characteristics

TABLE 5

Size of Target	2 dB	4 dB	6 dB
Mode of Attention			
Single	35·9 (14·8)	63·8 (11·4)	76·8 (19·6)
Select	42·1 (12·5)	72·9 (18·3)	88·6 (10·8)
XOR	32·9 (14·4)	62·6 (21·8)	67·7 (18·4)
IOR	25·2 (12·6)	57·7 (22·3)	73·4 (15·0)
AND	17·0 (15·3)	34·2 (21·5)	40·6 (27·8)
NAND	50·2 (10·2)	82·1 (14·2)	80·0 (14·8)
AND*	28·4 (16·6)	43·2 (20·2)	54·4 (15·5)

Mean percentage hits averaged over all conditions for five subjects. (Numbers in brackets are the standard deviations)

is available from both messages even in Select Mode. But the data on AND responses shows that this is not true. (The experiment usually cited in connection with the non-attenuation of simple signals is that of Lawson (1966), which showed that listeners could tap to pips when they occurred in XOR Mode in two messages while shadowing one; but, as we saw, since there was summation of the speech and pure tone signals, and since there was no information about the shaping of the waveform or the suppression of transients, this experiment cannot be taken as useful evidence.) Treisman's model does not then fit the data, and needs more

H

elaboration to state explicitly what the predictions are from it about performance in the AND Mode.

How does Deutsch and Deutsch's model fare? The crucial condition here appears to be XOR. The listeners in Moray's experiments were clearly told that the two messages were equally important. There was no *a priori* difference in the importance of the two signals. There are no simultaneous targets in the XOR Mode; therefore even though the listeners were monitoring both channels there could never be competition for responses since at any given time only the one or the other response was required. Yet performance on the XOR condition was significantly worse than on the Single Mode or the Select Mode, at least in some subjects. There is some effect of response selection, since AND* shows that when only ANDs are to be detected (single right or left targets being ignored), performance was better than when AND responses are made in the full IOR response mode. However the low level of performance in the XOR Mode, which is much more apparent when the data is available subject by subject rather than pooled (see the original papers), would not be predicted by the Deutsch model.

Where then do we look? Consider first the difficulty found in handling the AND Mode, where targets occur simultaneously in both messages. This has clearly been shown in four studies (Moray and O'Brien, and three experiments by Moray of which one has just been summarised). Also it has long been known in shadowing that when a listener was really required to respond to the rejected channel success on that task ruins performance on the 'primary' message. (See Mowbray, 1964, for a good example.) Treisman was led to postulate attenuation because of the evidence that some information appeared to be coming through from the rejected message—how else could the listener respond to his own name?—and also because of the evidence that simple stimuli were not affected. We now know that this last is not true, from the AND responses in the study mentioned above. Partial loss of information, we saw earlier, appearing as an ability to perform relatively crude, but not complex, discriminations, could result either from the *complete* loss of *some* information or from the *partial* loss of *all* information. Treisman has adopted the second alternative, but it runs into difficulties. Let us look at the former alternative, and, in doing so, three further facts need to be added to the list of items to be explained.

Item 11 AND configuration cannot be detected for weak signals.
Item 12 AND signals are better detected as signal strength increases.
Item 13 XOR and IOR Mode give poorer detection than Select Mode or Single Mode.

Let us start from Items 11 and 12. If two weak targets are presented simultaneously and for a duration of 100 msecs. very seldom are both detected. Let us assume that the observer's attention is directed wholly to one message at the moment they both begin. He samples that channel until he has determined that a target is present, and then switches to the opposite channel and begins to process the second signal. Now we know from the work of Plomp and Bouman (1959) and Taylor et al. (1967) that when a step function signal is applied information is gained about its presence not in a stepwise manner, but as a monotonically increasing function of time up to about 150 msecs. Hence it will be some time after the presentation of a signal that a listener decides that there is a target on that channel and is prepared to switch.

It follows that the listener, having handled the information on one channel, has only the remainder of the signal duration left to handle the second channel. The chance that the criterion for detecting the presence of a target on the second channel will be reached in the remaining time before the signal ends is slight for a small target, greater for larger targets. Hence even an all-or-none switch such as we are postulating here will show a rise in AND detections as a function of signal strength.

A natural conclusion would be that if we made the signals much longer the listener would have time to listen to the target on one side, make his decision, change over to the other side, and still have time to detect the second target. Moray's third experiment however varied the signal duration of tones whose targets were 4 dB increments from 25 to 250 msecs., and found that while there was a steady improvement in the detectability of ANDs, neither the ANDs nor the single targets in the IOR were nearly as detectable as the single channel condition even at the longest signals. Extrapolating from the data would seem to indicate that signals as long as many seconds would be required for perfect detection of ANDs, a result which seems absurd. At present, then, the psychophysics of time sharing is not sufficiently developed for us to do more than feel certain that it will lead to substantial changes in the picture as portrayed by present models. But although our information is incomplete, we can at least attempt a summary of the present position, and the groundwork for a new model.

ASSUMPTION 1   *At any moment a listener is sampling only one message. All others are totally rejected.*

This seems necessitated by the extreme difficulty which AND signals cause.

ASSUMPTION 2   *A running average of the level of activity in each 'channel' is kept (i.e. some kind of 'adaptation level' is monitored).*

During a run the observer will have a measure of what counts as the average level for the computation of the criterion mentioned above. This does not mean that information is available to conscious perception, but that it is computed *somewhere* in the system. It is the departure from this value that counts as a 'target'. Notice that it is not an average of signal energy but rather some transform of the value of each locus in signal space. Signal strength is measured as the distance of current values of the locus from the recent average value; therefore large decrements will count as large signals, as well as large increments.

ASSUMPTION 3   *A sudden departure from the current running average state of a locus will result in the switch being called to that locus for at least a short time (with the option of staying there longer once it is there) or after current processing on the accepted channel has reached a decision providing the accepted channel is then silent. If it is active the call will become effective at the next silent period, or when voluntarily switched.*

This allows the detection of a sudden change in a locus of input space which has been in a steady state, even though the switch is at that time pointed elsewhere (Item 6). The mechanisms which call the switch are rate-sensitive. It also, taken with Assumptions 1 and 2, explains why XOR and IOR performance is worse than Single or Select. When deliberately time sharing (switching between messages) the observer will be on the wrong channel for 50% of the signals in the XOR condition, and rather less than that in the IOR condition. Hence the target will have to call the switch in order to be detected. This situation is equivalent to the AND mode with no target in the first channel examined. The overall effect will be to suppress performance.

In the Select Mode the rejected message can be locked out completely *providing that the signals begin exactly synchronously.* If the rejected signals are randomly related in phase to the accepted signals, then some of them will call the switch, which will take at least one sample from the 'wrong' message; and performance on the accepted channel will decline slightly, with some information, but not much, being taken from the rejected message (Items 1 and 2). It will be apparent that strong predictions can be made on these assumptions about the effect of signal strength, duration, and phase relations.

ASSUMPTION 4 *Sampling may be continued on one channel indefinitely until the switch is 'called' by another channel. There is probably no quantal effect or upper limit on the sample duration.*

Performance in all the shadowing experiments now becomes intelligible. Upon selecting one message the switch will remain on that message until called by the rejected message. If we assume that the running average is based on a time constant of about 50 msecs. (for which value we might cite the 'tearing apart' phenomenon, which would actually give a rather lower value, nearer to 10 msecs.) then the onset of every word of the rejected message which begins slightly before an accepted message word will result in a short sample of the rejected message being taken. The content will not be available, but 'crude physical characteristics' will be heard, and *over a long run* enough information about them will be collected to let them be identified. This effect is directly testable by randomly sampling a single message at appropriate intervals. (See Huggins, 1964)

Thus Items 1 and 2 and part of 3 are explained. Item 8 is also covered because discontinuous sampling with short samples will result in a different probability of hits and misses in shared, compared with single channel, presentation. Item 9 is covered if we assume that so much time is taken to identify the first signal that not enough of the second remains to be useful after the switch is made. Item 10, as we saw, was probably spurious, or a special case of Assumption 3.

This leaves Items 3, 4, 5, and 7. To explain these we must invoke the interaction of the sampling mechanism with the probabilistic recognisers. It will be remembered that a listener does not always respond to his name in the rejected message. Let us assume along the lines outlined above that the occasions when he does are when it begins just before a word on the accepted channel, so that one sample of it is taken. The 'name' recogniser is set with a particularly low criterion for detecting sounds that are part of the name. (This argument is taken to apply to all 'important' signals.) The reception of one sample, therefore, results in the switch being kept on that channel to take a longer sample. As the evidence accumulates it is kept there more and more and a complete switch occurs; whereas for words which do not appear to be part of an 'important' signal, the switch reverts to its original setting as soon as possible. Thus 'importance' has the effect of lengthening the sample taken until a decision can be made. Hence the amount of interference caused by signals in the rejected message will depend both on their similarity to the important signals for a given observer, and also on where in the course of the signal the critical features for identification come. This covers Item 5. Item 4 would be dealt with in a similar way, assuming that context (signal probability) has the effect of acting to lengthen the duration of sample taken.

These factors increase the amount of sample taken, rather than, as in Treisman's and the Deutsch's models, altering directly the chances of a recogniser firing to a signal of a certain strength. The leading-lagging experiment would assume (Item 7) that the rate at which a fragmentary record of a signal becomes unrecognisable is greater than that at which a nearly perfect record fades, and therefore that the time during which cross-correlation of input with trace can detect the identity of the signals will be greater in one case than the other. This again is experimentally testable. Finally (Item 3) why do bilinguals often show a breakdown of attention when the rejected message is a translation into their second language of the accepted message? Here an arbitrary but testable assumption is that signals in the second language of a bilingual are especially 'important' because of their peculiar role in his psychological life. The argument for 'important' stimuli immediately follows.

It would be, therefore, fairly easy to cover the existing data using a discontinuous on-off switching model. The assumptions require a preliminary sorting of incoming stimuli at the receptors, resulting in the activation of appropriate loci in input signal space; cross-correlation of the loci with appropriate reduction in their number, auto-correlation of each resulting locus to establish a running average of the activity level at that locus, with a time average of about some tens of milliseconds and a probabilistic recogniser.

One major advantage of the model being developed in this chapter is that all the assumptions are easily testable. Some values should fit in with earlier psychophysical work. Even the rather arbitrary assumptions needed to handle verbal stimuli lead directly to experiments which are readily designed. The relations between the assumptions are clear cut and lead to direct predictions. Overall, it seems that, with minor changes, Broadbent (1958) was right.

Several problems, however, remain. Earlier in this chapter reference was made to the fact that response factors do make a difference in the AND Mode. Moreover the whole of Chapter 7 was concerned to show that attentional selectivity should not be regarded as only to do with the control of inflow of information but also with the allocation of processing capacity to input, output, transformations and calculations, and wherever it is required. Our supposed model has gone back on this insistence. Although experiments are under way on these problems at the time of writing it is not possible to show how this wider sense of switching would alter the details of the model. A generalised account of this notion will be found in Moray (1967) where arguments are presented for regarding the brain as a general purpose processor whose computing elements can be allocated indifferently to input, output, or transformation tasks: neurons, or groups of neurons, really are 'general purpose computing elements'. Such reorganisation of the functional anatomy of the brain must take time, probably substantially longer than switching between inputs (Kolers, 1968, on switching between languages and Neisser, 1967, on redirecting search processes).

To fill out the picture we need more information about vision and about intermodal continuous tasks. We need to link 'one shot' tasks to continuous tasks. We need more information about what happens with unbalanced probabilities of signals between the two inputs, and more experiments on the effect of payoff on attention distribution. We need experiments using different durations and types of precisely defined signals. The experiments are not difficult and out of such work a precise, quantitative theory seems quite likely to emerge.

One final warning should be made. What is not usually published is that it is common for experimenters in the field of attention to find after some time that they can achieve performance levels in competitive and selective tasks which far exceed the performance levels attained by their subjects. *All work reported in this book should be regarded as work on unpractised subjects, and the theories as theories of unpractised subjects.* No one has systematically investigated what happens with observers who have been practised over many thousands of trials, and it is most important that such work should be undertaken, since it is almost certain that the performance will differ by orders of magnitude from that reported in this book.

Attention is back again, respectable both in theory and in practice. But despite the considerable recent progress it is perhaps salutary to end with an ancient but still valid call to better things:

The discovery of a reliable measure of the attention would appear to be one of the most important problems that await solution by the experimental psychology of the future.

O. Kulpe, *Outlines of Psychology, 1895*

BIBLIOGRAPHY

ADAMTHWAITE, M. AND SCHAFFER, J. (1965) Assimilation and Attention in Form Perception, *Am. J. Psychol. 78*, 665–71.

ADRIAN, E., BREMER, F. AND JASPER, H. (1953) (eds.) *Brain Mechanisms and Consciousness*, Oxford: *Blackwell*.

ALLANSON, J. AND WHITFIELD, I. (1956) Cochlear Nucleus and its relation to theories of hearing, *3rd London Information Theory Symposium* (ed. C. Cherry), London: *Butterworths*.

ATTNEAVE, F. (1959) *Applications of Information Theory to Psychology*, New York: *Holt, Reinhart, and Winston*.

BABINGTON-SMITH, B. (1961a) Attention in Peripheral Vision, *Nature 189*, 776.

BABINGTON-SMITH, B. (1961b) Effect of attention in Peripheral Vision, *Nature 191*, 732–3.

BADDELEY, A. (1966) The capacity for generating information by randomisation, *Quart. J. exp. Psychol. 18*, 119–30.

BAKAN, P. (1968) *Attention*, New Jersey: *Van Nostrand Insight Books*.

BAKER, C. (1967) Target detection performed with a stationary radar sweep line, *Attention and Performance* (ed. Sanders, A.), Amsterdam: *North Holland*.

BASMAJIAN, J. V. (1963) Control and training of individual motor units, *Science 141*, 440–1.

BÉKÉSY, G. VON (1967) *Sensory Inhibition*, Princeton, New Jersey: *Princeton University Press*.

BERLYNE, D. (1960) *Conflict Arousal and Curiosity*, New York: *McGraw Hill*.

BERTLESON, P. (1966) Central Intermittency 20 years later, *Quart. J. exp. Psychol. 18*, 153–64.

BERTLESON, P. (1967) The refractory period of choice reactions with regular and irregular stimulus intervals, *Attention and Performance* (ed. Sanders, A.), Amsterdam: *North Holland*.

BOWMAN, A. (1920) Size vs. Intensity as a determiner of attention, *Am. J. Psychol. 31*, 87.

BRADSHAW, J. (1968) Pupil size and problem solving, *Quart. J. exp. Psychol. 20*, 116–23.

BROADBENT, D. (1952) Listening to one of two synchronous messages. *J. exp. Psychol. 44*, 51–5.

BROADBENT, D. (1954) The role of auditory localisation and attention in memory span, *J. exp. Psychol. 47*, 191–6.

BROADBENT, D. (1955) A note on binaural fusion, *Quart. J. exp. Psychol. 7*, 46–7.

BROADBENT, D. (1956) Listening between and during practised auditory distractions, *Brit. J. Psychol. 47*, 51–60.

BROADBENT, D. (1958) *Perception and Communication,* London: *Pergamon.*

BROADBENT, D. AND GREGORY, M. (1961) On the recall of stimuli presented alternately to two sense organs, *Quart. J. exp. Psychol. 13*, 103–10.

BROADBENT, D. AND GREGORY, M. (1962) Donders B- and C-reactions and S-R compatibility, *J. exp. Psychol. 63*, 575–9.

BROADBENT, D. AND GREGORY, M. (1963) Division of attention and the decision theory of signal detection, *Proc. Roy. Soc.* (B) (London) *158*, 222–31.

BROADBENT, D. AND GREGORY, M. (1964a) Stimulus set and Response set: the alternation of attention, *Quart, J. exp. Psychol. 16*, 309–18.

BROADBENT, D. AND GREGORY, M. (1965) On the interaction of S-R compatibility with other variables affecting reaction time, *Brit. J. Psychol. 56*, 61–9.

BROADBENT, D. AND HERON, A. (1962) Effects of a subsidiary task on performance involving immediate memory by younger and older men, *Brit. J. Psychol. 53*, 189–98.

BRYDEN, M. (1964) The manipulation of strategies of report in dichotic listening, *Canad. J. Psychol. 18*, 126–38.

BUCKNER, D. AND MCGRATH, J. (1963) *Vigilance: a symposium,* New York: *McGraw Hill.*

CARMEL, P. AND STARR, A. (1963) Acoustic and non-acoustic factors modifying middle-ear muscle activity in waking cats, *J. Neurophysiol. 26*, 598–616.

CHERRY, C. (1957) *On Human Communication,* London: *Wiley.*

CHERRY, C. (1953) Some experiments on the reception of speech with one and with two ears, *J. acoust. Soc. Amer. 25*, 975–9.

CHERRY, C. AND SAYERS, B. (1956) Human 'cross-correlator'—a technique for measuring parameters of speech perception, *J. acoust. Soc. Amer. 28,* 889–95.

CHERRY, C. AND TAYLOR, W. (1954) Some further experiments on the recognition of speech with one and with two ears, *J. acoust. Soc. Amer. 26,* 554–9.

CHOMSKY, N. (1957) *Syntactic Structures,* 's-Gravenhage: *Mounton.*

CORBIN, H., CARTER, J., REESE, E. AND VOLKMANN, J. (1958) *Experiments on Visual Search, 1956–7, Psychological Research Unit, Mount Holyoke.*

COWEY, A. AND WEISKRANTZ, L. (1963) A perimetric study of visual field defects in monkeys, *Quart. J. exp. Psychol. 15,* 91–116.

CRAIK, K. (1948) Theory of the human operator in control systems, *Brit. J. Psychol. 38,* 142–8.

CRAMER, P. (1965) Response entropy as a function of the affective quality of the stimulus, *Psychon. Sci. 3,* 347–8.

CREED, R. (1935) Observations on Binocular Fusion and rivalry, *J. Physiol. 84,* 381–92.

CROSSMAN, E. (1953) Entropy and choice time: the effect of frequency unbalance on choice responses, *Quart. J. exp. Psychol. 5,* 41–51.

CROSSMAN, E. (1955) The measurement of discriminability, *Quart. J. esp. Psychol. 7,* 176–95.

CURTIS, AND FOSTER (1917) Size vs. Intensity as a determiner of attention, *Am. J. Psychol. 28,* 293.

DALLENBACH, K. (1923) Gradient of importance in the visual field, *Am. J. Psychol. 34,* 282.

DAVIS, R. (1967) Intermittency and selective attention, *Attention and Performance* (ed. Sanders, A.), Amsterdam: *North Holland.*

DAVIS, R., MORAY, N. AND TREISMAN, A. (1961) Imitative responses and the rate of gain of information, *Quart. J. exp. Psychol. 13,* 79–91.

DAWSON, G. (1956) The relative excitability and conduction velocity of sensory and motor nerve fibres in man, *J. Physiol. 131,* 436–51.

DAY, R. (1967) Fusion in dichotic listening, *Paper to the Chicago Meeting of the Psychonomics Society.*

DENNY-BROWN, D. AND CHAMBERS, R. (1958) The parietal lobe and behaviour, *Res. Publ. Ass. Nerve. Ment. Dis. 36,* 37–117.

DEUTSCH, J. A. (1960) *The Structural Basis of Behaviour,* Cambridge: *Cambridge University Press.*

DEUTSCH, J. AND DEUTSCH, D. (1963) Attention: some theoretical considerations, *Psychol. Rev. 70*, 80–90.

DEUTSCH, J., DEUTSCH, D. AND LINDSAY, P. (1967) Comments on 'Selective Attention: stimulus or response', *Quart. J. exp. Psychol. 19*, 362–8.

DITCHBURN, R. (1959) Physical methods applied to the study of visual perception, *Bull. Inst. Physics (London)*, 121–5.

DURET-COSYNS, S. AND DURET, R. (1956) Contribution experimentale à l'étude de l'electrodermogramme et du reflex psychogalvanique chez l'homme, *Acta neurol. Psychiat. Belgica 56*, 213.

EGAN, J., CARTERETTE, E. AND THWING, E. (1954) Some factors affecting multichannel listening, *J. acoust. Soc. Amer. 26*, 774–82.

EGETH, H. (1967) Selective attention, *Psychol. Bull. 67*, 41–57.

EVANS, C. AND PIGGINS, D. (1963) A comparison of the behaviour of geometrical shapes when viewed under conditions of steady fixation, and with apparatus for producing a stabilised retinal image, *Brit. J. physiol. Optics 20*, 1–13.

FENDER, D. AND JULESZ, B. (1967) The extension of Panum's fusional area in binocularly stabilised vision, *J. opt. Soc., Amer. 57*, 819–30.

FITTS, P. AND DEININGER, R. (1954) S-R compatibility: correspondence among paired elements within stimulus and response codes, *J. exp. Psychol. 48*, 483–92.

FRENCH, J. AND HERNANDEZ-PEON, R. (1955) Projections from cortex to cephalic brain stem in monkeys, *J. Neurophysiol. 18*, 74–95.

FRENCH, J., LIVINGSTON, R. AND HERNANDEZ-PEON, R. (1953) Cortical influences upon arousal mechanism, *Trans. Amer. neurol. Ass. 78*, 57.

FRIEDLINE, M. AND DALLENBACH, K. (1929) Distance from point of fixation vs. intensity as a determiner of attention, *Am. J. Psychol. 41*, 464.

GALAMBOS, R. (1955) Suppression of the auditory nerve activity by stimulation of efferent fibres to the cochlea, *Fed. Proc. 14*, 53.

GALAMBOS, R. (1960) Studies in the auditory system with implanted electrodes, *Neural Mechanisms of Auditory and Vestibular Systems*, (ed. G. Rasmussen and W. Windle), Springfield, Illinois: *Charles Thomas*.

GARDNER, R. AND LOHRENZ, L. (1961) Attention and assimilation, *Am. J. Psychol. 74*, 607–11.

GARNER, W. (1962) *Uncertainty and Structure as Psychological Concepts,* London: *Wiley.*

GAZZANIGA, M. AND SPERRY, R. (1966) Simultaneous double discrimination response following brain bisection, *Psychon. Sci. 4* (7), 261–2.

GAZZANIGA, M. AND YOUNG, E. (1967) Effects of commisurotomy on the processing of increasing visual information, *Exp. Brain Res. 3,* 368–71.

GIBSON, J. (1941) A critical review of the concept of set in contemporary psychology, *Psychol. Bull. 38,* 781–817.

GOLDMANN-EISLER, F. (1958a) The predictability of words in context and the length of pauses in speech, *Lang. and Speech 1,* 226–31.

GOLDMANN-EISLER, F. (1958b) Speech production and the predictability of words in context, *Quart. J. exp. Psychol. 10,* 96–106.

GOTTSDANKER, R. (1967) Computer determination of the effects of superseding signals, *Attention and Performance* (ed. Sanders, A.), Amsterdam: *North Holland.*

GRANIT, R. (1955) *Receptors and Sensory perception,* Connecticut: *Yale U.P.*

GRAY, J. (1966) Attention, Consciousness and Voluntary Control, *In Present-day Russian Psychology* (ed. O'Connor, N.), London: *Pergamon Press.*

GRAY, J. AND WEDDERBURN, A. (1960) Grouping strategies with simultaneous stimuli, *Quart. J. exp. Psychol. 12,* 180–5.

GRINDLEY, G. AND TOWNSEND, V. (1968) Voluntary attention in peripheral vision and it effects on acuity and differential thresholds, *Quart. J. exp. Psychol. 20,* 11–20.

GUILDFORD, J. (1936) Varieties and levels of clearness correlated with eye movements, *Am. J. Psychol. 48,* 371–88.

GUZMAN-FLORES, C. (1961) Discussion in 'Brain and Behaviour' (ed. Brazier, M.), *Amer. Inst. Biol. Sci. 1,* 232.

HAYDECK, C., PETROVICH, L. AND ELLSWORTH, D. (1966) Feedback of speech muscle activity during silent reading: rapid extinction, *Science, 154,* 1467–8.

HEBB, D. (1949) *Organisation of Behaviour,* London: *Wiley.*

HERMAN, L. (1965) Study of the single channel hypothesis and input regulation within a continuous simultaneous task situation, *Quart. J. exp. Psychol. 17,* 37–47.

HERNANDEZ-PEON, R. (1966) Physiological Mechanisms in Attention in *Frontiers in Physiological Psychology* (ed. Russell,R.), New York: *Academic Press.*

HERNANDEZ-PEON, R. AND DONOSO, M. (1959) Influence of attention and suggestion upon subcortical evoked electric activity in the human brain, *1st Internat. Cong. neurol. Sci. Bruxelles,* Vol. III, London: *Pergamon Press* pp. 385–96.

HERNANDEZ-PEON, R. AND SCHERRER, H. (1955) 'Habituation' to acoustic stimuli in cochlear nucleus, *Fed. Proc. 14,* 71.

HERNANDEZ-PEON, R., SCHERRER, H. AND JOUVET, M. (1956) Modification of electrical activity in the cochlear nucleus during 'attention' in unanaesthetised cats, *Science 123,* 331–2.

HESS, E. (1965) Attitude and pupil size, *Sci. Amer. 212* (4), 46–54.

HILL, R. AND HORN, G. (1964) Responsiveness to sensory stimulation of cells in the rabbit midbrain, *Proc. Physiol. Soc.* (London) *175,* 40P–41P.

HOF, V. M. (1960) Open eye and closed eye occipitocortical response to photic stimulation of the retina, *Acta Physiol. Pharm. Neel. 9,* 443–51.

HORN, G. (1960) Electrical activity of the cerebral cortex of unanaesthetised cats during attentive behaviour, *Brain 83,* 57–76.

HORN, G. (1965) Physiological and psychological aspects of selective attention, *Advances in the Study of Behaviour* I (ed. Lehrman, D. S., Hinde, R. A., and Shaw, E.), London: *Academic Press.*

HORN, G. AND BLUNDELL, J. (1959) Evoked potentials in the visual cortex of the unanaesthetised cat, *Nature 184,* 173–4.

HORN, G. AND HILL, R. (1964) Habituation of the response to sensory stimuli of neurons in the brainstem of rabbits, *Nature 202,* 296–8.

HOWARTH, I. AND ELLIS, K. (1961) The relative intelligibility threshold for one's own and other people's names, *Quart. J. exp. Psychol. 13,* 236–40.

HOWARTH, I. AND TREISMAN, M. (1958) Lowering of an auditory threshold produced by a light signal occurring after the threshold stimulus, *Nature 182,* 1093–4.

HUBEL, D. AND WEISEL, T. (1962) Receptive fields, binocular interaction, and functional architecture in the cat's visual cortex. *J. Physiol. 160,* 106–54.

HUGGINS, A. F. (1964) Distortion of temporal pattern of speech: Interruption and Alternation, *J. acoust. Soc. Amer. 36,* 1055–65.

INGHAM, J. (1957) The effect upon monaural sensitivity of continuous stimulation of the opposite ear, *Quart. J. exp. Psychol. 9,* 52–4.

INGLIS, J. (1960) Dichotic stimulation and memory disorder, *Nature 186,* 181–2.

ITEK CORPORATION (1967) *Bibliography on Eye Movement Recording,* Cambridge, Mass.: *Itek corporation.*

KARSLAKE, J. (1940) The Purdue eye-camera. A practical apparatus for studying the attention value of advertisements, *J. appl. Psychol. 24,* 417–40.

KAUFMANN, L. AND PITBLADO, C. (1965) Further observation on the nature of effective binocular disparities, *J. exp. Psychol. 78,* 379–91.

KIANG, N. (1965) *Discharge Patterns of Single Fibres in the Cat's Auditory Nerve,* Boston: *M.I.T. Press.*

KIMURA, D. (1964) Left-right differences in the perception of melodies, *Quart. J. exp. Psychol. 16,* 355–9.

KOHLER AND ADAMS, (1958) Perception and attention, *Am. J. Psychol. 71,* 489–503.

KOLERS, P. (1968) Bilingualism and Information processing, *Sci. Amer. 218,* 78–90.

KRISTOFFERSON, A. (1967a) Attention and psychophysical time, *Attention and Performance* (ed. Sanders, A.), Amsterdam: *North Holland.*

KRISTOFFERSON, A. (1967b) Successiveness discrimination as a two-state quantal process, *Science 158,* 1337–40.

LADEFOGED, P. AND BROADBENT, D. (1960) Perception of sequence in auditory events, *Quart. J. exp. Psychol. 12,* 162–70.

LANDGREN, S. (1959) Thalamic and cortical perception of afferent impulses from the tongue, *Pain and Itch* (ed. G. Wolstenholme and M. O'Connor), CIBA Foundation Study Group No. 1, London: *Churchill.*

LATOUR, P. (1966) Cortical control of eye movements, *Institute for Perception RVO-TNO,* Soesterberg, Netherlands.

LAWRENCE, D. (1963) The nature of a stimulus: some relationships between learning and perception, *Psychology, Study of a Science* (ed. S. Koch), London: *McGraw Hill,* vol. 5.

LAWSON, E. (1961) Influence of different orders of approximation to the English language upon eye-voice span, *Quart. J. exp. Psychol. 13,* 53–6.

LAWSON, E. (1966a) Decisions concerning the rejected channel, *Quart. J. exp. Psychol. 18,* 260–5.

LAWSON, E. (1966b) Spontaneous speech generation, *Quart. J. exp. Psychol. 18*, 254–9.

LEONARD, J. (1959) Tactual choice reactions 1, *Quart. J. exp. Psychol. 11*, 76–83.

LEVELT, W. (1965a) Binocular brightness averaging and contour information, *Brit. J. Psychol. 56*, 1–15.

LEVELT, W. (1965b) On binocular rivalry, *Institute for Perception RVO-TNO,* Soesterberg, Netherlands.

LEVELT, W. (1966) The alternation process in binocular rivalry, *Brit. J. Psychol. 57*, 225–39.

LEVELT, W. (1967) Note on the distribution of dominance times in binocular rivalry, *Brit. J. Psychol. 58*, 143–7.

LICKLIDER, J. (1959) Three auditory theories, *Psychology: Study of a Science* (ed. Koch, S.), London: *McGraw Hill,* vol. 1.

LICKLIDER, J. (1961) On Psychophysiological models, *Sensory Communication* (ed. Rosenblith, W.), London: *M.I.T. and Wiley.*

MACKINTOSH, N. (1964) Overtraining and transfer within and between dimensions in the rat, *J. exp. Psychol. 16*, 250–6.

MACKINTOSH, N. (1965) Incidental cue learning in rats, *Quart. J. exp. Psychol. 17*, 292–301.

MACMILLAN, J. (1941) Eye movements and attention, *Am. J. Psychol. 54*, 373–84.

MACKWORTH, N. (1967) *Paper to the Chicago Meeting of the Psychonomics Society.*

MACKWORTH, N. AND MORANDI, A. (1968) The gaze selects informative details within pictures, *Percept. & Psychophys. 2*, 547–52.

MAGOUN, H. (1954) The ascending reticular system and wakefulness, *Brain Mechanisms and Consciousness* (eds. Adrian, E. D., Bremer, F. & Jasper, H.), Oxford: *Blackwell.*

MCCULLOCH, W. (1949) Why the mind is in the head, *Cerebral Mechanisms and Behaviour* (ed. Jeffress), New York: *Wiley.*

MCDOUGALL, W. (1928) *Outlines of Psychology,* London: *Methuen.*

MCFARLAND, J. (1965) Sequential part presentation: a method for studying visual form perception, *Brit. J. Psychol. 56*, 439–47.

MEADS, L. (1915) Form vs. intensity as a determiner of attention, *Am. J Psychol. 26*, 150.

MELZACK, R. AND CAREY, K. (1968) Sensory, motivational, and central control determinants of pain, *The Skin Senses* (ed. Kenshalo), Springfield, Illinois: *Charles Thomas.*

MILLER, G. (1951) Language and communication. London: *McGraw Hill.*

MILLER, G., GALANTER, E. AND PRIBRAM, K. (1960) *Plans and the Structure of Behaviour,* New York: *Henry Holt.*

MILLER, G. AND LICKLIDER, J. (1950) The Intelligibility of Interrupted Speech, *J. acoust. Soc. Amer. 22,* 167–72.

MILLER, G. AND SELFRIDGE, J. (1950) Verbal context and the recall of meaningful material, *Am. J. Psychol. 63,* 176.

MORAY, N. (1958) The effect of the relative intensities of messages in dichotic shadowing, *Language and Speech 1,* 110–13.

MORAY, N. (1959) Attention in dichotic listening: affective cues and the influence of instructions, *Quart. J. exp. Psychol. 9,* 56–60.

MORAY, N. (1960a) *Studies in Selective Listening,* unpubli shed doctora thesis for University of Oxford.

MORAY, N. (1960b) Broadbent's filter theory; postulate H and the problem of switching time, *Quart. J. exp. Psychol. 12,* 214–21.

MORAY, N. (1961) Perceptual defence and filter theory, *Nature 191,* 940.

MORAY, N. (1966) Cultural differences in statistical approximations to English, *Psychon. Sci. 5* (12), 467–8.

MORAY, N. (1967) Where is capacity limited? A survey and a model, *Attention and Performance* (ed. Sanders, A.), Amsterdam: *North Holland.*

MORAY, N. (1969a) *Listening and attention,* Harmondsworth: *Penguin Books.*

MORAY, N. (1969b) Introductory experiments in auditory time-sharing: detection of intensity increments (in preparation).

MORAY, N. (1969c) Introductory experiments in auditory time-sharing: detection of frequency increments (in preparation).

MORAY, N. (1969d) Introductory experiments in auditory time-sharing: effect of signal duration (in preparation).

MORAY, N. (1969e) Computer simulation of some visual functions, *Proceedings of AGARD, Brussels Bionics Conference, 1968.*

MORAY, N. AND BARNETT, T. (1965) Stimulus presentation and methods of scoring in short term memory experiments, *Acta Psychol. 24,* 253–63.

MORAY, N., BATES, A. AND BARNETT, T. (1965) Experiments on the four-eared man, *J. acoust. Soc. Amer. 38,* 196–201.

MORAY, N. AND JORDAN, A. (1966) Practice and compatability in 2-channel short-term memory, *Psychon. Sci. 4* (12), 427.

MORAY, N. AND O'BRIEN, T. (1967) Signal detection theory applied to selective listening, *J. acoust. Soc. Amer. 42,* 765–72.

MORAY, N. AND REID, A. (1967) Two-channel immediate memory span, *Psychon. Sci. 8* (6), 249–50.

MORAY, N. AND TAYLOR, A. (1958) The effect of redundancy on shadowing one of two dichotic messages, *Language and Speech 1,* 102–9.

MORTON, J. (1964a) A model for continuous language behaviour, *Language and Speech 7,* 40–70.

MORTON, J. (1964b) The effects of context upon speed of reading, eye movements, and eye-voice span, *Quart. J. exp. Psychol. 16,* 340–55.

MOUNTCASTLE, V. (ed.) (1962) *Interhemispheric relations and cerebral dominance,* Baltimore: *Johns Hopkins Press.*

MOUSHEGIAN, G., RUPERT, A. AND WHITCOMB, M. (1964) Medial superior olivary-unit response to monaural and binaural clicks, *J. acoust. Soc. Amer. 36,* 196–202.

MOWBRAY, G. (1952) Simultaneous vision and audition: the detection of elements missing from over learned sequences, *J. exp. Psychol. 44,* 293–300.

MOWBRAY, G. (1953) Simultaneous visions and audition: the comprehension of prose passages with varying levels of difficulty, *J. exp. Psychol. 46,* 365–72.

MOWBRAY, G. (1954) The perception of short phrases presented simultaneously for auditory and visual reception, *Quart. J. exp. Psychol. 6,* 86–92.

MOWBRAY, G. AND RHOADES, M. (1959) On the reduction of choice reaction times with practice, *Quart. J. exp. Psychol. 11,* 16–23.

MOWBRAY, G. (1964) Perception and retention of verbal information presented during auditory shadowing, *J. acoust. Soc. Amer. 36,* 1459–65.

MURDOCK, B. (1965) Effects of a subsidiary task on short-term memory, *Brit. J. Psychol. 56,* 413–19.

NEFF, D. (1958) The neural basis of auditory discrimination, *Biological and Biochemical Bases of Behaviour,* Madison-Wisconsin: *Wisconsin University Press.*

NEISSER, U. (1967) *Cognitive Psychology,* New York: *Appleton Century Crofts.*

NORMAN, D. AND LINDSAY, P. (1967) *Paper to the Chicago Meeting of the Psychonomics Society.*

ODENTHAL, D. (1961) Simultaneous dichotic frequency discrimination, *J. acoust. Soc. Amer. 33*, 357.

OSWALD, I. (1962) *Sleeping and Waking*, Amsterdam: *Elsevier*.

OSWALD, I., TAYLOR, A. AND TREISMAN, M. (1960) Discriminative responses to stimulation during human sleep, *Brain, 83*, 440–53.

PAYNE, W. (1967) Visual reaction times on a circle about the fovea, *Science 155*, 481–2.

PERRY, N. (1966) Signal vs. noise in the evoked potential, *Science 153*, 1022.

PLOMP, R. (1964) Rate of decay of auditory sensation, *J. acoust. Soc. Amer. 36*, 227–83.

PLOMP, R. AND BOUMAN, M. (1959) Relation between hearing thresholds and the duration of tone pulses, *J. acoust. Soc. Amer. 31*, 749–58.

POLLACK, I. (1952) The information of elementary auditory displays, *J. acoust. Soc. Amer. 24*, 745–9.

POLLACK, I. AND FICKS, L. (1954) Information of elementary multidimensional displays, *J. acoust. Soc. Amer. 26*, 155–8.

POLLACK, I. (1959) Message uncertainty and message reception, *J. acoust. Soc. Amer. 31*, 1500–8.

POLLACK, I., JOHNSON, L. AND KNAFF, P. (1959) Running memory span, *J. exp. Psychol. 57*, 137–46.

POSNER, M. (1964) Information reduction in the analysis of sequential tasks, *Psychol. Rev. 71*, 491–504.

POULTON, E. G. (1953) Two channel listening, *J. exp. Psychol. 46*, 91–6.

POULTON, E. C. (1956) Listening to overlapping calls, *J. exp. Psychol. 52*, 334–9.

RABBITT, P. (1962) Short term retention of more than one aspect of a series of stimuli, *Nature 195*, 102.

RATLIFF, F. (1965) *Mach Bands: quantitative studies on neural networks in the retina*, New York: *Holden Day*.

REYNOLDS, D. (1964) Effects of double stimulation: Temporary inhibition of response, *Psychol. Bull. 62*, 333–47.

ROSENSWEIG, M. AND SUTTON, D. (1958) Binaural interaction in the lateral lemniscus of the cat, *J. Neurophysiol. 21*, 17.

ROSENSWEIG, M. AND WYERS, E. (1955) Binaural interaction at the inferior colliculi, *J. Comp. Physiol. Psychol. 48*, 426.

SAMPSON, H. (1964) Immediate memory and simultaneous visual stimulation, *Quart. J. exp. Psychol. 16,* 1–10.

SAMPSON, H. AND HORROCKS, J. (1967) Binocular rivalry and immediate memory, *Quart. J. exp. Psychol. 19,* 224–31.

SAMPSON, H. AND SPONG, P. (1961a) Binocular fixation and immediate memory, *Brit. J. Psychol. 52,* 239–48.

SAMPSON, H. AND SPONG, P. (1961b) Handedness, eye dominance and immediate memory, *Quart. J. exp. Psychol. 13,* 173–80.

SAMUELS, I. (1959) Reticular mechanisms and behaviour, *Psychol. Bull. 56,* 1–25.

SANDERS, A. (1963) The selective process in the functional visual field, *Institute for Perception, RVO-TNO,* Soesterberg, Netherlands.

SANDERS, A. (ed). (1967) *Attention and Performance,* Amsterdam: *North Holland* (vol. 27 of *Acta Psychologica*).

SATTERFIELD, J. (1964) Evoked cortical potential correlates of attention in human subjects, *EEG, clin. Neurophysiol. 19,* 470–5.

SAVIN, H. (1967) On the successive perception of simultaneous stimuli, *Percept. & Psychophys. 2* (10), 479–82.

SAYRE, K. (1965) *Recognition: a Study in the Philosophy of Artificial Intelligence,* Indiana: *Univ. of Notre Dame Press.*

SCHILLER, P. AND CHOROVER, S. (1968) Annual report 1967–68, *Massachusetts Institute of Technology Department of Psychology.*

SCHUBERT, E. AND PARKER, C. (1955) Additions to Cherry's findings on switching speech between the two ears, *J. acoust. Soc. Amer. 27,* 792–4.

SENDERS, J. (1966a) The estimation of pilot workload, *Research report,* Cambridge, Mass.: *Bolt, Beranek, and Newman, Inc.*

SENDERS, J. (1966b) A re-analysis of pilot eye movements data, *IEEE Transactions on Human Factors in Electronics HFE-7,* 103–6.

SENDERS, J. (1967) On the distribution of attention in a dynamic environment, *Attention and Performance* (ed. Sanders, A.), Amsterdam: *North Holland.*

SENDERS, J., WEBB, J. AND BAKER, C. (1955) The peripheral viewing of dials, *J. appl. Psychol.* 433–6.

SHANNON, C. AND WEAVER, W. (1949) *The Mathematical Theory of Communication,* Urbana: *Univ. of Illinois Press.*

SHARPLESS, S. AND JASPER, H. (1956) Habituation of the arousal reaction, *Brain, 79,* 655–80.

SPERLING, G. (1960) The information available in brief visual presentations, *Psychol. Monog. 74,* 11.

SPERRY, R. (1964) The great cerebral commisure, *Sci. Amer. 210,* 42–52.

SPIETH, W., CURTIS, J. AND WEBSTER, J. (1954) Responding to one of two simultaneous messages, *J. acoust. Soc. Amer. 26,* 391–6.

SPRAGUE, J. (1966) Interaction of cortex and superior colliculus in mediation of visually guided behaviour in the cat, *Science 153,* 1544–7.

STEWART, G. AND HOVDA, O. (1918) The intensity factor in binaural localisation: an extension of Weber's Law, *Psychol. Rev. 25,* 242–51.

STOCKHAM, T. (1967) Personal Communication.

STROUD, J. (1956) The fine structure of psychological time, *Information Theory in Psychology* (ed. H. Quastler), *Illinois Glencoe Free Press.*

SUTHERLAND, N. (1964) The learning of discrimination by animals, *Endeavour 23,* 148–54.

SWETS, J. (1963) Central Factors in Auditory Frequency Selectivity, *Psychol. Bull. 60,* 429–40.

TAYLOR, A. AND MORAY, N. (1960) Statistical approximations to English and French, *Language and Speech 3,* 7–10.

TAYLOR, M. (1967) Detectability theory and the interpretation of vigilance data, *Attention and Performance* (ed. Sanders, A.), Amsterdam: *North Holland.*

TAYLOR, M., LINDSAY, P. AND FORBES, S. (1967) Quantification of shared capacity processing in auditory and visual discrimination, *Attention and Performance* (ed. Sanders, A.), Amsterdam: *North Holland.*

TAYLOR, W. (1956) Recent developments in the use of 'cloze' procedure, *Journalism Quarterly 33,* 99.

TEUBER, H. L. (1959) Some alterations in behaviour after cerebral lesions in man, *Evolution of Nervous Control from Primitive Organisms to Man, Amer. Assoc. Advance. Sci. Publ.* No. 5.

THOMSON, A. (1961) Effect of attention in peripheral vision, *Nature 191,* 732–3.

TINBERGEN, N. (1951) *The Study of Instinct: Oxford University Press.*

TITCHENER, E. (1903) *The Psychology of Feeling and Attention.* London: *Macmillan.*

TOLHURST, G. AND PETERS, R. (1956) The effect of attenuating one channel of a dichotic circuit upon the word reception of dual messages, *J. acoust. Soc. Amer. 28*, 602–5.

TREISMAN, A. (1960) Contextual cues in selective listening, *Quart. J. exp. Psychol. 12*, 242–8.

TREISMAN, A. (1961) *Attention and Speech,* Unpublished doctoral thesis, University of Oxford.

TREISMAN, A. (1962) Binocular rivalry and stereoscopic depth, *Quart. J. exp. Psychol. 14*, 23–38.

TREISMAN, A. (1964a) Verbal cues, language and meaning in attention, *Amer. J. Psychol. 77*, 206–14.

TREISMAN, A. (1964b) The effect of irrelevant material on the efficiency of selective listening, *Am. J. Psychol. 77*, 533–46.

TREISMAN, A. (1964c) Selective attention in man, *Brit. Med. Bull. 20*, 12–16.

TREISMAN, A. (1965) The effects of redundancy and familiarity on translating and repeating back a foreign and a native language, *Brit. J. Psychol. 56*, 369–79.

TREISMAN, A. (1966) Our limited attention, *Adv. Sci.,* 600–11.

TREISMAN, A. (1967) Reply to comments on 'Selective listening: perception or response', *Quart. J. exp. Psychol. 19*, 362–8.

TREISMAN, A. AND GEFFEN, G. (1967) Selective attention: perception or response? *Quart. J. exp. Psychol. 19*, 1–18.

TULVING, E. AND LINDSAY, P. (1967) Identification of simultaneously presented simple visual and auditory stimuli, *Attention and Performance* (ed. Sanders, A.), Amsterdam: *North Holland.*

TUNE, G. (1964) Sequential errors in a time-sharing task, *Brit. J. Psychol. 55*, 415–19.

TUNTURI, A. (1960) Anatomy and physiology of the auditory cortex, *Neural Mechanisms of the auditory and vestibular systems* (ed. G. Rasmussen and W. Windle), Springfield: *Charles Thomas.*

UTTLEY, A. (1955) The conditional probability of signals in the nervous system, *Radar Research Establishment,* Memo. No. 1109.

VINCE, M. (1950) Medical Research Council Applied Psychology Unit Report, No. 124/50.

VORONIN, L. AND SOKOLOV, E. (1960) Cortical mechanisms of the orienting reflex and its relation to the conditioned reflex, *EEG, clin. Neurophysiol. Suppl. 13*, 335–46.

WALL, P. (1961) Two transmission systems for skin sensations, *Sensory Communication* (ed. Rosenblith, W.), New York: *M.I.T. Press and Wiley.*

WALL, P. AND SWEET, W. (1967) Temporary abolition of pain in man, *Science,* 1955, 108–9.

WALTER, G. (1964) The convergence and interaction of visual, auditory, and tactile responses in human non-specific cortex, *Ann. N.Y. Acad. Sci. 112,* 320–61.

WARRINGTON, E. (1965) The effect of stimulus configuration on the incidence of the completion phenomenon, *Brit. J. Psychol. 56,* 447–54.

WELFORD, A. (1967) Single channel operation in the brain, *Attention and Performance* (ed. Sanders, A.), Amsterdam: *North Holland.*

WHELAN, E. (1968) Visual Perception and Cerebral Dominance, unpublished Ph.D. Thesis, Univ. of Sheffield.

WHITE, C. AND FORD, A. (1960) Eye movements during simulated radar search, *J. opt. Soc. Amer. 50,* 909–13.

WILKINSON, R. (1967) Evoked response and reaction time, *Attention and Performance* (ed. Sanders, A.), Amsterdam: *North Holland.*

WILKINSON, R. AND MORLOCK, H. (1966) Evoked cortical response and performance, *Bull Brit. Psychol. Soc. 19,* 10A.

WILLIAMS, L. (1967) The effect of target specification on objects fixated during visual search, *Attention and Performance* (ed. Sanders, A.), Amsterdam: *North Holland.*

WITTENBORN, J. (1943) Factorial equations for tests of attention, *Psychometrika 8,* 19–35.

WITTGENSTEIN, L. (1953) *Philosophical Investigations,* Oxford: *Blackwell.*

WORDEN, F. (1967) Attention and auditory electrophysiology, *Prog. Physiol. Psychol. 1,* London: *Academic Press.*

YATES, A. (1963) Delayed auditory feedback, *Psychol. Bull. 60,* 213–32.

YNTEMA, D., WOZENCRAFT, F. AND KLEM, L. (1964) Immediate recall of digits presented at very high speeds, *Paper to the Psychonomics Society.*

YOUNG, L. R. AND STARK, L. (1963) Variable feedback experiments testing a sampled data model for eye tracking, *IEEE Trans. on Human Factors in Electronics HFE-4:* 38–46.

ZWISLOCKI, J. (1953) Acoustic attenuation between the ears, *J. acoust. Soc. Amer. 25,* 743–52.

AUTHOR INDEX

This index does not include last-minute material added at the end of chapters.

SUBJECT INDEX

This index does not include last minute material added at the end of chapters.